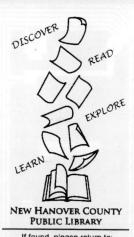

Crisps, Cobblers, Custards & Creams

For information about permission to reproduce selections
from this book, write to trade.permission@hmhco.com
or to Permissions, Houghton Mifflin Harcourt Publishing
Company, 3 Park Avenue, 19th Floor, New York,
New York 10016.

www.hmhco.com

Library of Congress Cataloging-in-Publication Data
Anderson, Jean.
Crisps, cobblers, custards & creams / by Jean Anderson ;
photography by Jason Wyche.
pages cm
ISBN 978-0-544-23075-0 (paper over board) —
ISBN 978-0-544-23076-7 (ebook)
1. Desserts. I. Title. II. Title: Crisps, cobblers,
custards & creams.
TX773.A4226 2016
641.86 — dc23
2015019992

Book design by Shubhani Sarkar

Printed in China
C&C 10 9 8 7 6 5 4 3 2 1

Crisps, Cobblers, Custards & Creams

Jean Anderson

Photography by JASON WYCHE

Houghton Mifflin Harcourt

Boston   New York

2016

For all lovers of crisps, cobblers,
custards & creams

Contents

ACKNOWLEDGMENTS xi

INTRODUCTION xiii

PUDDING PRIMER xv

BAKEWARE/COOKWARE xvii

HELPFUL EQUIPMENT, COOK'S TOOLS & MORE xix

HANDY TABLE OF EQUIVALENTS xxxiii

Crisps & Cobblers 1

Blueberry-Oatmeal Crumble 6   October Pudding 25   Apple-Cheddar Crisp 26
Golden Delicious–Butter Crumb Betty 35
Pick-Your-Own-Peaches Crumble with Ginger Shortbread 46   Cherry Clafoutis 57
Roasted Rhubarb Cobbler with Whole-Wheat Topping 58
Green Tomato Crumble with Apples and Raisins 64   *plus dozens more*

Custards & Creams 69

Baked Vanilla Bean Custard 72   Blue Ridge Jam Custards 76   River of Gold Flan 81
Sericaia (Cinnamon-Dusted Baked Custard) 82   Rice Pudding 85
Mama's Tapioca Pudding 89   Old-Timey Tar Heel Banana Pudding 93   Kheer (Indian Rice Pudding) 95
Feliciana Parish Sweet Potato Crème Caramel 100   Dulce de Leche Pots de Crème 107
Fresh Peach Soufflé 110   Showstopper Bavarian Cream 116
Sweet Potato Panna Cotta with Clementines in Lemongrass Syrup 119
Bill Smith's Butterscotch Pudding 126   Chocolate Mousse 128   *plus dozens more*

Bread Puddings & Steamed Puddings 161

The Best Chocolate Bread Pudding 164   Rum-Raisin Bread Pudding 167

Lemon Meringue Bread Pudding 169   Summer Pudding 172

Buttermilk-Biscuit Pudding 176   Capirotada (New Mexican Bread Pudding) 179

Queen of Puddings 181   French Bread Pudding with Whiskey Sauce 183

Maple Bread Pudding 184   Noodle Pudding 191   Steamed Applesauce Pudding 193

Steamed Cocoa–Brown Sugar Pudding 197   Christmas Pudding 198

Steamed Fig and Cranberry Pudding 204   *and many more*

Miscellaneous Puddings 209

Indian Pudding 210   Woodford Pudding 212   Food for the Gods 213   Sticky Toffee Puddings 223

Wild Persimmon Pudding 225   Iron Skillet Sweet Potato Pudding 230   Heavenly Hash 249

Eton Mess 251   Pudim Molotov 252   Finnish Cranberry Pudding 254

and many more

Sauces & Toppings 261

Homemade Biscuit Mix 262   Butter Crumb Streusel 263   Gluten-Free Granola Topping 264

Gluten-Free Streusel Topping 266   Butterscotch Sauce 268   Thin Chocolate Sauce 269

Crème Anglaise (Custard Sauce) 270   Mock Devonshire Cream 273   Frothy Egg Sauce 277

Nutmeg Sauce 283   Quick Cardinal Sauce 284   Brown Sugar Hard Sauce 289   *and more*

SOURCES 291

Where to buy unusual ingredients, bakeware, and cook's tools

INDEX 293

ACKNOWLEDGMENTS

First of all, deepest thanks to New York friend and colleague Joanne Lamb Hayes for a heroic assist in developing and testing recipes for this book. No one is more professional than Joanne, more painstaking, or more knowledgeable thanks to her experience in the test kitchens of major magazines (*McCall's* and *Family Circle*) not to mention her fifteen years as Food Editor of *Country Living*.

For sharing pudding ideas, revered family recipes, and ingredient sources, I owe a debt of gratitude to these friends, colleagues, and relatives: Luis Abilio, Judy Berek, Sylvia Carter, Barbara Fairchild, Barbara Gillam, Sandra Gutierrez, Enca Mello Lameiro, Ronni Lundy, Dea Martin, Sally Massengale, Mike Moore, Sara Moulton, Moreton Neal, Lisa Prince, Bill Smith (extra thanks to you, Bill, for sharing your precious wild persimmon pulp), Kathy McDonald Snead, Brenda Sutton, Dotty Tookey, Betsy Wade, Andrea Weigl, and Susan O'Haver Young.

I'd be remiss if I didn't thank my eagle-eyed friend Margaretta Yarborough who reads proof after I've had a go at it and invariably catches typos I missed. Thanks, too, to Robert Holmes, friend and hobby cook both accomplished and devout, who'll try a just-tested recipe and let me know what he thinks.

A big salute to my editor, Justin Schwartz, who has now shepherded four of my cookbooks into print with grace, patience, style, and skill.

Finally, ongoing thanks to my agent David Black who, no matter how busy, always takes time to listen and advise. You are the best, David, my rock and voice of reason in today's increasingly iffy world of book publishing.

INTRODUCTION

Soothing, nourishing, uplifting, puddings are quintessential comfort food. But what exactly *is* a pudding? Merriam-Webster gives three definitions: (1) "a thick, sweet, soft, and creamy food that is usually eaten cold at the end of a meal . . ." (2) "a sweet, soft food that is made of rice, bread, etc. . . ." or (3) "a hot dish like a pie that has a mixture of meat or vegetables inside of it."

In my own family, and in my corner of the South, puddings included *Webster's* first two definitions as well as a fruit-based version of the third. And these are the puddings you will find in the pages that follow.

As toddlers, cool and creamy is what we craved—custards, cornstarch puddings, and gelatins whipped into fluffs. But before long we'd graduated to crisps and cobblers, then bread puddings, then sophisticated charlottes and crème caramels.

My mother made them all and welcomed me into her kitchen when I was barely tall enough to see into her mixing bowl. Soon I was lending a hand—buttering pans and casseroles, crumbling bread for toppings, and of course licking the bowl.

I remember picking the blueberries and rhubarb my father grew, all the while dreaming of the cobblers, crisps, and crumbles to come. I remember dodging brambles when asked to gather blackberries, also racing into the woods after "first frost" to scoop up wild persimmon windfalls before the raccoons and deer could devour them. Not easy.

Early each summer, we'd pile into the family Ford and drive an hour or so down U.S. Highway 1 to the Sandhills, where peach orchards rippled across every horizon. Then come autumn, we'd head for the nearest apple orchard and pick a bushel or more. I still like to pick my own. Or buy at my farmers' market because no fruits shipped across the country, let alone across the world, can match the home-grown for succulence and flavor.

My mother loved to improvise with the pudding recipes she'd picked up at her book club and sewing circle as well as the North Carolina State College Woman's Club and AAUW. These meetings, it seemed to me, were mostly recipe swaps. I now have the foot-long metal card file my mother filled with recipes, each one neatly written on a three-by-five index card with source and date noted in the upper right-hand corner. Whenever Mother hosted one of her club meetings, I played "fly on the wall" just so I could listen in on discussions that nearly always focused on food, particularly desserts.

When I began working on this book, I e-mailed friends, relatives, and colleagues to ask if they'd be willing to share a cherished family pudding recipe or two, and was startled to learn how many of them admitted to having grown up on instant puddings and Jell-O. Really?

Were their mothers too busy to do anything more than open a box of Might-T-Fine? Did they never learn how easy, how economical, how delicious crisps and cobblers can be? Never discover the magic of floating island? Or the mystery of a pan of batter that emerges from the oven as a two-layered pudding, soft and creamy underneath a layer of cake? Did they never swoon over the delicacy of vanilla bean custard? Or marvel at the loft and glamour of a soufflé?

These were all so integral to my own childhood they remain delicious memories to this day, memories I'd like to share. My mission, then, is simply to give puddings their due—make that their long overdue due.

So, what I've assembled here is a global collection of the puddings I like best, all-time family favorites retrieved from dusty attics plus dozens of unusual recipes that caught my fancy while traveling at home and abroad. Things like Capirotada (a cheese-and-raisin-rich bread pudding I enjoyed in Santa Fe), a refreshingly tart Finnish Cranberry Pudding made with Cream of Wheat that I picked up in Helsinki, Britain's Sticky Toffee Puddings (rumored to be the Duchess of Cambridge's favorite), and Portugal's positively celestial Pudim Abade de Priscos, a 24-karat egg-yolk custard made with bacon. That's right, bacon.

The variety of puddings is staggering, greater by far than the different kinds of cake or pie or cookies, even greater, perhaps, than all three combined. You'll find more than 150 of the best, each meticulously tested, in the chapters that follow: Crisps & Cobblers . . . Custards & Creams . . . Bread Puddings & Steamed Puddings . . . Miscellaneous Puddings. There's a fifth chapter too: Sauces & Toppings, most of which can be made ahead and stashed in the refrigerator or freezer.

Come to think of it, many of the puddings, themselves, are make-aheads—easy, economical, accommodating. May they become new family favorites.

Jean Anderson
Chapel Hill, NC
www.jeanandersoncooks.com

PUDDING PRIMER

Before you begin, review this introduction carefully. It discusses bakeware, ingredients, techniques, the "dos" and "don'ts" for each type of pudding, and also passes along professional tips and tricks that will save you time, trouble, and possibly money as well.

RECIPE "DOS" AND "DON'TS"

Never begin a recipe until you've read it—several times, if necessary. Only then will you understand what you're to do and know what ingredients and implements you'll need.

- Measure each recipe ingredient at the outset and do as much pre-prep as possible (peeling, coring, slicing, etc.) so you don't have to pause mid-recipe. Having everything at-the-ready saves no end of time.

- Never substitute one ingredient for another unless a recipe offers that option and names acceptable substitutions.

- Always use freshly squeezed citrus juice—orange, lemon, lime. No canned juice, no reconstituted frozen juice can match their flavor.

- Always use pure extracts—almond, butterscotch, coconut, hazelnut, orange, rum, vanilla, whatever. Artificial flavorings are, well, artificial, taste unpleasantly "perfume-y," and can ruin a custard or other delicate cream.

- Never double or triple a recipe—you're courting disaster. When I was a recipe tester/developer at *Ladies' Home Journal* in New York, the majority of recipe complaints came from readers who decided to double or triple one of our carefully tested recipes—this, mind you, the first time they tried the recipe.

- Never use one casserole, baking dish, or pan in place of another unless I suggest alternatives. The size and shape of a baking dish, casserole, or pan, indeed the very material from which it's made, can mean success or failure.

Note: Because many puddings contain highly acidic fruits, I call for nonreactive baking dishes whenever needed. "Nonreactive"? That simply means that the baking dish—usually ovenproof glass, ceramic, or earthenware—is unaffected by high-acid ingredients and will not impart a "tinny" taste to the puddings baked in them. Not so for anything made of aluminum, cast iron, or copper. Stainless-steel pans are considered nonreactive though in my opinion they don't do as well by puddings as ovenproof glass, ceramic, and earthenware.

Tip: Dark or darkly coated metal pans (the kind many supermarkets sell) are likely to overbrown anything baked in them and for that reason I never use them. I also do not use pans with nonstick coatings because I worry that anything acidic may "eat" into the coating over time and possibly emit fumes of questionable safety.

- Make sure your oven is spot-on. Our *Ladies' Home Journal* test kitchen ovens were calibrated every two weeks. Most home ovens run high or low—often by as much as 50 degrees—which of course can ruin a recipe. Some utility companies will calibrate your oven for you or can suggest someone who will. To know whether your oven is accurate, keep an oven thermometer in the oven and place it where the manufacturer recommends. Also make sure that the thermometer, itself, is accurate.

- Remember that "to cool" means to bring something to room temperature, usually on a wire baking rack so that air can circulate on all sides. And that "to chill" means to refrigerate or set in an ice bath until uniformly cold. Caution: Never chill a hot pudding in the freezer because you not only risk thawing the frozen foods stored there but also raising the freezer's interior temperature to unsafe levels.

- Allow 20 minutes for an oven to preheat to the desired temperature and 15 minutes for a broiler. For this reason, I routinely call for preheating the oven in Step 1 of most pudding recipes.

BAKEWARE/COOKWARE

Casseroles & Baking Dishes: The sizes I consider essential for puddings: 13 x 9 x 2-inch . . . 9 x 9 x 2-inch . . . 8 x 8 x 2-inch. Also necessary: two of each of the following three casserole sizes (one deep, one shallow): 1½-quart (6-cup) . . . 2-quart (8-cup) . . . 2½-quart (10-cup). I prefer those made out of ovenproof glass (Pyrex), porcelain, or earthenware.

Cast-Iron Skillet: Every now and then a pudding recipe calls for two-part cooking—an initial stove-top sautéing, then a longer stint in the oven (see Iron Skillet Sweet Potato Pudding, page 230). The iron skillet, it goes without saying, should be well seasoned. If you have no cast-iron skillet, a heavy enameled metal one works equally well. Best size? I use my 10-inch skillet more than any other.

Custard Cups & Ramekins: Choose sturdy ones made of ovenproof glass, porcelain, or earthenware. Best sizes: 5 ounces (which holds about ⅔ cup) and 6 ounces (¾ cup). I keep a dozen ramekins on hand because one sometimes slips and breaks. But more important, these little containers are perfect for softening a packet or two of unflavored gelatin in cold water as well as for mixing small quantities of ingredients: a bit of sugar and cornstarch or flour, for example, a few ground spices. I find ramekins and custard cups endlessly useful.

Double Boiler: Thanks to new-generation ranges with precise heat control from tepid to intense,

experienced cooks have learned to cook egg mixtures over very low direct heat, stirring constantly until thickened. Beginners, however, should cook custardy mixtures (custards, hollandaise, zabaglione, etc.) over simmering water—in the top of a double boiler because the mixture never boils and thus never curdles. Our grandmothers had several sizes of double boilers, but today's cook needs only one—a middle size one with a 1½-quart (6-cup) insert or a 2-quart (8-cup) one. Buy a stainless-steel double boiler that is largely nonreactive, meaning anything acidic (intensely lemony, for example) will not end up tasting metallic. There used to be flameproof glass double boilers, in fact my mother had one. But as far as I can tell, they're no longer available. All-Clad, however, makes the next best thing: a 2-quart stainless-steel saucepan with a white porcelain insert. But it's expensive—at last look, nearly $200.

Pie Pans: I suppose I should say pie "plates" because those I recommend are made of ovenproof glass, earthenware, or porcelain. Handiest sizes: 8-inch (holds 1½ quarts or 6 cups), 9-inch (2 quarts or 8 cups), and 10-inch (2¾ quarts/11 cups if 2 inches deep, 12 cups/3 quarts if 3 inches deep). These pie plates can be substituted for shallow casseroles of matching volume.

Rimmed Baking Sheets: Ones sturdy enough to hold 8, 10, even 12 filled ramekins on trips to and from the refrigerator as well as overnight stays there.

Ring Molds (also called Savarin Molds): You'll need three sizes for the recipes in this book: 1-quart (4-cup), 1½-quart (6-cup), and 2-quart (8-cup). Choose fluted or plain (or splurge on one of each for the three sizes), preferably nonreactive molds meaning stainless steel, ovenproof glass, or ceramic. But I must admit that the tinned copper molds I bought in France have worked splendidly over the years for puddings both bland and tart.

Note: Avoid floppy molds made of silicone, ditto any molds with nonstick coatings.

Roasting Pans: Have both a medium and large pan on hand. They are just the thing when a pudding (almost always an egg-thickened one) must be baked in a water bath.

Steamed Pudding Molds: The majority of these are metal and fluted. All have central tubes and lids that snap on tight. Sizes needed: 1-quart (4-cup), 1½-quart (6-cup), and 2-quart (8-cup).

Tube or Angel Food Cake Pan: At least one of my pudding recipes calls for a 10-inch tube pan (Pudim Molotov, page 252) and it must be a one-piece pan, not one with a removable bottom because the batter is sure to leak out as the pudding bakes. Use a sturdy bright stainless-steel pan without a nonstick coating.

HELPFUL EQUIPMENT, COOK'S TOOLS & MORE

Beyond such kitchen essentials as mixing bowls, measuring cups and spoons, electric blenders, electric hand and stand mixers, you should have the following on hand.

Chef's Butane Torch: Also called a crème brûlée torch, this mini "flame thrower" has come to the home kitchen and is widely available at moderate cost in kitchen shops and online (see Sources, page 291). Far better at caramelizing the sugar atop Crème Brûlée (page 87) than an oven broiler, this torch's clean blue flame can also brown meringue toppings, though they may not reach the 160°F internal temperature the American Egg Board deems safe. For that reason, use pasteurized eggs (see Eggs, page xxv) whenever you brown meringues by butane torch.

Cherry Pitter: You'll save yourself no end of time, energy, and exasperation if you buy one of these little miracle workers. There's a huge variety of cherry pitters out there, most of them sold in kitchen shops and online with prices ranging from a few dollars up to $30 or more (see Sources, page 291).

Electric Spice Grinder: A mini food processor that's equally adept at grinding whole spices, grating small amounts of hard cheese, chopping a handful of nuts as fine as cornmeal, puréeing a bit of marmalade or "seed-y" jam, and combining a tablespoon or two of ingredients both wet and dry.

Food Mill: Pre-processor, this sturdy implement with a crank that went round and round forcing fruits and vegetables through a perforated metal plate is what our mothers and grandmothers used to make purées. It's still useful if you need to "sieve" out the seeds and skins as you do with wild persimmons. See Wild (Native) Persimmons, page xxi.

Instant-Read Thermometer: Introduced years ago as a way to determine the doneness of turkeys and large roasts, the instant-read thermometer, now more sensitive and accurate, can be used to check the internal temperature of egg-thickened puddings and sauces, even meringues (important in this age of salmonella food poisoning; only when egg mixtures have reached an internal temperature of 160°F are they safe to eat). Often as skinny as a skewer, instant-read probes may show temperatures in a graduated scale or digital readout. Fancier ones have Celsius-Fahrenheit buttons that allow you to switch from one to the other—invaluable if you're using a European cookbook. Instant-read thermometers are sold in all good kitchen shops, even in high-end groceries, and of course, online. Choose a brand you know and trust. Prices vary hugely—from about $10 up to ten times that.

Large Food Processor: By large, I mean a processor with a 12- to 14-cup work bowl, a variety of shredding and slicing disks, and a motor with plenty of process. There are wimpy machines out there—a waste of money in my opinion. Powerful, well-designed, well-made food processors are endlessly versatile. I use mine to crumb bread both soft and hard, to grate Parmigiano-Reggiano by the pound, to shred Cheddar, to blend, purée, knead, and emulsify. For a discussion of the new generation of food processors, check out my *Process This!*, which won the James Beard Award for Best Cookbook, Tools and Techniques category. In it I show how easy it is to turn your food processor into everything from a bread machine to an ice cream maker and, of course, into a pudding virtuoso.

Mandoline Slicer/Shredder: If you do much slicing and shredding, you may want to splurge and buy one of these impressive manual "machines." Don't waste money on a cheap plastic version; instead, go for a sturdy metal chef's model that will serve you well for years. Good kitchen shops sell mandolines and you will also find them online (see Sources, page 291).

Microplane: Designed as a revolutionary new carpenter's tool, this razor-sharp stainless-steel rasp is every cook's must-have. But its detour to the kitchen some twenty years ago was both sudden and unexpected, most of all to inventors Richard and Jeff Grace of Russellville, Arkansas. It seems that the owner of an Ottawa hardware store took one of their new Microplanes home to give it a try in his shop. But his wife, faced with a dull shredder and a pile of oranges to zest for a favorite cake, grabbed her husband's new Microplane and presto! The zest began flying off the oranges in perfect shreds. Word spread and before long cooks everywhere had discovered what a whiz this new kitchen gadget was. I grate citrus zest by Microplane, ditto Parmigiano-Reggiano, fresh ginger, whole nutmegs—all integral to many recipes in this book. Microplanes now come in a variety of lengths, widths, and

degrees of coarseness. Every good kitchen shop sells them—I've even seen them at my supermarket.

FRUIT PREPARATION (SORTING, WASHING, STEMMING, HULLING)

Note: If you'd like to freeze fresh fruits for off-season puddings, you'll find every detail spelled out in *Jean Anderson's Preserving Guide* (University of North Carolina Press, 2012).

Apples and Pears: Because these two fruits are so similar, structurally speaking, they can be prepared the same way. Wash well; I use mild dish soap and tepid water to rinse away any residual chemicals. Pat fruits dry on paper toweling, then quarter lengthwise and cut out cores. Last job: Peel each quarter using a swivel-bladed vegetable peeler, if indeed the recipe calls for peeling (some don't). Your apples or pears are now ready to use as recipes direct.

Berries:

- Blueberries, Cranberries, Gooseberries: Refrigerate immediately in original container—do not wash (refrigerated fresh-picked berries will keep 10 to 14 days). When ready to use, sort berries, remove stems, then wash in a large fine sieve or colander under cool running water. Pat dry on several thicknesses of paper toweling, then use as recipes direct.

- Strawberries, Blackberries, Dewberries, Raspberries: Far more fragile than blueberries or cranberries, these berries should be used as soon as possible. Just before using, remove any caps or "hulls," wash well in a large fine sieve or colander set under cool running water, then empty onto several thicknesses paper toweling and pat dry. Slice or dice strawberries as recipes direct; other berries are nearly always used whole.

Figs: Old-timers always gather figs in the cool of the morning, knowing that these fragile fruits are at their peak of flavor then. Figs require little more than a gentle wash in cool water before using. Each recipe will tell what else is required.

Mangoes: Such delicious fruits but difficult to prepare because their long flat seeds are almost impossible to remove. One old hand taught me that once a mango is washed and dried, it should be stood on its side on a cutting board. Next, he said, "Insert a sharp paring knife into the mango just to one side of center. You should hit the seed. Next draw your knife straight down following the line of the seed until you've cut clear through the mango, then remove that half of the fruit." The giant seed will be exposed, stuck to the remaining mango half. Just repeat the process and lift out the seed. Also cut off any bits off fruit clinging to it and discard the seed. Peeling a mango is only slightly easier, in fact it's rather like skinning a fish. Place mango half, skin side down, on cutting board, slide knife along the skin the length of the mango. Discard skin, then repeat with remaining mango half. Now the fruit can be sliced or diced as recipe directs.

Rhubarb: Of course, rhubarb is a vegetable, not a fruit, but when its scarlet stalks are trimmed of all leaves (necessary because of their high oxalic acid content), sliced, and sugared, it's a crisp and cobbler favorite. Preparation couldn't be simpler. Once all leaves have been removed, trim coarse ends from stalks and discard, then gently wash rhubarb in cool water and pat dry. From this point on, follow recipe directions.

Stone Fruits: So-called because their pits are as hard as stones.

- Apricots, Nectarines, Peaches: Wash in cool water, then blanch for 20 to 30 seconds in boiling water. Remove from water and slip off skins. Halve fruits, lift out and discard pits.

  Tip: When buying peaches, look for freestone varieties, meaning their pits will slip right out. Not so, cling-stone peaches. Once these fruits have been blanched and pitted, they're ready to use as individual recipes direct, which invariably includes mixing the sliced or diced fruits with a little lemon or other citrus juice to keep them from turning brown (oxidizing).

- Cherries: Sort berries and stem, then wash in a large fine sieve or colander under cool running water. Pat dry on several thicknesses of paper toweling, then using cherry pitter, pop out the seeds. Proceed as recipes direct.

Wild (Native) Persimmons: Only the persimmon pulp is used and the 'simmons must be ripe—soft and orange with a "haze" of purple. Remove stems and caps, then slosh persimmons up and down in a sink of cold water. Next, using a slotted spoon, scoop persimmons onto several thicknesses of paper toweling, cover with more toweling, and pat dry. Now force persimmons through a food mill, leaving the skins and seeds behind. Spoon the persimmon pulp into a refrigerator container, cover tight, and use within several days to make Wild Persimmon Pudding (page 225). Or, if you prefer, freeze the pulp.

- How to Freeze Persimmon Pulp: To prevent discoloring, mix ⅛ teaspoon powdered ascorbic acid (vitamin C) into each 1 quart persimmon pulp. Pack in 1-pint freezer containers leaving ½-inch head room at top. Snap on lids, date, label, and set in freezer. Storage Time: One year.

OTHER INGREDIENTS

I concentrate here on the more unusual ingredients as well as familiar ones that need clarification or explanation. You'll also find useful information in the recipe headnotes.

Almond Extract: See Extracts/Flavorings.

Almond Meal (also called Natural Almond Flour): Ground from either whole blanched or unblanched almonds, almond meal not only brims with mono-unsaturated fats and vitamin E but also contains a modicum of protein, calcium, and iron. Unlike wheat flour, almond meal is low in carbohydrates, blessed with delicate nut flavor, and gluten-free. It's a little coarser than regular almond flour (always ground from blanched almonds), and it can be substituted for some of the wheat flour in certain puddings (see Steamed Orange Pudding, page 201). It is also integral to Gluten-Free Streusel Topping (page 266). Most health food stores sell almond meal; so, too, many high-end groceries. It can also be ordered online (see Sources, page 291).

Almond Milk: A staple among vegans, this ivory-hued beverage made from finely ground blanched almonds has recently become more popular than soy milk. Brimming with minerals but less protein-rich than cow's milk, almond milk can be substituted for cow's milk in a few creamy puddings (see Rice à l'Impératrice, page 96). You can buy sweetened or unsweetened almond milk as well as vanilla, chocolate, and plain. My choice: Plain almond milk—unsweetened.

Amaretti: Almond macaroons are as crisp as meringue cookies and a good substitute for them (see Eton Mess, page 251). Amaretti are made by several companies, but the best known come from Lazzaroni, a venerable Italian firm that still prepares them according to the original 1718 recipe. Look for amaretti in specialty food shops, in high-end groceries, or order online (see Sources, page 291). Lazzaroni amaretti are packed in scarlet tins so decorative I use them as colorful accents in my kitchen.

Beef Suet: This delicate, brittle fat encasing the kidneys of beef cows is what gives steamed puddings their voluptuousness. So where can you buy suet? A local butcher who doesn't depend on cuts prepackaged halfway across the country is your best source. Can other fats be used in place of suet? Butter? Lard? Vegetable shortening? Only if the recipe gives you that option. In such classics as Christmas Pudding (page 198) and Colonial Suet Pudding (page 194), however, suet is the only fat to use.

Black Walnuts: Native to America, this member of the hickory family grows wild across much of the North, South, and Midwest and rains fleshy fruits down upon the ground every autumn. But it's the meaty nuts inside that cooks prize because of their unique flavor: sweet, mellow, and, I might add, slightly musky. Black walnuts taste nothing like their better known cousins, English walnuts. Because extracting the nuts from their rock-hard shells is hellish, buy ready-to-use black walnut nutmeats (see Sources, page 291).

Bread: Breads have always been a frugal way to "plump up" puddings just as they have been for meatloaves. In fact, bread is so integral to puddings I devote most of a chapter to them. The best bread to use is firm-textured bread (also called "home-style") and that goes for white bread, whole-wheat bread, and even raisin bread, though richer puddings may call for richer bread—brioche, for example, or challah (see Maple Bread Pudding, page 184). Some recipes specify bread crumbs, others bread cubes (see Handy Table of Equivalents, page xxxiii), and still others whole slices of bread (see Summer Pudding, page 172).

Butter: Recipes in this book call for unsalted, old-fashioned stick butter. Do not substitute salted butter (unless you also reduce the amount of salt in the recipe); do not substitute soft butter, faux butter, or margarine unless those options are given. Apart from the differences in flavor, each fat behaves differently when used as a shortening for baked goods.

Tip: Several of my puddings call for melted butter. The microwave, I find, is the quickest, surest way to do the job. Using the tablespoon demarcations on a stick of butter wrapper, I slice off what I need, drop into a spouted 1-quart ovenproof glass measuring cup, and microwave uncovered on DEFROST. It takes about 5 minutes to melt ¼ cup (½ stick) butter in my 650-watt oven. You'll soon learn what works best for you.

Buttermilk: Once a by-product of butter churning, today's commercial buttermilk is "cultured," meaning fermented with bacterial cultures that convert the lactose (milk sugar) into lactic acid. That's what gives buttermilk its tang and makes it a welcome addition to many puddings. Although my Georgia colleague Rebecca Lang tells me that her Publix supermarket now sells full-fat buttermilk (the Marburger Farm Dairy brand), I've never seen it. Around here and, I suspect, in most of the country,

you have two choices: low-fat (regular) buttermilk or fat-free. For pudding recipes, regular is my preference.

Butterscotch Extract: See Extracts/Flavorings.

Candied Fruits: Say "Christmas," and fruitcakes spring to mind, some dark, some light, each strewn with mixed candied or glacéed fruits—citron, orange and lemon rind, red and green cherries. Candied fruits are also integral to a number of puddings (see Christmas Pudding, page 198). Fortunately, these are winter desserts to be made when candied fruits are readily available. Still, much to my surprise, candied fruits can be ordered online—off-season (see Sources, page 291).

Cardamom: My first encounter with cardamom took place in Sweden where so many breads and pastries are scented with it, my second in India where cardamom is integral to certain curries, and my third in Jordan where the oversize spouts of copper coffee pots are stuffed with green cardamom pods (and yes, cardamom-infused coffee is delicious). For some reason, however, cardamom is unappreciated here. Time to change that. When ground, the little black seeds inside the chickpea-size cardamom pods are deeply aromatic—a bit minty, a bit smoky, a bit citrusy. Several of my puddings call for cardamom and I think you'll like them: See "Dutch Baby," page 23, and Kheer (Indian Rice Pudding), page 95.

Cheese: Cheese in a pudding? Absolutely. Even a small amount of Cheddar, Monterey Jack, or Parmigiano-Reggiano—especially Parmigiano-Reggiano—can point up the flavor and add a note of mystery. And ricotta can form the foundation of supremely creamy fillings. See also Ricotta and Quark, pages xxx–xxxi.

- When it comes to grating hard and semi-hard cheeses, I always do the job myself, because packaged grated cheeses never seem to melt smoothly and also lack flavor. For shredding small amounts of Cheddar, a coarse-toothed Microplane will do, but if more is needed, I use the food processor shredding disk.

- How to Grate Parmigiano-Reggiano: Buy it by the pound, cut into 1-inch chunks, then drop into a food processor fitted with the metal chopping blade. Alternately pulse and churn until as fine as you like; it takes only 30 seconds or so. Scoop into a 1-pint or 1-quart preserving jar, screw the lid down tight, and store in the refrigerator; the cheese will taste freshly grated for several weeks.

  Tip: If Italian Parmigiano-Reggiano is beyond your budget, substitute a Wisconsin Parmesan or an Argentine one. Both are good.

Citrus Juices: Whenever a pudding calls for orange, lemon, or other citrus juice, only freshly squeezed will do because only it has fresh fruit flavor. For small amounts (a tablespoon or two), I use a wooden reamer. For larger amounts, my little electric juicer. I place a 1-cup glass measuring cup underneath the spout to catch the juice and instantly know when I have the amount that I need.

- Citrus Zest: Nothing boosts fresh orange or lemon flavor like a bit of finely grated zest (colored part of the rind). Puddings rarely call for more than a teaspoon or two and if you use a fine-toothed Microplane, the grating's done in seconds.

Clementines: A variety of Mandarin orange, in fact the smallest and sweetest of them, clementines are virtually seedless. Indigenous to Asia, they have only recently made an impact here. They come to market in early fall and are available right through Christmas. A cinch to peel and section, clementines make attractive, edible garnishes (see Sweet Potato Panna Cotta with Clementines in Lemongrass Syrup, page 119). I also think they would make a dandy substitute for oranges in Syllabub (page 157).

Coconut: Unlike coconut cakes that require gobs of grated coconut, puddings need so little there's no need to wrestle with a fresh coconut. So I simply grab a packet of frozen flaked or grated coconut or one from the baking aisle of my supermarket. Grated and flaked coconut are available both sweetened and unsweetened—my choice is unsweetened.

- Coconut Milk: Now that nearly every supermarket sells canned coconut milk—sweetened, unsweetened, full-fat, low-fat, and fat-free—I've been improvising with it and discovered that it's superb in certain puddings (see Coconut Custards, page 75).

  Note: One 13.5- or 13.66-ounce can coconut milk = about 1⅔ cups.

Coffee, Instant Espresso: Nothing, I find, deepens the flavor of chocolate like a tablespoon or so of instant espresso powder. And nothing is faster when it comes to turning chocolate into mocha—a robust mix of coffee and chocolate (see the Mocha Pots de Crème variation to Chocolate Pots de Crème, page 99).

Cornmeal: There'd be no Indian Pudding (page 210) without cornmeal, but I also use it to perk up cobblers (see Red, White, and Blue Berry–Corn Bread Cobbler, page 11). Indian Pudding calls for the supermarket staple, big-brand granular yellow cornmeal, but my cobbler uses the more flavorful stone-ground, which contains both the husk and germ. Ubiquitous across the South, stone-ground cornmeal is difficult to find north of the Mason-Dixon and west of the Mississippi. Fortunately, it's sold online (see Sources, page 291). Unfortunately, it has a short shelf life, so should be stored in an airtight container in the refrigerator or freezer.

Cornstarch: Gluten-free, cornstarch has twice the thickening power of flour but it's tricky. Like flour, it's usually mixed with a liquid (often milk or cream) in a saucepan, set over direct heat, then stirred constantly until the mixture begins to thicken. After 3 minutes, the cornstarch mixture will have thickened fully and turned translucent. Remove from the heat at once—you've reached the point of no return. Further cooking will break the cornstarch down and the mixture will thin out. Often dramatically.

Cream: There's a reason satiny puddings are called *creams*. But which cream is the right cream? I list them here in ascending order of richness, beginning with half-and-half, which has the lowest butterfat content.

Note: The lower its butterfat content, the faster a cream will curdle when overheated, so pay attention and take care.

- Half-and-Half: A 50/50 blend of whole milk and cream that's 10 to 12 percent butterfat. I use half-and-half to enrich custards and creams without sending the calorie count sky-high.

- Light Cream: Though light cream's butterfat content varies somewhat from brand to brand, the average is about 20 percent.

- Whipping Cream: You'll get softer, more billowing peaks from whipping cream than from heavy cream because its butterfat content is slightly lower (30 to 36 percent). But make a note, whipped whipping cream deflates faster on standing than stiffly whipped heavy cream.

   Note: Though whipping cream's butterfat content is somewhat lower than that of heavy cream, the two can be used interchangeably.

- Heavy Cream: With 36 to 40 percent butterfat, heavy cream whips to Alpine peaks that are slow to deflate, especially when beaten with a little confectioners' (10X) sugar.

   Note: Ultra-pasteurized heavy cream takes somewhat longer to whip.

Dulce de Leche: See Sweetened Condensed Milk under Milk.

Eggs: Use LARGE eggs unless recipes specify otherwise. Many old pudding recipes call for raw eggs or ones not cooked long enough to reach the 160°F internal temperature deemed necessary to avoid the risk of salmonella food poisoning by both the American Egg Board and the U.S. Department of Agriculture. Always test the doneness of egg-thickened puddings by inserting an instant-read thermometer midway between the rim of the baking dish and the center. On the other hand, if a pudding calls for raw eggs or egg whites, use pasteurized eggs or eggs from a local source you trust.

- Pasteurized Eggs: Now increasingly available (Davidson is the brand my supermarket carries), pasteurized eggs can be used in place of raw eggs in any recipe. Their whites are slightly cloudy and take longer to whip to stiff peaks than raw egg whites. Otherwise, I see no difference between pasteurized and unpasteurized eggs. Whenever I think it wise to use pasteurized eggs in a particular recipe, I say so.

- Meringues: Here's the American Egg Board's recommendation for browning a three-egg meringue: Make sure the filling is hot before swirling a meringue on top of a pudding or pie. Slide onto the middle oven shelf of a preheated 350°F oven and bake for 15 minutes or until an instant-read thermometer reaches 160°F. It should be inserted horizontally into the center of the meringue just as you would do when testing the doneness of a burger.

Evaporated Milk: See Milk.

Extracts/Flavorings: When buying any extract or flavoring, look for "pure" on the label. Those marked "artificial" are exactly that and so "perfume-y" they can never approximate the true flavor of almond, butterscotch, coconut, hazelnut, maple, orange, rose water, rum, vanilla, etc. In my opinion, they're more likely to obscure it than enhance it. The rarer extracts — butterscotch and coconut, to name two — can be ordered online (see Sources, page 291).

- Hazelnut Extract: Not an extract many groceries carry, even many specialty food shops. Fortunately it can be ordered online (see Sources, page 291). Also see Extracts/ Flavorings discussed above.

  Note: Though I've made pure hazel-nut extract an optional ingredient in my Chocolate-Hazelnut Panna Cotta (page 105), it boosts the hazelnut flavor of the pudding so I, myself, always add it.

- Rose Water: Back in the Middle Ages, Muslims learned to capture the flavor of roses by steaming their petals, then allowing the vapor to condense into water. To this day rose water is widely used throughout India and the Middle East to flavor a variety of dishes and Kheer (Indian Rice Pudding, page 95) is one of the best. Unlike alcohol-based extracts, rose water contains no alcohol or spirits of any kind. High-end groceries and specialty food shops usually carry rose water and it can also be ordered online (see Sources, page 291).

- Vanilla Beans: Vanilla was utterly unknown in the Old World until Spanish Conquistadors saw the Aztecs flavoring their hot chocolate (another unknown) with this skinny black bean. It's the fruit of a Mexican orchid, but in truth, it's not the bean that exudes that heavenly vanilla flavor as much as the tiny black seeds inside it. Cortez carried vanilla beans and cacao (chocolate) back to Spain in the 1520s and until the mid-nineteenth century, all vanilla came from Mexico and Central America. Today, even though Madagascar and the East Indies grow significant amounts of vanilla, it remains one of earth's priciest flavorings, second only to saffron. But to chefs and devout hobby cooks, vanilla beans are worth a splurge because vanilla extract, no matter how pure, can never duplicate their flavor. High-end groceries routinely carry vanilla beans as do online suppliers (see Sources, page 291).

Flour:

- All-Purpose Flour: A good balance of soft and hard wheat, bleached all-purpose flour is my preference for cakes, puddings, and pastries — *not* self-rising, and *not* "pre-sifted" because flour compacts in transit and storage. Spoon sifted flour lightly into a dry-cup measure (these are the nested cups in 1-cup, ½-cup, ⅓-cup, and ¼-cup sizes), then level off the top with the edge of a small, thin-blade spatula.

Note: Like the big gasoline companies that vary their blends now and then, so, too, do some of the "big brand" millers (usually tipping the ratio of hard and soft wheat in favor of the protein-and-gluten-rich hard wheat). So, before you buy all-purpose flour, check the ingredient list. If the flour contains more than 2 grams of protein per ¼ cup, its higher ratio of hard wheat won't deliver the feathery cakes or flaky biscuits and pastries you expect. Luckily, there's an easy fix: Use a 50/50 mix of all-purpose flour and cake flour (with only 7 percent protein, Swans Down is my choice). Sift the two flours together several times to combine, transfer to your flour canister, and sift again *before* measuring. I now use this softer 50/50 blend (about 8.5 percent protein) for cake- and pastry-like puddings and so far, it's been perfect.

- Almond Flour: See Almond Meal.

- Soy Flour: Ground from toasted soybeans, this fine-textured flour is gluten-free but protein- and mineral-rich. The "natural" or full-fat soy flour can be used in place of some of the all-purpose flour in a variety of pudding toppings (see Gluten-Free Streusel Topping, page 266). Most high-end groceries and even a few supermarkets sell soy flour. And of course it can be ordered online (see Sources, page 291). Sift or not as recipes direct.

- Whole-Wheat Flour: Do not sift. Few people associate this protein-, vitamin-, mineral-, and fiber-rich flour with puddings. But why

not boost the texture, flavor, and nutritive value of a crisp or cobbler with a whole-wheat topping? (See Roasted Rhubarb Cobbler with Whole-Wheat Topping, page 58.) And why not use whole-wheat bread in a bread pudding? (See Bread-and-Butter Blackberry Pudding, page 174.) You should have no problem finding whole-wheat flour at upscale supermarkets and specialty groceries. But if you do, you can always order whole-wheat flour online (see Sources, page 291).

Gelatin: Each little envelope of plain (unflavored) gelatin weighs 0.25 ounces. But because we sometimes measure gelatin by the teaspoon, I measured the contents of one envelope. It contains between 2¼ and 2½ level teaspoons gelatin, enough to set up (congeal) 2 cups of liquid. Also see Handy Table of Equivalents (page xxxiii).

Ginger: Whenever possible, I use finely grated fresh ginger to flavor cakes, cookies, and puddings because ground ginger cannot duplicate, or even approximate, the lemony-spicy taste of the fresh. The implement to use for grating: a fine-toothed Microplane.

Gluten-Free Flours & Meals: What, exactly, is gluten? The protein in wheat, barley, and rye flours, so these three are off-limits to those with gluten-intolerance or celiac disease. Not so for gluten-free Almond Meal (page xxii) and Soy Flour (left, under Flour).

Note: Though rolled oats (AKA oatmeal) are naturally gluten-free, they may be contaminated in the milling process by residual bits of wheat, barley, or rye flour ground in the same mill. Only oat products labeled "pure" and/or "uncontaminated" are truly gluten-free. See Sources, page 291.

Helpful Equipment, Cook's Tools & More

Note: Rice flour is also gluten-free, but because it is now known to contain varying amounts of arsenic, I have used no rice flour in any of my recipes.

Hazelnuts: Also called filberts, these brown-skinned nuts the size of chickpeas are delicious in certain puddings (see Grandma Anna Weigl's Rum Pudding with Fruits and Nuts, page 136). But if their flavor is to develop, the hazelnuts must be toasted.

- How to Toast Hazelnuts: Spread shelled nuts on an ungreased rimmed baking sheet, set on the middle shelf of a preheated 350°F oven, and toast until the skins blister and nuts smell irresistible — 10 to 12 minutes. Bundle the hot nuts in a clean, dry dish towel and rub vigorously. Most of the skins will slake off. Any that don't will add color and texture.

Hickory Nuts: Hickories are New World nuts, first cousins to pecans, and the two can be used interchangeably in recipes, though I find hickories a little stronger as befits nuts from a tree that grows wild over the eastern half of this country. Unlike pecans, hickory nuts are hard-shelled and extracting their meat is exhausting. Fortunately, shelled hickory nuts can be ordered online (see Sources, page 291).

Honey: I find some honeys too dark and too strong for puddings, so always choose a light, well-balanced one. There's no need to splurge on such trendy honeys as Tupelo; any good commercial blend works well — though I, myself, use Appalachia's golden sourwood if I'm lucky enough to have some on hand.

Tip: Honey will slide out of your measuring cups or spoons more easily if they've been spritzed with nonstick cooking spray.

Ladyfingers: Whatever happened to ladyfingers, those little finger-shaped sponge cakes every grocery used to sell? My mother lined her charlotte molds with ladyfingers and used them in other puddings, too. Lately, however, they've become a rarity. Fortunately, crisp Italian ladyfingers are taking up the slack and can be used in place of the soft American variety. Many supermarkets now sell Italian ladyfingers, but if not, they can be ordered online. So, too, I just discovered, can old-timey soft ladyfingers (see Sources, page 291).

Tip: You can substitute store-bought sponge cake as well as thawed frozen pound cake for soft ladyfingers in any recipe. All you have to do is cut them into "fingers."

Lemon Geranium: Must sprigs of mint garnish every dessert? I find lemon geranium's lacy leaf a more attractive, more aromatic alternative. Best of all, lemon geranium couldn't be easier to grow. I keep a pot of it in my south-facing kitchen window. Top sources: Your farmers' market or a local nursery that specializes in herbs.

Lemongrass: The key ingredient in citronella, the bug repellant our mothers used to "shoo" bees, flies, and mosquitoes, lemongrass, at first the darling of chefs, is now so routine that my supermarket sells it. I find its grassy-lemony flavor particularly suited to creamy puddings (see Sweet Potato Panna Cotta with Clementines in Lemongrass Syrup; page 119). Only the fleshy inner white stalks are used. Usually they're pounded or minced, then boiled into an infusion that's strained, leaving the lemongrass solids behind.

Tip: For maximum flavor, buy lemongrass that is absolutely fresh. The tops should be green and the stalks moist with no trace of drying or browning.

Lemon Verbena: Another exquisitely lemony herb. Integral to herbal teas, lemon verbena—or lemon beebrush, as it's also called—is used to season an impressive variety of savories as well as a world of sweets. To my mind, however, there's no better culinary marriage than lemon verbena with a custard or cream (see Lemon Verbena Panna Cotta, page 123). Finally, lemon verbena is a more appealing dessert garnish than mint. Best source? The same as for Lemon Geranium (opposite page).

Liquor/Liqueur: Puddings often contain whiskey—usually bourbon, brandy, or rum—to add oomph and flavor (see Feliciana Parish Sweet Potato Crème Caramel, page 100). Soufflés and fluffy creams, even berries, may call for a bit of Grand Marnier or other orange liqueur to improve the flavor (see Sara's Snow Pudding, page 158).

Maple Syrup/Sugar: For cooking, the maple syrup to use is extra-dark grade B because only its deep maple flavor is strong enough to "shine through." Grade B is by no means inferior, just more assertive than the golden grade A maple syrup we spoon over waffles and pancakes. Granulated maple sugar is another way to inject maple flavor into puddings and dessert sauces. Both it and grade B maple syrup are available online (see Sources, page 291).

Meringue Cookies/Nests: Like ladyfingers, packages of crisp meringue cookies are disappearing, and that's a shame because they're essential to a number of puddings (see Eton Mess, page 251). I have substituted the more readably available Italian amaretti with good results (see Amaretti). Still, plain old-fashioned meringue cookies—the supercrisp ones that many supermarkets sell—work best in my opinion. You can also use commercially baked meringue nests, which to my surprise can be ordered online, as can meringue cookies and amaretti (see Sources, page 291).

Milk (Canned): People are forever confusing these two types of canned milk, so let me clarify things once and for all:

- Evaporated Milk: Fresh milk that's had about 60 percent of the water removed. It's unsweetened, pasteurized, and a must for every pantry. Originally only full-fat evaporated milk was available, but now there are low-fat and fat-free options. I like the faintly caramel flavor of evaporated milk and the way it enriches puddings, so I use it often, each time specifying which type of evaporated milk to use—full-fat, low-fat, or fat-free.

- Sweetened Condensed Milk: The foundation of key lime pie and dulce de leche, this intensely sweet canned milk is as thick as library paste—well almost. It was created more than 150 years ago by Gail Borden, Jr., who, dismayed by the number of children being killed by the spoiled milk they drank, vowed to develop a safe non-perishable milk. By 1858, his Eagle Brand sweetened condensed milk was known for its "purity, durability, and economy." At first, only full-fat sweetened condensed milk was available, but today there are low-fat and fat-free versions. I use the original for Dulce de Leche Pots de Crème (page 107), and in that recipe also show how to make your own dulce de leche, nothing more than caramelized sweetened condensed milk. You can also buy dulce de leche online (see Sources, page 291).

Note: Also see Almond Milk and Coconut Milk, discussed earlier in this list of ingredients.

Helpful Equipment, Cook's Tools & More

Molasses: Several of my puddings call for molasses and the best one to use is medium-brown, unsulfured, and the consistency of corn syrup. I keep a popular brand in my pantry and it has served me well. Under no circumstances substitute blackstrap molasses. It's too sludgy, too dark, too intensely flavored for any pudding.

Tip: Molasses will slide out of a measuring cup or spoon more easily if it's been spritzed with non-stick cooking spray.

Nutmeg: Once you've tasted the exquisite lemony-ness of freshly grated nutmeg, there's no going back to the sometimes bitter commercially ground. Our grandmothers always grated whatever nutmeg they needed, but their little grinders weren't the handiest gadgets. How they would have loved today's Microplanes.

Parmigiano-Reggiano: See Cheese.

Pecans: The all-American nut, all-American on two counts. Pecans are indigenous to this country and they are the nuts we Americans use the most in cooking. Delicious raw, pecans are even better if lightly toasted because a brief spell in the oven accentuates their flavor.

- How to Toast Pecans: Spread shelled pecan halves on an ungreased rimmed baking sheet, slide onto the middle shelf of a preheated 350°F oven, and toast until a pecan aroma begins to fill the air—6 to 8 minutes. Cool the nuts until easy to handle, then chop, or not, as individual recipes direct.

Pistachios: Not a nut we usually associate with puddings and yet Kheer (Indian Rice Pudding, page 95), wouldn't be Kheer without them.

Pistachios are easy enough to shell—just push the two halves apart and pop out the nuts. But blanching? That's something else again. Moreover, blanched pistachios tend to be soggy. My solution is to buy shelled, blanched pistachios (see Sources, page 291).

Quark: A creamy, fresh, unripened cheese popular in Germany that's gaining favor here (I recently saw it in Walmart's Wellness Center; I also discovered that there are online sources for it, among them amazon.com; see Sources, page 291). Quark resembles fine-curd ricotta, which can be substituted for it though quark is a bit tarter, a bit saltier. You can easily buzz up your own version of it.

- How to Make Quark: Empty 1 (15-ounce) carton small-curd, full-fat ricotta cheese into food processor work bowl or electric blender, add 2 tablespoons sour cream, and alternately pulse and churn until consistency of whipped cream cheese—10 seconds should do it. If the mixture seems a little thick, add another tablespoon sour cream and buzz until smooth. Makes about 2 cups. Scoop into 2-cup container, cover, and store in refrigerator; use within three to five days. Use in any recipe that calls for quark.

Rice: Most rice puddings are judged by their creaminess, and the best way I know to achieve that is to use long-grain (Carolina) rice. Kheer (Indian Rice Pudding, page 95) is also made with long-grain rice, but a more delicate variety of slender grain called basmati (most supermarkets sell it). Basmati is indigenous to the north of India and its Sanskrit name means "fragrant."

Note: I would be remiss if I did not add a cautionary note about the arsenic now known to be present in rice. There are two types of arsenic that occur naturally in the soil and water in which rice is grown—inorganic arsenic (the more toxic and carcinogenic) and the less toxic organic arsenic (which, by the way, has nothing to do with whether the rice is organically grown or not). Ongoing scientific analyses have shown that rice grown in Texas, Louisiana, and Arkansas tends to contain the most inorganic arsenic; Californian, Indian, and Pakistani rice, particularly basmati, contain the least. Still, most nutritionists would agree, there's no harm in enjoying an occasional rice pudding. To learn more about the arsenic in rice, visit consumer-reports.org.

Ricotta: You might call ricotta "the Italian cottage cheese," but that doesn't do justice to this creamy fresh (un-aged) cheese. Its flavor is faintly sweet, lightly salty, and far mellower than any cottage cheese. In Italy, ricotta can be made of goat's milk, cow's milk, or water buffalo milk, the most highly prized of all. Domestic ricottas, on the other hand, are invariably made of cow's milk. They are finer-textured than cottage cheese, even creamier than cream-style cottage cheese. Today, several brands of ricotta are sold in nearly every supermarket and each of these in full-fat, low-fat, and fat-free versions. In Italy, ricotta forms the foundation of a vast repertoire of classic recipes, and this includes desserts. Try the Ricotta Pudding with Dark Sweet Red Cherries (page 244)—not an Italian classic but a creation of my own.

Rose Water: See Extracts/Flavorings.

Salt: I use un-iodized table salt because kosher and other coarse salts do not dissolve as quickly or completely as table salt, particularly in custards and creams where smoothness is the mark of perfection.

Why un-iodized salt? Because the iodized tastes faintly of iodine.

Soy Flour: See Flour.

Sugar: Always use a dry-cup measure when measuring sugars, meaning one designed for dry ingredients. These come in little nests of four (¼ cup, ⅓ cup, ½ cup, 1 cup), may be metal or plastic, and have no pouring spouts.

- Brown Sugar: There are two types of brown sugar: light brown and dark brown. I prefer light brown sugar; the dark, in my opinion, is too "molasses-y" for most puddings. To measure brown sugar, spoon into a dry-cup measure, packing as you go, then level off the top with the broad side of a small thin-blade spatula, exerting light pressure.

- Confectioners' (10X) Sugar: Also sometimes called powdered sugar, this is the one to use for glazes, heavy cream to be whipped, and of course, for dusting all manner of baked goods. Sift or not as individual recipes direct, then spoon lightly into a dry-cup measure and level off the top with the edge of a small thin-blade spatula.

  Note: Confectioners' sugar contains an anti-caking agent, usually cornstarch or tapioca, both gluten-free. A few, however, may contain wheat flour, so if gluten intolerance is an issue, scrutinize the ingredient list.

- Granulated Sugar: Essential to almost every pudding. If it and it alone is used in a recipe, *granulated* is not specified. However, if a recipe calls for more than one kind of sugar, each one is identified. To measure, spoon sugar into a dry-cup measure and level off top with the edge of a small thin-blade spatula.

Helpful Equipment, Cook's Tools & More

- Maple Sugar: See Maple Syrup/Sugar.

- Raw Sugar: I think of this as granulated light brown sugar because it has the same faint caramel flavor and is handier to use than heavier, stickier brown sugar. Measure just as you would granulated sugar (page xxxi).

Tapioca: Tapioca is a gluten-free starch extracted from the roots of cassava, a plant native to South America. Back when my mother made tapioca pudding (page 89), she'd buy a box of small- or medium-pearl tapioca, little white pellets that had to be softened in cold water before they could be cooked and that, to an eager little girl, took *forever*. Today every supermarket sells quick-cooking tapioca. No soaking needed.

Vanilla Beans: See Extracts/Flavorings.

Walnuts: Next to pecans, these are the nuts I use most. Unlike pecans, walnuts are better raw than toasted because oven heat seems to bring out their incipient bitterness. However, you'll find that they're lightly roasted for Noodle Pudding (page 191) and no harm done. Also see Black Walnuts.

Wild Persimmons: Native persimmons, as botanists and horticulturists prefer to call them, are Ping-Pong ball–size fruits that begin dropping to the ground in early autumn—"after first frost," old timers say. And woes to anyone who bites into one before it's ripe. I did that long ago and felt my mouth turning inside-out. But when soft, orange, and hazed with purple, wild persimmons have lost their "pucker power" and are sweeter than a ripe peach. Unfortunately, with housing developments overtaking field and forest, persimmon trees are being axed at a rate so alarming that lovers of wild persimmons have begun keeping their sources

secret—though raccoons and white-tailed deer have no trouble finding them. Fortunately, you can buy frozen wild persimmon purée online (see Sources, page 291), but only in season. You may be happier looking for canned or frozen wild persimmon purée at your local farmers' market—or even baskets of wild persimmons. For directions on how to purée and freeze wild persimmons, see Wild (Native) Persimmons under FRUIT PREPARATION (page xx). And for one of my favorite recipes, see Wild Persimmon Pudding (page 225).

Wines: It's not unusual for puddings to be spiked with a fortified sweet wine like port or Madeira. But a few puddings contain table wine instead (see Rote Grütze [Red Berry Pudding], page 246).

NOTE: These equivalents can only be approximate at best, still they will suggest what to buy for a particular recipe. Amounts given for sliced and diced fruits are for those that have been peeled and pitted or cored.

HANDY TABLE OF EQUIVALENTS

	VOLUME	WEIGHT	NUMBER
FRESH FRUITS			
Apples/Pears	2 cups sliced, or 2½ cups diced	1 pound	2 large or 3 medium
Blackberries/Blueberries	3½ cups whole berries	1 pound	
Cherries	1¾–2 cups, pitted	1 pound	
Lemons, 1 medium	2 tablespoons juice, 1 teaspoon grated zest	1 pound	3–4 medium
Oranges, 1 medium	⅓–½ cup juice, 1 tablespoon grated zest	1 pound	3 medium or 2 large
Peaches, 2 medium	1 cup sliced, or ⅞ cup diced	1 pound	4 medium or 3 large
Strawberries	2⅔ cups sliced, or 2½ cups diced	1 pound	3 cups whole berries
GELATIN			
Plain (unflavored)	2¼–2½ level teaspoons	0.25 ounces	1 envelope
	3⅓–3¾ level teaspoons	0.375 ounces	1½ envelopes
	1½–1⅔ level tablespoons	0.5 ounces	2 envelopes
SHELLED NUTS			
ALMONDS			
Blanched, whole	3½–4 cups	1 pound	
Chopped	3–3½ cups	1 pound	
Sliced	5–5¼ cups	1 pound	
Slivered	4 cups	1 pound	
HAZELNUTS			
Skinned, whole	3–3⅓ cups	1 pound	
Chopped	2⅔–3 cups	1 pound	
PECANS/WALNUTS/BLACK WALNUTS			
Halves	4–4½ cups	1 pound	
Chopped	3½–4 cups	1 pound	
BREADS/CRACKERS/COOKIES			
Bread (home-style white), 1 slice	½ cup crumbs, or ⅓ cup ½-inch cubes	1 pound loaf	16 slices
Graham Crackers (2.5-inch squares), 13–14	1 cup crumbs	14.25-ounce box	104 crackers
Vanilla Wafers, 28	1 cup crumbs	11-ounce box	88 cookies
CHEDDAR, MONTEREY JACK, AND OTHER SEMI-HARD CHEESES			
	½ cup, shredded	2 ounces	
	1 cup, shredded	4 ounces/¼ pound	
	2 cups, shredded	8 ounces/½ pound	
	3 cups, shredded	12 ounces/¾ pound	
	4 cups, shredded	16 ounces/1 pound	
PARMIGIANO-REGGIANO AND OTHER HARD CHEESES			
	4 cups, processor-grated	16 ounces/1 pound	

Crisps

&

Cobblers

So Easy Blueberry-Pecan Crunch

Makes 12 Servings

I bumped into this unusual pudding eons ago at a Home Demonstration picnic—one of the many held every August in Iredell County, NC, where I worked right after college. This was also my first encounter with natural-born cooks, country women all, and I will always be grateful for the many things they taught me. But what I didn't realize until recently was that what made the recipe so easy was the fact that it began with a yellow cake mix. I've substituted a homemade biscuit mix (handy to have on hand—an instant topping that's perfect for a variety of crisps and crunches). If you're in a tearing hurry, use a commercial biscuit mix but, in my opinion, your crunch won't be as good.

1. Preheat oven to 350°F. Lightly spritz 13 x 9 x 2-inch baking dish with nonstick cooking spray.

2. Toss blueberries with orange zest, spread over bottom of baking dish, and drizzle with orange juice. Sprinkle dry biscuit mix–sugar mixture evenly on top, then drizzle melted butter evenly over pudding and scatter with pecans.

3. Slide onto middle oven shelf and bake until lightly browned—45 to 50 minutes.

4. Serve at once—as is—or, if you prefer, with drifts of whipped cream or scoops of vanilla ice cream. Good, too, with Mock Devonshire Cream (page 273) or Crème Fraîche (page 274).

1½ quarts (6 cups) fresh or solidly frozen blueberries

1 teaspoon finely grated orange zest

½ cup fresh orange juice

2⅔ cups Homemade Biscuit Mix (page 262) or commercial biscuit mix, either one combined with ¾ cup sugar

¾ cup (1½ sticks) unsalted butter, melted

1 cup moderately coarsely chopped pecans

OPTIONAL TOPPING:

1 cup heavy cream, whipped to soft peaks, or 1 pint vanilla ice cream

Down East Blueberry Buckle

Makes 8 to 10 Servings

You might call this a three-layer cobbler — yellow cake on the bottom, blueberries in the middle, then a crunchy topping aromatic of cinnamon and freshly grated nutmeg. Fresh blueberries make the best buckle, but off-season you can make a perfectly good one with frozen blueberries as long as they are not sweetened.

Note: As with many crisps, crumbles, crunches, and cobblers, it's best to make the topping first so that it's ready to sprinkle on the filling the instant it's in the baking dish, in this case the first two layers — yellow cake batter and blueberries.

TOPPING (SEE NOTE ABOVE):

½ cup granulated sugar or raw sugar or ¼ cup of each

½ cup unsifted all-purpose flour

½ teaspoon ground cinnamon

½ teaspoon freshly grated nutmeg

½ cup (1 stick) refrigerator-cold unsalted butter, diced

CAKE BATTER:

2 cups sifted all-purpose flour

2½ teaspoons baking powder

½ teaspoon salt

½ cup (1 stick) unsalted butter

½ cup granulated sugar

1 large egg

1 teaspoon vanilla extract

½ cup milk

BERRIES:

1 pint (2 cups) fresh or solidly frozen blueberries (see headnote)

1. Preheat oven to 375°F. Butter 9 x 9 x 2-inch ovenproof glass baking dish well or spritz with nonstick cooking spray and set aside.

2. Topping: Whisk sugar, flour, cinnamon, and nutmeg together in small bowl, add butter, then with pastry blender, cut in until crumbly and texture of lentils; set aside.

3. Cake Batter: Sift flour, baking powder, and salt onto piece of wax paper. Cream butter and sugar in large electric mixer bowl at moderately high speed until light — about 2 minutes. Beat in egg and vanilla, then with mixer at low speed, add sifted dry ingredients alternately with milk, beginning and ending with the dry and beating after each addition only enough to combine. Pour into baking dish and spread to corners.

4. Berries: Scatter blueberries on top of batter in baking dish, distributing evenly, then sprinkle topping over all, again distributing as evenly as possible.

5. Slide buckle onto middle oven shelf and bake until puffed and nicely browned— 1 to 1¼ hours.

6. Remove buckle from oven, set on wire baking rack, and cool 10 minutes.

7. To serve, scoop buckle onto bright dessert plates, making sure everyone gets some of each layer—cake, blueberries, and topping. Resist the temptation to smother each portion with whipped cream or to add a scoop of vanilla ice cream. I don't find either necessary because this buckle is rich enough to stand alone.

Blueberry-Oatmeal Crumble

Makes 6 Servings

Such an easy recipe and a nutritious one, too. Because I like a lot of crunch to contrast with the softness of the berries, I use old-fashioned rolled oats here. I've tried the quick-cooking and the crumble was soft, bordering on mushy.

1. Preheat oven to 350°F. Lightly butter shallow 2-quart baking dish or spritz with nonstick cooking spray.

2. Toss blueberries with flour and lemon zest in medium mixing bowl, then spread over bottom of baking dish and set aside.

3. Crumble: Combine all but final ingredient (butter) in same mixing bowl (now wiped clean), then gradually stir in melted butter—mixture will be crumbly. Sprinkle evenly over berries.

4. Slide onto middle oven shelf and bake until bubbling and nicely browned—about 45 minutes.

5. Serve hot or warm or even at room temperature topped, if you like, with whipped cream or ice cream. Good, too, with Mock Devonshire Cream (page 273) or Crème Fraîche (page 274).

---

1 quart (4 cups) fresh or solidly frozen blueberries

2 tablespoons all-purpose flour

¼ teaspoon finely grated lemon zest

CRUMBLE:

1 cup uncooked old-fashioned rolled oats (see headnote)

1 cup sifted all-purpose flour

¾ cup firmly packed light brown sugar

¼ teaspoon freshly grated nutmeg

¼ teaspoon salt

½ cup (1 stick) unsalted butter, melted

OPTIONAL TOPPING:

1 cup heavy cream, whipped to soft peaks with 2 tablespoons confectioners' (10X) sugar and ½ teaspoon vanilla extract, or 1 pint vanilla or dulce de leche ice cream

Yankee Berry Slump or Grunt

Makes 6 Servings

Said to date back to Colonial America when women tried to bake the fruit pies of England in open hearths, the recipe that emerged was a dumpling-topped pudding made of local fruits (usually berries but sometimes apples or stone fruits). It's called a "slump" in some parts of New England and a "grunt" in others. Though usually known as a grunt in Massachusetts, *Little Women* author Louisa May Alcott was so fond of this humble sweet that she named her Concord, Massachusetts, home "Apple Slump" (see recipe, page 20).

Note: If you have Homemade Biscuit Mix (page 262) on hand, just stir 5 teaspoons granulated sugar into 1¼ cups of the mix and you are ready to add the milk and vanilla and proceed as directed.

BISCUIT TOPPING (SEE NOTE ABOVE):

1 cup + 2 tablespoons sifted all-purpose flour

2 tablespoons granulated sugar

1½ teaspoons baking power

¼ teaspoon salt

2½ tablespoons cold unsalted butter, diced

½ cup milk

1 teaspoon vanilla extract

1 tablespoon confectioners' (10X) sugar (to sift on top)

BERRIES:

1 quart (4 cups) ripe blackberries, blueberries, or raspberries, or an equal mixture of two or all three

½ to 1 cup granulated sugar, depending on sweetness of berries

½ teaspoon finely grated lemon or orange zest

OPTIONAL TOPPING:

1 cup heavy cream, whipped to soft peaks with 2 tablespoons confectioners' (10X) sugar, or 1 pint vanilla ice cream

1. Biscuit Topping: Place flour, granulated sugar, baking powder, and salt in large bowl and whisk well to combine. Add butter, then using pastry blender, cut butter into flour mixture until texture of lentils. Add milk and vanilla and whisk only enough to combine; specks of flour should still be visible. Set aside.

2. Berries: Place all ingredients in deep, heavy nonreactive 10-inch skillet, set over moderate heat, cover, and cook until berries release liquid and liquid bubbles—about 3 minutes.

3. Drop biscuit dough by rounded tablespoon on top of bubbling berries, spacing as evenly as possible.

4. Reduce heat to low. Simmer uncovered 10 minutes, then cover and simmer until biscuit dumplings are cooked through—about 10 minutes longer.

5. To serve, sift confectioners' sugar on top of dumplings, then dish up making sure that everyone gets plenty of dumplings and berries. Accompany, if you like, with a bowl of softly whipped cream or top each portion with a scoop of vanilla ice cream. Good, too, with Mock Devonshire Cream (page 273) or Crème Fraîche (page 274).

Red, White, and Blue Berry–Corn Bread Cobbler

Makes 6 Servings

For some reason, we neglect cranberries when it comes to crisps and cobblers. Ditto corn bread toppings. So I've rectified things here in a cobbler that's as delicious as it is unusual.

Note: Use fresh blueberries and cranberries, if in season. If not, the frozen work just fine—and there's no need to thaw them.

BERRIES:

1 pint (2 cups) fresh or solidly frozen cranberries (see Note above)

¾ cup granulated sugar mixed with 1½ tablespoons cornstarch

1 pint (2 cups) fresh or solidly frozen blueberries

1 tablespoon unsalted butter

1 teaspoon finely grated lemon zest

TOPPING:

⅔ cup sifted all-purpose flour

⅓ cup unsifted white stone-ground cornmeal

⅓ cup sugar

¾ teaspoon baking powder

¼ teaspoon baking soda

¼ teaspoon ground ginger

⅛ teaspoon salt

½ cup buttermilk (not fat-free)

1 large egg, lightly beaten

3 tablespoons unsalted butter, melted

OPTIONAL ACCOMPANIMENT:

1 cup heavy cream, softly whipped with 1 tablespoon confectioners' (10X) sugar, or 1 pint vanilla ice cream

1. Preheat oven to 350°F. Butter 9 inch round baking dish about 3 inches deep or spritz with nonstick cooking spray and set aside.

2. Berries: Place cranberries in heavy nonreactive medium saucepan set over low heat and cook, stirring frequently, until just beginning to burst—about 3 minutes. Stir in sugar mixture and continue to cook, stirring, just until mixture thickens—about 3 minutes. Stir in blueberries, butter, and lemon zest. As soon as mixture begins to bubble, pour into baking dish and set aside.

3. Topping: Combine first seven ingredients (flour through salt) in medium bowl and make well in center. Whisk buttermilk, egg, and melted butter until frothy in small bowl. Pour into well in dry ingredients and stir just until combined—no matter if a few floury specks show.

Recipe continues

4. Carefully spoon topping over berries, distributing evenly, and spread to edge of dish; berries should be completely covered.

5. Slide onto middle oven shelf and bake until bubbling and lightly browned—about 35 minutes.

6. Remove cobbler from oven, set on wire baking rack, and cool 10 minutes.

7. To serve, carry warm cobbler to table and dish up. Accompany, if you like, with whipped cream or vanilla ice cream. Good, too, with Mock Devonshire Cream (page 273) or Crème Fraîche (page 274).

Berries of Summer Cobbler with Rye Biscuit Topping

Makes 6 to 8 Servings

Almost any summer berries (except raspberries and strawberries, which don't take kindly to oven heat) work well in this cobbler. Try blackberries, blueberries, and if you can find them, loganberries, boysenberries, even red currants. My mother often baked loganberries and boysenberries into crisps and cobblers, but both of these berries seem to have vanished from our lives. Too bad. I remember their being plump and juicy and sweet; red currants, of course, are tarter and should be seeded (a pesky job). To add flavor and interest to the biscuit topping, I decided to use both all-purpose and rye flour—a light or medium whole-grain one; dark rye and pumpernickel flours are too strong for this recipe.

BERRIES:

2 quarts (8 cups) firm-ripe berries (any berry or mix of berries you fancy, see headnote), washed, stemmed, and patted dry on paper toweling

½ cup granulated sugar, or to taste

½ cup raw sugar

⅓ cup unsifted cornstarch

½ teaspoon freshly grated nutmeg

1 tablespoon finely grated fresh ginger

1 teaspoon finely grated lemon or orange zest

RYE BISCUIT TOPPING:

1 cup sifted all-purpose flour

½ cup unsifted whole-grain rye flour (light or medium, see headnote) or ½ cup unsifted whole-wheat flour or ¼ cup of each

2 teaspoons baking powder

½ teaspoon ground cinnamon

¼ teaspoon salt

½ cup (1 stick) refrigerator-cold unsalted butter, diced

½ cup milk

TOPPING:

1 cup heavy cream, whipped to soft peaks with 2 tablespoons confectioners' (10X) sugar and 1 teaspoon vanilla extract, or 1 recipe Crème Fraîche (page 274) or Mock Devonshire Cream (page 273)

Recipe continues

1. Preheat oven to 400°F. Lightly butter 3-quart casserole or spritz with nonstick cooking spray.

2. Berries: Mash 1½ cups berries. Whisk two sugars, cornstarch, and nutmeg together in large mixing bowl. Add the mashed berries along with remaining 6½ cups whole berries, the ginger, and zest and toss well to mix. Taste for granulated sugar and adjust as needed, then scoop into casserole and let stand 30 minutes at room temperature.

3. Rye Biscuit Topping: Whisk first five ingredients (all-purpose flour through salt) together in medium bowl. Using pastry blender, cut butter in until crumbly and texture of lentils. Forking mixture briskly, drizzle in milk and continue forking just until soft dough forms.

4. Stir berries in casserole well, then drop rounded tablespoons of biscuit dough on top of berries, distributing evenly.

5. Slide onto middle oven shelf and bake until berries bubble and topping is tipped with brown — 25 to 30 minutes.

6. Transfer casserole to wire baking rack and cool cobbler at least 30 minutes.

7. To serve, scoop cobbler onto bright dessert plates and drift each portion with whipped cream, Crème Fraîche (page 274), or Mock Devonshire Cream (page 273).

Apple-Pecan Scallop

Makes 6 Servings

Being a faculty wife, my mother belonged to the North Carolina State College Woman's Club in Raleigh. Even though I was a little girl at the time, I remember well the cookbook that club members published because my mother had a hand in its production. I still have a copy of *The North Carolina State College Woman's Club Cook Book*. This easy recipe comes from that long-ago book, its pages now dog-eared and splattered.

1. Preheat oven to 400°F. Spritz shallow 1½-quart casserole or gratin dish with nonstick cooking spray and set aside.

2. Combine first five ingredients (flour through salt) in medium mixing bowl, add butter, and work in with fingers until uniformly crumbly. Add pecans, toss well.

3. Place apples and lemon juice in casserole, toss lightly, then spread over bottom. Sprinkle pecan mixture on top, covering apples completely.

4. Slide onto shelf in lower third of oven and bake until bubbly and nicely browned—about 45 minutes.

5. Remove pudding from oven and cool on wire baking rack 20 to 30 minutes.

6. To serve, spoon warm pudding onto colorful dessert plates and drift each portion with whipped cream topping. I've also served this scallop with Mock Devonshire Cream (page 273), and on occasion, with Crème Fraîche (page 274).

1 cup sifted all-purpose flour

½ cup firmly packed light brown sugar

1 teaspoon ground cinnamon

½ teaspoon freshly grated nutmeg

¼ teaspoon salt

½ cup (1 stick) cold butter, diced

½ cup coarsely chopped pecans

4 large Golden Delicious or Gala apples (about 2 pounds), peeled, cored, quartered, and each quarter thinly sliced

2 tablespoons fresh lemon juice

TOPPING:

1 cup heavy cream, whipped to soft peaks with 2 tablespoons confectioners' (10X) sugar and 1 teaspoon vanilla extract

Berry Patch Cobbler with Pecan Shortbread Crust

Makes 6 Servings

One of the joys of summer Down South was to go blackberrying. Brambles of them grew wild all over our Raleigh neighborhood, and whenever the call went out — "blackberries ripe!" — my brother and I would set forth, buckets in hand. Dodging thorns, we managed to fill our buckets in short order, then Mother went to work making blackberry cobblers, pies, and jams. Her cobbler topping was a drop biscuit dough sweetened with a bit of sugar. I've played around with her recipe over the years and like this shortbread crust better.

Note: If fresh blackberries — either wild or home-grown — are unavailable, substitute solidly frozen blackberries.

Tip: For directions on how to toast pecans — and they should be toasted before they're chopped — see page xxx.

1. Preheat oven to 350°F. Lightly butter shallow 2-quart nonreactive baking dish at least 9 inches across or spritz with nonstick cooking spray and set aside.

2. Berries: Place all ingredients in heavy nonreactive medium saucepan and mix well. Set over moderately low heat and bring to boil, stirring constantly — about 5 minutes. Remove from heat, pour into baking dish, and set aside.

3. Shortbread: Cream butter and brown sugar in small bowl with hand electric mixer at high speed about 1 minute. With mixer at low speed, beat in flour, then fold in pecans. Between sheets of wax paper, roll dough into 7-inch square and cut into 16 squares of equal size. Arrange randomly, slightly overlapping, on top of berries.

4. Slide cobbler onto middle oven shelf and bake until berry mixture bubbles, shortbread is lightly browned and feels fairly firm when touched — about 35 minutes.

5. Remove cobbler from oven, set on wire baking rack, and cool 10 minutes.

6. To serve, carry cobbler to table and spoon onto dessert plates, making sure everyone gets plenty of berries and shortbread. No sauce needed, no whipped cream, no ice cream.

BERRIES:

3 pints (6 cups) fresh blackberries (see Note above)

1 cup sugar blended with 3 tablespoons cornstarch

1 tablespoon fresh lemon juice

½ teaspoon finely grated lemon zest

SHORTBREAD:

½ cup (1 stick) unsalted butter, slightly softened

¼ cup firmly packed light brown sugar

1¼ cups sifted all-purpose flour

⅓ cup coarsely chopped lightly toasted pecans (see Tip above)

Biscuits 'n' Berries

Makes 6 Servings

My inspiration for this cobbler is my mother's strawberry shortcake. Unlike neighbors who simply spooned a few berries into store-bought sponge-cake cups, Mama always baked a batch of biscuits, split them, buttered them, and sandwiched them together with the strawberries my father grew by the acre. Of all the berries out there, strawberries would never be my choice for crisps and cobblers because they tend to bake poorly. But this upside-down cobbler, I'm pleased to say, rivals Mama's best strawberry shortcake. Yes, the strawberries do go squishy as they bake, but inverting the cobbler on a serving plate turns them into a sauce that's just right for the biscuit topping underneath.

1. Preheat oven to 400°F. Lightly butter shallow 2½-quart ovenproof glass or ceramic casserole at least 9 inches across or spritz with nonstick cooking spray.

2. Berries: Spoon sliced strawberries into casserole. Blend preserves and orange juice mixture, then fold into berries in casserole.

3. Slide onto middle oven shelf and bake uncovered until berry mixture bubbles and thickens slightly—about 10 minutes, stirring well at half-time. Remove from oven, stir well, and set aside.

4. Topping: Whisk biscuit mix and sugar together in medium mixing bowl, then forking briskly, drizzle in milk and continue forking just until soft dough forms. Drop dough by rounded tablespoons on top of berry mixture, spacing evenly.

5. Slide cobbler onto middle oven shelf and bake just until biscuit topping is cooked through and dappled with brown—30 to 35 minutes.

6. Remove cobbler from oven, set on wire baking rack, and cool 30 minutes.

7. To serve, loosen still-warm cobbler around edge, invert on large round rimmed dessert platter, and dish up at table. Accompany, if you like, with bowl of softly whipped cream or Crème Fraîche so that everyone can help himself.

BERRIES:

1 quart (4 cups) medium-large red-ripe strawberries, hulled and cut lengthwise into slices about ½ inch thick

½ cup strawberry preserves

½ cup fresh orange juice blended with 2 tablespoons cornstarch

TOPPING:

2 cups Homemade Biscuit Mix (page 262)

2 tablespoons sugar

1 cup milk

OPTIONAL ACCOMPANIMENT:

1 cup heavy cream, whipped to soft peaks, or 1 recipe Crème Fraîche (page 274)

Apple Slump

Makes 6 Servings

Was this author Louisa May Alcott's favorite pudding? It may be so because it's lemony, gingery, and delicious (see Yankee Berry Slump or Grunt headnote, page 8).

Note: If you have Homemade Biscuit Mix (page 262) on hand, just stir 5 teaspoons granulated sugar into 1¼ cups of the mix along with the cinnamon and nutmeg called for in the recipe and you are ready to add the milk and proceed as directed.

BISCUIT TOPPING (SEE NOTE ABOVE):

1 cup + 2 tablespoons sifted all-purpose flour

2 tablespoons sugar

1½ teaspoons baking powder

½ teaspoon ground cinnamon

¼ teaspoon freshly grated nutmeg

¼ teaspoon salt

2½ tablespoons cold unsalted butter, diced

½ cup milk

APPLES:

2 cups moderately thinly sliced peeled and cored Granny Smith apples (about 1 pound)

2 cups moderately thinly sliced peeled and cored Golden Delicious apples (about 1 pound)

½ to ¾ cup sugar, depending on sweetness of apples

1 tablespoon fresh lemon juice

1 teaspoon finely grated fresh ginger

½ teaspoon finely grated lemon zest

OPTIONAL TOPPINGS:

½ teaspoon sugar mixed with ⅛ teaspoon ground cinnamon (cinnamon sugar) and/or 1 cup heavy cream, whipped to soft peaks with 2 tablespoons confectioners' (10X) sugar, or 1 pint vanilla ice cream

1. Biscuit Topping: Place first six ingredients (flour through salt) in large bowl and whisk well to combine. Add butter, then using pastry blender, cut butter into flour mixture until texture of lentils. Add milk and whisk only enough to combine; specks of flour should still be visible. Set aside.

2. Apples: Place all ingredients in deep, heavy nonreactive 10-inch skillet, set over moderate heat, cover, and cook until apples release liquid and liquid bubbles—about 5 minutes.

3. Drop biscuit dough by rounded tablespoon on top of bubbling apples, spacing as evenly as possible.

4. Reduce heat to low. Simmer uncovered 10 minutes, then cover and simmer until dumplings are cooked through—about 10 minutes longer.

5. To serve, sprinkle dumplings with cinnamon sugar, if desired, then dish up making sure that everyone gets plenty of dumplings and apples. Accompany, if you like, with a bowl of softly whipped cream or top each portion with a scoop of vanilla ice cream. Good, too, with Mock Devonshire Cream (page 273) or Crème Fraîche (page 274).

"Dutch Baby"

Makes 4 to 6 Servings

Is it a pancake? A dessert pizza? A buckle? A grunt? A clafoutis? I call it a cobbler, a unique one that's popular in Germany, Holland, and other northern European countries.

Note: For best results, bake in a nonreactive 10-inch skillet with an ovenproof handle, one that's deep enough to hold 10 cups. Do not use cast iron; it will react with the acidity of the apple, making your pudding taste faintly of rust.

APPLE MIXTURE:

¼ cup (½ stick) refrigerator-cold unsalted butter, cut into pats

1 large Golden Delicious apple (about 8 ounces), peeled, cored, and thinly sliced

¼ cup sugar blended with 1 teaspoon ground cinnamon and ¼ teaspoon ground cardamom or freshly grated nutmeg (spiced sugar)

BATTER:

⅔ cup sifted all-purpose flour

2 tablespoons sugar

½ teaspoon baking powder

½ teaspoon ground cinnamon

¼ teaspoon ground ginger

¼ teaspoon salt

3 large eggs, well beaten

1 cup milk

2 tablespoons unsalted butter, melted

OPTIONAL TOPPING:

1 cup heavy cream, whipped to soft peaks, or 1 pint vanilla ice cream

1. Preheat oven to 425°F.

2. Apple Mixture: Melt butter in heavy nonreactive 10-inch skillet with oven-proof handle (see Note above) over moderate heat, then swirl to coat skillet sides with butter. Layer apple slices in butter, cover, and cook over low heat until almost tender—about 5 minutes. Sprinkle spiced sugar evenly on top of apples and set aside.

3. Batter: Whisk first six ingredients (flour through salt) together in large electric mixer bowl, add eggs, milk, and melted butter, and beat first at low mixer speed, then at high until well blended—about 3 minutes.

Recipe continues

Crisps & Cobblers

4. Pour batter evenly over apples in skillet. Slide onto middle oven shelf and bake uncovered until apples are tender and top is puffed and richly browned — 15 to 20 minutes.

5. Serve hot accompanying, if you like, with softly whipped cream or scoops of vanilla ice cream. Good, too, with Crème Anglaise (page 270), Frothy Egg Sauce (page 277), and Mock Devonshire Cream (page 273).

October Pudding

Makes 6 Servings

Why October? Because that's when apples hang heavy on the branch, when bushels of home-grown apples crowd farmers' markets, and when pick-your-own orchards set out "Y'all come" or "Come 'n' get 'em" signs by the side of the road. I'm partial to tart-sweet Gala apples that hold their shape when baked, ditto the sweeter Golden Delicious. Grannies are good but they tend to cook down to mush. For a good balance of tart and sweet, firm and soft, I often use one Gala or Golden Delicious and one Granny Smith.

1. Preheat oven to 350°F. Butter 9 x 9 x 2-inch baking pan or spritz with non-stick cooking spray and set aside.

2. Whisk flour, baking powder, cinnamon, and salt together in small bowl and set aside.

3. Place sugar, egg, vanilla, and lemon zest in medium bowl, then using hand electric mixer, beat at high speed until color and consistency of mayonnaise — about 2 minutes.

4. Add flour mixture and stir only enough to combine — it's good if a few specks of flour show. Finally, fold in apples and nuts.

5. Scoop batter into pan, spreading to corners and smoothing top.

6. Slide onto middle oven shelf and bake until pudding begins to pull from sides of pan and cake tester inserted midway between rim and center comes out clean — about 30 minutes.

7. Transfer pudding to wire baking rack and cool 20 minutes.

8. To serve, cut warm pudding into large rectangles and, if you like, drift each portion with whipped cream topping. I also sometimes skip the whipped cream and accompany this pudding with a pitcher of Butterscotch Sauce (page 268) or Nutmeg Sauce (page 283).

¼ cup unsifted all-purpose flour

1 teaspoon baking powder

¼ teaspoon ground cinnamon

¼ teaspoon salt

⅔ cup sugar

1 large egg

1 teaspoon vanilla extract

¼ teaspoon finely grated lemon zest

2 cups coarsely chopped peeled and cored apples (about 1 pound; see headnote)

½ cup coarsely chopped walnuts, black walnuts, or pecans

OPTIONAL TOPPING:

1 cup heavy cream, whipped to soft peaks with 2 tablespoons confectioners' (10X) sugar

Apple-Cheddar Crisp

Makes 8 Servings

To be honest, all the years I've been making apple crisp, it never occurred to me to add a grated sharp Cheddar to the topping mixture. Or as I've done here, a combination of Cheddar and freshly grated Parmigiano-Reggiano to enrich the flavor. So where did I get the idea? From one of my many spiral-bound community fund-raiser cookbooks. The recipe below, however, is my own invention.

Note: I like to use Golden Delicious apples for this recipe because they don't lose their shape when baked. Moreover, they're widely available and reasonably inexpensive.

Tip: Grate the Cheddar cheese for the topping yourself and make sure the cheese you buy isn't dry; packaged pre-grated cheeses are sometimes so dry that when baked, they never meld properly with the other topping ingredients.

4 large Golden Delicious apples (about 2 pounds), peeled, quartered, cored, and cut into eighths

¼ cup apple cider

1 tablespoon all-purpose flour

½ teaspoon finely grated lemon zest

1 tablespoon fresh lemon juice

TOPPING:

¾ cup sugar

⅔ cup sifted all-purpose flour

½ teaspoon ground cinnamon

½ teaspoon freshly grated nutmeg

¼ teaspoon salt

¼ cup (½ stick) refrigerator-cold unsalted butter, cut into pats

½ cup moderately finely grated sharp Cheddar cheese (see Tip above)

¼ cup freshly grated Parmigiano-Reggiano

OPTIONAL TOPPING:

1 cup heavy cream, whipped to soft peaks, or 1 pint vanilla ice cream

1. Preheat oven to 350°F. Lightly butter shallow 2-quart casserole.

2. Arrange apples in casserole. Combine cider, flour, lemon zest, and lemon juice in a small bowl. Pour cider mixture evenly over apples.

3. Topping: Combine sugar, flour, cinnamon, nutmeg, and salt in small bowl and scatter butter pats on top. With pastry blender, cut butter into dry ingredients until texture of coarse meal. Add Cheddar and Parmigiano-Reggiano and toss well to mix. Sprinkle topping evenly over apples.

4. Slide onto middle oven shelf and bake until apples are tender and top is lightly browned—about 45 minutes.

5. Serve hot or warm, topping each portion, if you like, with whipped cream or ice cream. Good, too, with Mock Devonshire Cream (page 273) or Crème Fraîche (page 274).

Antebellum Apple Brown Betty

Makes 6 Servings

Though called "pandowdy" in the little 1950s fund-raiser where it first appeared *(North Carolina Kitchens, Favorite Recipes Old & New),* this pudding is definitely a brown betty. Here's the recipe, exactly as it appeared in that long-ago spiral-bound cookbook—maddeningly vague like the majority of recipes in early club fund-raisers. But that very vagueness is part of these books' charm.

> *Pare, core, and slice thin some juicy sour apples. Butter a deep baking dish or pan and put in a layer of apples; sweeten with brown sugar and flavor with lemon peel; strew over a layer of bread crumbs and bits of butter. Repeat this until dish is nearly full, finishing with a layer of bread crumbs, bits of butter, and a sprinkle of brown sugar. Bake till apples are soft. Copied from my mother's cookbook published in 1860.*
> —Mrs. Jesse Gardner, Warren County, NC

Here now, my thoroughly tested version of that 156-year-old recipe, which fills in all the blanks. You'll note that I use a 50/50 mix of tart apples (Granny Smiths) and sweet (Golden Delicious). The Golden Delicious, unlike the Grannies, hold their shape when baked and that, I think, makes for a better brown betty.

Tip: I use my food processor to crumb the bread and it couldn't be easier: Tear slices of bread—crusts and all—into work bowl then pulse briskly until crumbs are about as coarse as uncooked oatmeal. For the record: 1 slice bread (with crust) = ½ cup crumbs.

2 large Granny Smith apples (about 1 pound), peeled, cored, and thinly sliced

2 large Golden Delicious apples (about 1 pound), peeled, cored, and thinly sliced

½ cup + 1 tablespoon firmly packed light brown sugar

½ teaspoon finely grated lemon zest

1 tablespoon fresh lemon juice

3 cups moderately coarse soft white bread crumbs (you'll need 6 slices firm-textured white bread, crusts and all; see Tip above)

½ cup (1 stick) unsalted butter, melted

OPTIONAL TOPPING:

1 cup heavy cream, whipped to soft peaks, or 1 pint vanilla ice cream

1. Preheat oven to 350°F. Butter deep 2-quart casserole or spritz with nonstick cooking spray and set aside.

2. Place apples in large mixing bowl, add ½ cup brown sugar, the lemon zest and juice, and toss well to mix.

3. Layer one-third apple mixture in casserole, top with one-third crumbs, and drizzle with 2 tablespoons melted butter. Repeat layers once, then top with remaining apples and crumbs and drizzle with remaining 4 tablespoons melted butter. Crumble remaining 1 tablespoon brown sugar on top, distributing evenly.

4. Cover casserole snugly with buttered sheet of aluminum foil, arranging buttered side down. Slide onto middle oven shelf and bake 30 minutes.

5. Remove foil and continue baking until apples are tender and crumbs nicely dappled with brown — 30 to 40 minutes longer.

6. Serve hot, warm, or even at room temperature — straight up or, if you prefer, drift each portion with whipped cream or top with scoop of vanilla ice cream. Good, too, with Mock Devonshire Cream (page 273) or Crème Fraîche (page 274). I've also been known to accompany this particular betty with Nutmeg Sauce (page 283).

Spicy Apple Brown Betty

Makes about 6 Servings

Nothing fussy or fancy about this recipe, which I learned to make before I could read — it's a good bit spicier than the Antebellum Apple Brown Betty that precedes. Many of the betties you find online are so gussied up they're barely recognizable. And a few are totally over-the-top. I prefer my mother's no-nonsense recipe.

Note: As with most apple puddings, I like to use a 50/50 mix of tart and sweet apples — Galas, for example, and Granny Smiths or Greenings.

Tip: For 1 quart bread cubes, you'll need about 8 slices firm-textured white bread, crusts and all. Day-old bread is perfect.

1 quart (4 cups) stale ½-inch bread cubes (see Tip above)

5 tablespoons unsalted butter, melted

1 quart (4 cups) thinly sliced peeled and cored apples (about 1¾ pounds; see Note above)

⅔ cup firmly packed light brown sugar

2 tablespoons fresh lemon juice

1 teaspoon finely grated lemon zest

1 teaspoon ground cinnamon

½ teaspoon ground ginger

¼ teaspoon freshly grated nutmeg

¼ teaspoon ground allspice

¼ teaspoon salt

¼ cup apple juice or apple cider

OPTIONAL TOPPING:

1 cup heavy cream, whipped to soft peaks, or 1 pint vanilla ice cream

1. Preheat oven to 400°F. Butter 2-quart casserole or spritz with nonstick cooking spray and set aside.

2. Place bread cubes and melted butter in large mixing bowl and toss until cubes are nicely buttered.

3. Place apples and next eight ingredients (brown sugar through salt) in second large bowl and toss well to combine.

4. Layer bread cubes and apple mixture into casserole, beginning and ending with bread cubes. Drizzle apple juice evenly over all and cover casserole with lid or foil.

5. Slide onto middle oven shelf and bake 45 minutes. Remove cover and continue baking until bubbling and nicely browned — 10 to 15 minutes longer.

Recipe continues

6. Serve hot, accompanying, if you like, with softly whipped cream or scoops of vanilla ice cream. I personally prefer to put out a pitcher of Crème Anglaise (page 270) or Frothy Egg Sauce (page 277) so that everyone can top their betty with one of these delicate sauces.

Variations:

Peach Betty: Prepare as directed, substituting thinly sliced peeled and pitted dead-ripe peaches for the apples and water for the apple juice. Omit the allspice. For a change of pace, try serving with Nutmeg Sauce (page 283). Makes about 6 servings.

Apple-Blueberry Betty: Prepare as directed, substituting 2 cups fresh blueberries (or thawed and drained frozen blueberries) for 2 cups of the sliced apples. Omit the nutmeg and allspice. Good with Mock Devonshire Cream (page 273) or Crème Fraîche (page 274). Makes about 6 servings.

Apple-Cranberry Betty: Prepare as directed, substituting 1 cup coarsely chopped fresh or frozen cranberries for 1 cup of the sliced apples. Increase the brown sugar to 1 cup, substitute orange zest for the lemon, and finally, omit the lemon juice, nutmeg, and allspice. Good with Mock Devonshire Cream (page 273) or Crème Fraîche (page 274). Makes about 6 servings.

Handy Dandy Pear Pudding

Makes 6 Servings

Not a cobbler, not a crisp, this pudding's topping is a mix of flour, sour cream, leavening, and salt. You need a pear that holds its shape when baked and that means the ubiquitous Bartlett. Choose big ones that are firm-ripe and loaded with flavor (a sniff at the blossom end will tell you).

1. Preheat oven to 350°F. Butter 1½-quart baking dish or spritz with nonstick cooking spray.

2. Place sliced pears in large nonreactive bowl, sprinkle with lemon juice, and toss lightly to mix. Add raw and granulated sugars, flour, and cinnamon and toss lightly again. Scoop into baking dish, spread to edge, and dot top evenly with diced butter.

3. Topping: Whisk flour, sugar, baking powder, and salt together in small bowl, add sour cream, and stir only enough to combine. Spread topping over pears in baking dish. Sprinkle with sliced almonds.

4. Slide pudding onto middle oven shelf and bake until bubbly and lightly browned—40 to 45 minutes.

5. Serve hot—or if you prefer, let pudding cool about 20 minutes before dishing up.

Variations:

Handy Dandy Apple Pudding: Prepare basic recipe as directed, substituting 6 large tart apples (Granny Smiths, for example) for the pears and adding ¼ teaspoon freshly grated nutmeg to the topping. Makes 6 servings.

Handy Dandy Peach Pudding: Prepare basic recipe as directed, substituting 6 large firm-ripe peaches for the pears and adding ¼ teaspoon almond extract to the topping. Makes 6 servings.

6 large firm-ripe Bartlett pears (about 3 pounds), peeled, cored, and quartered, then each quarter sliced about ½ inch thick

2 tablespoons fresh lemon juice

¼ cup raw sugar

2 tablespoons granulated sugar

1 tablespoon unsifted all-purpose flour

½ teaspoon ground cinnamon

1 tablespoon refrigerator-cold unsalted butter, diced

TOPPING:

3 tablespoons unsifted all-purpose flour

2 tablespoons granulated sugar

½ teaspoon baking powder

⅛ teaspoon salt

1 cup firmly packed sour cream

3 tablespoons sliced almonds

Crisps & Cobblers

Golden Delicious–Butter Crumb Betty

Makes 6 Servings

What's unusual about this betty is that the apples are grated—skins and all—which adds welcome texture. Although I've used both Gala and Jonathan apples for this recipe, I've decided that Golden Delicious work best because they hold their shape as they bake, even when grated.

Note: For variety you might use a 50/50 mix of Golden Delicious and tart Granny Smiths. You also might try the gluten-free variation that follows.

Tip: The easiest way to grate the apples is on a mandoline slicer/shredder; failing that, try the second coarsest side of a box grater provided the grater is super-sharp. The food processor is too powerful and rips the skins to smithereens. If you're unable to grate the apple skins, you've two options: Either eliminate them altogether or chop with a sharp chef's knife—a moderately coarse chop is the texture you're after.

6 medium to large (about 3 pounds) Golden Delicious apples (see Note above), cored and quartered but not peeled, then each quarter coarsely grated (see Tip above)

1 tablespoon fresh lemon juice

½ cup granulated sugar

2 tablespoons all-purpose flour

¾ teaspoon ground cinnamon

¼ teaspoon salt

2 cups Butter Crumb Streusel (page 263), thawed if frozen

TOPPING:

1 cup heavy cream, whipped to soft peaks with 2 tablespoons confectioners' (10X) sugar and 1 teaspoon vanilla extract, or 1 recipe Crème Fraîche (page 274)

1. Preheat oven to 400°F. Lightly butter 9 x 9 x 2-inch ovenproof glass baking dish or spritz with nonstick cooking spray and set aside.

2. Place grated apples in large nonreactive bowl, add lemon juice, and toss well. Add sugar, flour, cinnamon, and salt and toss well again.

3. Scoop apple mixture into baking dish and crumble streusel evenly on top.

4. Slide onto middle oven shelf and bake 10 minutes. Reduce oven temperature to 375°F and continue baking until apples are bubbly and streusel is golden brown—about 30 minutes longer.

Recipe continues

Crisps & Cobblers

5. Remove betty from oven, set on wire baking rack, and cool 30 minutes.

6. To serve, dish betty onto bright dessert plates and top each portion with dollop of whipped cream or Crème Fraîche.

Variation:

Gluten-Free Golden Delicious–Butter Crumb Betty: Prepare as directed, but use 1 tablespoon cornstarch instead of the 2 tablespoons flour in the apple filling and substitute Gluten-Free Streusel Topping (page 266) for the Butter Crumb Streusel. Makes 6 servings.

Old Pennsylvania Apple Pandowdy

Makes 6 Servings

There are scores of recipes masquerading as pandowdies, but this early Pennsylvania dowdy topped with a butter cake batter is the real thing.

3 large Granny Smith apples (about 1⅓ pounds), peeled, cored, and thinly sliced

2 large Golden Delicious apples (about 1 pound), peeled, cored, and thinly sliced

½ cup firmly packed light brown sugar mixed with ½ teaspoon ground cinnamon

and ¼ teaspoon freshly grated nutmeg (spiced brown sugar)

BATTER:

1¼ cups sifted all-purpose flour

1½ teaspoons baking powder

¼ teaspoon salt

½ cup (1 stick) unsalted butter

½ cup granulated sugar

1 large egg

½ cup milk

OPTIONAL TOPPING:

1½ cups heavy cream (do not whip)

1. Preheat oven to 350°F. Butter 2-quart casserole well or spritz with nonstick cooking spray.

2. Place all apples and spiced brown sugar mixture in large mixing bowl, toss well, and scoop into casserole. Slide onto middle oven shelf and bake uncovered, stirring once or twice, until apples are soft—about 30 minutes.

3. Batter: After apples have baked 20 minutes, sift flour, baking powder, and salt onto piece of wax paper. Using hand electric mixer, cream butter and granulated sugar in small mixing bowl at high speed until fluffy—about 2 minutes. Reduce mixer speed to low and beat in egg. With mixer still at low speed, add combined dry ingredients alternately with milk, beginning and ending with dry and beating after each addition only enough to incorporate.

4. Remove baked apples from oven and spread batter evenly on top. Slide back onto middle oven shelf and continue baking uncovered until dowdy begins to pull from sides of casserole and top is nicely browned—35 to 40 minutes longer.

5. Remove dowdy from oven and let stand 10 minutes to allow juices to settle.

6. To serve, dish up at table and, if you like, pass a pitcher of heavy cream so that everyone can trickle a bit of it over their apple pandowdy.

Eve's Pudding

Makes 4 to 6 Servings

I first tasted this apple pudding while traveling about Wales one autumn on assignment for *Bon Appétit* magazine. I kept my steno pad at-the-ready, trying to crack the recipe as I'd learned to do while a young food editor at *The Ladies' Home Journal* in New York. Then, browsing one day in a tiny bookstore, I came upon a shelf of local cookbooks and found *Pwdin Efa* (Welsh for "Eve's Pudding") in a slim paperback. Welsh, by the way, is still spoken in Wales and for me, wholly impenetrable despite a bit of DNA passed down from Welsh ancestors. I've altered the recipe a bit for American ingredients and implements, but the taste's the same. Do try the variation that follows—equally popular in Wales.

Tip: The maple syrup to use is grade B because of its rich flavor (see Maple Syrup/ Sugar, page xxix, and Sources, page 291).

½ pound (about 1 large) Golden Delicious apple, peeled, cored, and thinly sliced

½ pound (about 1 large) Granny Smith apple, peeled cored, and thinly sliced

¼ cup golden syrup or pure maple syrup (see Tip above)

¼ cup water

3 tablespoons fresh lemon juice

2 tablespoons unsalted butter

3 tablespoons all-purpose flour

1½ cups milk

2 large eggs, separated

2 tablespoons sugar

1 teaspoon vanilla extract

¼ teaspoon salt

1. Preheat oven to 350°F. Butter shallow 1½-quart casserole or deep 9-inch oven-proof glass pie plate or spritz with nonstick cooking spray.

2. Arrange apples over bottom of casserole, then, in order listed, drizzle syrup, water, and lemon juice evenly over apples.

3. Slide casserole onto middle oven shelf and bake uncovered until apples begin to soften—about 20 minutes.

4. Meanwhile, melt butter in heavy medium saucepan over moderate heat. Blend in flour and cook and stir 1 minute. Whisking briskly, add milk slowly and continue whisking until thickened—3 to 5 minutes.

5. Beat egg yolks and sugar in small bowl until frothy, then whisking hard, slowly add 1 cup hot milk mixture. Stir back into pan and cook, whisking constantly, until mixture again thickens—2 to 3 minutes. Do not allow mixture to boil or it will curdle. Remove from heat and mix in vanilla. Set aside, but stir occasionally to prevent skin from forming on top.

6. Place egg whites and salt in medium bowl and beat to soft peaks. Fold about ½ cup beaten whites into hot sauce, then fold in balance until no streaks of white or yellow remain.

7. Spoon hot batter evenly over apples, slide onto middle oven shelf, and bake until puffy and tipped with brown—about 45 minutes.

8. To serve, rush casserole to table just as you would a soufflé.

Blueberry Variation:

Prepare as directed, using ½ pound fresh or solidly frozen blueberries and ½ pound thinly sliced peeled and cored Gala apple. Makes 4 servings.

Cran-Apple Casserole with Oatmeal Crust

Makes 6 Servings

Red-skinned apples are best for this recipe because the apples are not peeled. Also best, a variety that does not bake down to mush. My choices? Cortlands, Galas, or Jonathans. Because I like a crust with plenty of crunch, I used old-fashioned rolled oats (oatmeal). The quick-cooking works well but delivers a somewhat softer crust.

Note: Make the crust first so it's ready to use the minute the apples and cranberries are in the dish.

CRUST:

1½ cups uncooked old-fashioned rolled oats (see headnote)

½ cup firmly packed light brown sugar

½ cup moderately coarsely chopped pecans or walnuts

2 tablespoons wheat germ

1 tablespoon all-purpose flour

¼ teaspoon salt

½ cup (1 stick) refrigerator-cold unsalted butter, diced

FRUIT:

2 large (about 1 pound) apples (see headnote), halved, and cored, then each half cut into ½-inch dice

2 cups (8 ounces) fresh or solidly frozen cranberries

¾ cup granulated sugar

½ teaspoon finely grated orange zest

TOPPING:

1 recipe Mock Devonshire Cream (page 273) or Crème Fraîche (page 274), or 1 pint vanilla or dulce de leche ice cream

1. Preheat oven to 350°F. Lightly butter 9 x 9 x 2-inch ovenproof glass baking dish or spritz with nonstick cooking spray and set aside.

2. Crust: Combine first six ingredients (oats through salt) in large bowl, add butter, and work in with fingers until uniformly crumbly.

3. Fruit: Place apples, cranberries, sugar, and orange zest in baking dish and toss lightly to mix. Sprinkle combined crust ingredients evenly on top.

4. Slide onto middle oven shelf and bake until bubbly and nicely browned—about 45 minutes.

5. Remove pudding from oven and cool on wire baking rack 20 to 30 minutes.

6. To serve, spoon warm pudding onto bright dessert plates, then add topping of your choice—don't be stingy.

Pear 'n' Apple Crumble with Pecan-Oatmeal Crust

Makes 8 Servings

Though our grandmothers didn't hesitate to combine various fruits in a single cobbler, crisp, or crumble—fruits other than berries, that is—few cooks do so today. It's a good way to use up a few apples and pears. But this particular recipe, I think, justifies buying both apples and pears.

Tip: Make the crust first so it's ready to use as soon as the fruits are in the baking pan.

CRUST:

1 cup moderately coarsely chopped pecans

⅔ cup raw sugar

⅓ cup unsifted all-purpose flour

¼ teaspoon ground cinnamon

¼ teaspoon freshly grated nutmeg

¼ teaspoon salt

6 tablespoons (¾ stick) refrigerator-cold unsalted butter, diced

1 cup uncooked quick-cooking rolled oats

FILLING:

¼ cup unsifted all-purpose flour

¼ cup firmly packed light brown sugar

1 tablespoon finely grated fresh ginger

¼ teaspoon finely grated lemon or orange zest

3 large Golden Delicious apples (about 1½ pounds), peeled, quartered lengthwise, then each quarter cored and sliced crosswise about ⅛ inch thick

3 large firm-ripe Bartlett pears (about 1½ pounds), peeled, quartered lengthwise, then each quarter cored and sliced crosswise about ⅛ inch thick

2 tablespoons fresh lemon juice

⅓ cup cold water or apple cider

TOPPING:

1 cup heavy cream, whipped to soft peaks with 2 tablespoons confectioners' (10X) sugar and ½ teaspoon vanilla extract, or 1 recipe Mock Devonshire Cream (page 273)

1. Preheat oven to 400°F. Lightly butter 13 x 9 x 2-inch nonreactive baking pan or spritz with nonstick cooking spray and set aside.

Recipe continues

2. Crust: Place first six ingredients (pecans through salt) in medium mixing bowl. Add butter and using pastry blender, cut in until crumbly and texture of lentils. Add rolled oats, toss well to mix, and set aside.

3. Filling: Whisk flour, brown sugar, ginger, and lemon zest together in large bowl. Add apples, pears, and lemon juice and toss well. Add water and toss well again.

4. Spread fruit mixture over bottom of baking pan and scatter crust evenly over all.

5. Slide onto middle oven shelf and bake until bubbling and nicely browned—40 to 45 minutes.

6. Transfer pan to wire baking rack and cool pudding 20 to 30 minutes.

7. To serve, scoop pudding onto bright dessert plates and top each portion generously with whipped cream or Mock Devonshire Cream.

Variation:

Three-Fruit Pecan-Oatmeal Crumble: Prepare as directed, but use equal parts peeled, cored, and sliced apples; peeled, cored, and sliced pears; and peeled, pitted, and sliced large purple or black plums—about 3½ pounds in all or a little more than 1 pound of each fruit. Also, if you like, add ¼ teaspoon almond extract to the filling. Makes 8 servings.

Pear-Amaretti Crisp

Makes 6 to 8 Servings

Amaretti, those crisp Italian almond cookies, can be crumbled atop a variety of crisps and crumbles and are particularly good with pears and peaches (see variation that follows). Once sold only in New York and other metropolitan areas with Little Italy communities, amaretti have come to high-end groceries, even to supermarkets. There are several brands, but the best known is *Lazzaroni Amaretti di Saronno.* Look for the bright red tins — tins so decorative I use them as colorful accents in my kitchen.

Note: If amaretti are not available in your area, order them online (see Sources, page 291).

Tip: The best pears to use? I like Bartletts, which hold their shape as they bake better than softer pear varieties.

PEAR FILLING:

6 large (about 3 pounds) ripe pears (see Tip above), quartered, peeled, cored, and thinly sliced

2 tablespoons fresh lemon juice

½ cup sugar

6 tablespoons all-purpose flour

¼ teaspoon salt

1 cup heavy cream, at room temperature, mixed with ½ teaspoon almond extract

AMARETTI CRUST:

1½ cups coarsely crumbled amaretti cookies (see Note above), about 36 (1½-inch) cookies, broken into ¼-inch pieces

3 tablespoons all-purpose flour

3 tablespoons unsalted butter, melted

OPTIONAL ACCOMPANIMENT:

1 pint vanilla ice cream

1. Preheat oven to 350°F. Lightly butter 9-inch square ovenproof glass baking dish or spritz with nonstick cooking spray and set aside.

2. Pear Filling: Place pears and lemon juice in large nonreactive bowl and toss well. Whisk sugar, flour, and salt together in small bowl.

3. Arrange 2 cups sliced pears in bottom of baking dish and sprinkle with ½ cup sugar mixture. Layer 2 cups sliced pears on top, sprinkle with remaining sugar mixture, and add final layer of sliced pears. Pour cream mixture evenly over all.

Recipe continues

Crisps & Cobblers

4. Loosely cover with a sheet of baking parchment or oiled aluminum foil. Slide onto middle oven shelf and bake until pear filling is bubbly and surface is set—25 to 30 minutes.

5. Amaretti Crust: Meanwhile, place crumbled cookies and flour in small mixing bowl, toss well, and set aside. Do not add melted butter yet.

6. Carefully remove pudding from oven. Quickly add melted butter to amaretti mixture, toss well, then scatter over pears.

7. Return pudding to oven and bake uncovered until filling is bubbly and crust nicely browned—15 to 20 minutes longer.

8. Remove crisp from oven, set on wire baking rack, and cool 30 minutes.

9. To serve, carry crisp to table and dish up, topping each portion, if you like, with scoop of ice cream.

Variation:

Peach-Amaretti Crisp: Prepare recipe as directed, substituting peeled, pitted, and sliced firm-ripe Redhaven peaches (or other free-stone variety) for the pears. Makes 6 to 8 servings.

Peach Tree Cobbler

Makes 6 Servings

Peach orchards ripple across much of the South, indeed can even be found as far north as Michigan and as far west as California. For me, however, the best peaches to use for crisps and cobblers are those I pick myself. For obvious reasons, I prefer free-stone varieties with pits that pop right out. And across much of this country, this means the golden-fleshed Redhaven, a variety that has replaced the Elberta as a favorite. Fortunately, they are widely available.

3 pounds ripe peaches (see headnote), peeled, pitted, and thinly sliced

¼ cup raw sugar mixed with 2 tablespoons cornstarch and ¼ teaspoon freshly grated nutmeg

¼ cup granulated sugar

2 tablespoons fresh lemon juice

1 tablespoon unsalted butter

¼ teaspoon almond extract

TOPPING:

1½ cups Homemade Biscuit Mix (page 262)

¼ cup granulated sugar

¼ teaspoon freshly grated nutmeg

½ cup milk combined with ½ teaspoon almond extract

OPTIONAL ACCOMPANIMENT:

1 cup heavy cream, softly whipped, or 1 pint vanilla or dulce de leche ice cream

1. Preheat oven to 375°F. Lightly butter 2½-quart casserole or spritz with nonstick cooking spray and set aside.

2. Combine peaches, raw sugar mixture, and granulated sugar in large nonreactive saucepan. Set over moderate heat, and then cook, stirring constantly, until juices thicken and clear—about 3 minutes. Remove from heat, mix in lemon juice, butter, and almond extract, then scoop into casserole and set aside.

3. Topping: Place biscuit mix in large bowl; add granulated sugar and nutmeg and whisk briefly to combine. Forking briskly, drizzle in milk mixture to make a soft dough—no matter if a few floury specks show. Drop dough by rounded teaspoons on top of peaches, spacing evenly.

4. Slide cobbler onto middle oven shelf and bake until bubbling and lightly browned—40 to 45 minutes.

5. To serve, carry cobbler to table and serve hot accompanying, if you like, with whipped cream or vanilla ice cream—or even better, dulce de leche ice cream.

Pick-Your-Own-Peaches Crumble with Ginger Shortbread

Makes 4 Servings

I've always been partial to shortbread, especially this unusual recipe given to me by Scottish friends that contains both ground ginger and crystallized ginger. I've turned things upside down by crumbling the shortbread dough over thinly sliced fresh-as-can-be peaches. Pick-your-own orchards proliferate wherever peaches grow, so next time you buy them, don't settle for what your supermarket sells. They will not be as fresh or full of flavor — even those labeled "local."

SHORTBREAD:

1¼ cups sifted all-purpose flour

¼ teaspoon ground ginger

¼ teaspoon salt

½ cup (1 stick) unsalted butter, slightly softened

¼ cup sugar

¼ cup finely diced crystallized ginger

PEACHES:

3 cups very thinly sliced peeled and pitted fresh peaches (4 to 5 large peaches, about 1¾ pounds)

1 tablespoon fresh lemon juice

¼ cup sugar

1 tablespoon cornstarch

¼ teaspoon salt

TOPPING:

1 cup heavy cream (do not whip) or 1 recipe Frothy Egg Sauce (page 277) or Crème Anglaise (page 270).

1. Preheat oven to 350°F. Butter 8-inch square baking dish or spritz with nonstick cooking spray and set aside.

2. Shortbread: Whisk flour, ground ginger, and salt together in small bowl. Using hand electric mixer, beat butter and sugar until fluffy in medium bowl—1 to 2 minutes. With mixer at slow speed, gradually beat in flour mixture. Using fork, stir in crystallized ginger.

3. Peaches: Toss peaches with lemon juice in large bowl. Blend together sugar, cornstarch, and salt, add to peaches, and toss well to mix. Spread evenly over bottom of baking dish. Crumble shortbread mixture evenly on top of peaches, spreading to edge of baking dish.

4. Slide pudding onto middle oven shelf and bake until bubbling and lightly browned—40 to 45 minutes.

5. Transfer pudding to wire baking rack and cool 20 minutes.

6. To serve, spoon warm pudding onto bright dessert plates. Top each portion with a little heavy cream (pass any remaining cream in a small pitcher), or top with Frothy Egg Sauce or Crème Anglaise.

Pinehurst Peach Pudding

Makes 6 Servings

Pinehurst? Golfers know that name because Pinehurst, one of this country's top golfing communities, frequently hosts the U.S. Open. What many people don't know, however, is that the village of Pinehurst, North Carolina, was designed at the turn of the twentieth century by Frederick Law Olmsted, who's better known for having designed New York City's Central Park. And here's something else few people know: Pinehurst is located deep in the Sandhills of North Carolina. Translation: peach country. Firm-ripe peaches just off the tree make the best pudding, but I've substituted frozen unsweetened sliced peaches with success.

2 cups thinly sliced peeled and pitted fresh peaches (about 1 pound) or solidly frozen unsweetened sliced peaches

1 cup sifted all-purpose flour

1 teaspoon baking powder

¼ teaspoon salt

¼ cup (½ stick) unsalted butter

⅓ cup sugar

½ cup milk

TOPPING:

⅓ cup sugar blended with 1 tablespoon cornstarch

¾ cup boiling water

1. Preheat oven to 325°F. Butter 8 x 8 x 2-inch ovenproof glass baking dish or spritz with nonstick cooking spray. Arrange sliced peaches over bottom and set aside.

2. Whisk flour, baking powder, and salt together in small bowl.

3. Place butter and sugar in second small bowl and using hand electric mixer, cream at high speed until light—about 1 minute. By hand, add flour mixture alternately with milk, beginning and ending with dry ingredients and mixing after each addition only enough to combine. It's OK if a few floury specks show. Spread batter over peaches in baking dish.

4. Topping: Sift sugar-cornstarch mixture evenly on top of batter, then pour boiling water evenly over all.

5. Slide pudding onto middle oven shelf and bake until lightly browned and center springs back when pressed—about 1 hour.

6. Transfer pudding to wire baking rack and cool 20 minutes.

7. To serve, spoon warm pudding onto bright dessert plates—nothing more needed.

Orange-Almond-Apricot Crisp

Makes 6 Servings

Most of us give fresh apricots short shrift, maybe because their season is relatively short (mid-summer to early fall), but also because the majority come from California where droughts are increasingly commonplace. Supplementing the dwindling supply and stretching the season, however, are shipments from Turkey, South Africa, Argentina, and Chile. Next time you see fresh apricots at your supermarket or greengrocer, buy several pounds — preferably a free-stone variety like Blenheim or Flora Gold. Then try this unusual crisp.

Note: For this recipe, quick-cooking rolled oats (uncooked, of course) work better than old-fashioned.

Tips: Prepare the topping first so it's ready to scatter over the apricots. The fastest way to grate almond paste? On the second coarsest side of a box grater.

TOPPING (SEE TIPS ABOVE):

½ (7-ounce) package almond paste, coarsely grated (see Tips above)

1 cup uncooked quick-cooking rolled oats

⅓ cup unsifted all-purpose flour

2 tablespoons granulated sugar

1 teaspoon finely grated orange zest

½ teaspoon ground cinnamon

¼ teaspoon salt

¼ cup (½ stick) refrigerator-cold unsalted butter, diced

APRICOTS:

1½ pounds ripe apricots (about 8 to 10 large) peeled, pitted, and moderately thinly sliced (you should have about 3½ cups sliced apricots)

½ cup firmly packed light brown sugar mixed with 2 tablespoons cornstarch

¼ cup fresh orange juice

OPTIONAL ACCOMPANIMENT:

1 cup heavy cream, whipped to soft peaks (no sugar needed), or 1 recipe Crème Fraîche (page 274)

1. Preheat oven to 375°F. Lightly butter shallow 1½-quart nonreactive baking dish (at least 9 inches across) or spritz with nonstick cooking spray and set aside.

2. Topping: Combine first seven ingredients (almond paste through salt) in large mixing bowl, add butter, then using fingers, work in until uniformly crumbly and set aside.

Recipe continues

3. Apricots: Place apricots and brown sugar mixture in heavy nonreactive medium saucepan and mix well. Add orange juice and mix well again. Set over moderately low heat, bring to a boil, then cook, stirring constantly, just until mixture thickens and clears—about 3 minutes. Do not cook further or mixture may thin out.

4. Scoop apricot mixture into baking dish, then scatter topping evenly over apricots, covering them completely.

5. Slide crisp onto middle oven shelf and bake until bubbling and lightly browned—about 25 minutes.

6. Remove crisp from oven, set on wire baking rack, and cool 20 minutes.

7. To serve, spoon crisp onto colorful dessert plates and top, if you like, with whipped cream or Crème Fraîche.

Fresh Fig–Granola Crumble

Makes 6 Servings

With the topping waiting in the freezer—"frozen assets," so to speak—this pudding could not be easier. But wait till fresh figs are in season and at their peak of flavor. Is any variety of fig preferable? Yes. One that can be grilled or baked without turning to mush, and that means the South's beloved "sugar fig" (or Celeste to give its proper name), or the Brown Turkey, or the Black Mission, planted nearly 250 years ago in San Diego by the Franciscans. Fig season? Summer and fall—don't miss it.

Note: This is a gluten-free recipe.

1. Preheat oven to 425°F. Spritz 9 x 9 x 2-inch ovenproof glass baking dish with nonstick cooking spray.

2. Whisk honey, lime juice, and melted butter together in small nonreactive bowl until smooth. Using pastry brush, coat each fig—cut sides only—with mixture. Arrange figs, cut sides up and shoulder to shoulder, in baking dish.

3. Slide onto middle oven shelf and bake uncovered just until figs are heated through, about 10 minutes. Remove from oven and scatter granola evenly on top. Reduce oven temperature to 375°F.

4. Return figs to oven and bake just until bubbly and tipped with brown—about 15 minutes longer.

5. To serve, spoon onto bright dessert plates as soon as figs come from oven, making sure everyone gets plenty of figs and granola topping.

3 tablespoons honey

2 tablespoons fresh lime juice

2 tablespoons unsalted butter, melted

15 large (about 1½ pounds) firm-ripe figs (see headnote), stemmed and halved lengthwise

2 cups Gluten-Free Granola Topping (page 264)

Fresh Plum Cobbler
with Whole-Wheat Topping

Makes 6 to 8 Servings

When it comes to cobblers, we tend to forget plums — a shame, because when ripe and full of juice, they make a splendid cobbler, maybe even better than apple and peach cobbler. The plums I like best? Big purple or black ones measuring about 2½ inches in diameter. The Japanese varieties come to market in late spring and last until early fall; European plums arrive a little later and are available all autumn long. The small Italian prune plums are a poor choice for this recipe because once they're peeled and pitted, there's not much left.

Tip: Make the topping first so it's ready to use as soon as the plums are prepared.

TOPPING:

½ cup unsifted whole-wheat flour

½ cup sifted all-purpose flour

1½ tablespoons raw sugar

1½ teaspoons baking powder

⅛ teaspoon salt

6 tablespoons (¾ stick) refrigerator-cold unsalted butter, diced

½ cup milk

PLUMS:

1 quart (about 2¼ pounds) large black or purple plums (see headnote), pitted, peeled, and thinly sliced

½ cup sugar mixed with 2 tablespoons cornstarch

1 teaspoon finely grated lemon zest

1 tablespoon refrigerator-cold unsalted butter, diced

1. Preheat oven to 400°F. Butter 2-quart baking dish or spritz with nonstick cooking spray and set aside.

2. Topping: Combine first five ingredients (whole-wheat flour through salt) in large mixing bowl. Add butter and using pastry blender, cut into flour mixture until uniformly crumbly. Forking briskly, drizzle in milk and continue forking just until soft dough forms.

3. Plums: Place plums, sugar mixture, and lemon zest in large bowl and toss well. Transfer to baking dish, spreading to edge, and dot with butter. Spoon topping over plums, covering completely.

Recipe continues

4. Slide cobbler onto middle oven shelf and bake 10 minutes. Reduce heat to 350°F and continue baking until bubbling and nicely browned—about 35 minutes longer.

5. Remove cobbler from oven, set on wire baking rack, and cool 30 minutes.

6. To serve, carry warm cobbler to table and dish up. I like to accompany with a small pitcher of heavy cream, though this cobbler can certainly stand alone.

Cherry Cobbler

Makes 6 Servings

Wherever I travel, whether on vacation or article assignment, I always spend time in the cookbook aisles of the local book store. And I rarely fail to buy several club or community fund-raisers — but only if the recipes are local. If I'm in Reidsville, NC, as I was when I picked up the *Rockingham County Home Demonstration Cook Book,* a spiral-bound yellow cookbook (8th printing 1973), it's old family recipes I'm after, ones that have passed the test of time. Like this cherry cobbler submitted by Mrs. J.W. Bartee of the Midway Home Demonstration Club. Here's what she has to say about it: "I use this batter often for a variety of fruits. It is easy and quickly made, therefore I use it much oftener than lining with regular pie pastry. I use blackberries, dewberries or soft peaches, chopped, which are also good with this type batter." Though she's specific about the ingredients needed for this cobbler, her directions are vague, which adds to the book's charm: "Put butter in casserole or baking pan to melt. Mix together sugar, flour, baking powder, salt and milk. This is a thin batter. Pour into baking dish then pour cherries on top. Cook in moderate oven until batter rises through the fruit and browns a golden brown." I've tested the recipe and have filled in all the blanks.

1. Preheat oven to 350°F. Place butter in 1½- to 2-quart casserole, tilting this way and that to cover bottom evenly.

2. Combine flour, sugar, baking powder, and salt in small bowl and make well in center. Add milk and stir only enough to combine — batter should be slightly lumpy. Pour batter into casserole, spoon cherries and all syrup on top. Don't stir.

3. Slide onto middle oven shelf and bake until cherries sink through batter and top is lightly browned — about 40 minutes.

4. Serve hot or warm, topping each portion, if you like, with whipped cream. Good, too, with Mock Devonshire Cream (page 273) or Crème Fraîche (page 274).

6 tablespoons (¾ stick) unsalted butter, melted

¾ cup sifted all-purpose flour

½ cup sugar

2 teaspoons baking powder

¼ teaspoon salt

1 (5-ounce) can evaporated milk

1 (15- or 16-ounce) can pitted dark sweet cherries packed in heavy syrup (do not drain)

OPTIONAL TOPPING:

1 cup heavy cream, whipped to soft peaks

Cherry Clafoutis

Makes 6 Servings

If you don't know this French classic, it's a cake-batter-topped cherry cobbler from the south-central Limousin, an area famous for its Limoges porcelain as well as the Limousin oaken barrels in which fine Cognacs, produced just next door, must age. Traditionalists frown upon today's trendy chefs who slip everything from apples to grapes into desserts they call clafoutis (pronounced kla-foo-TEE), insisting that a true clafoutis must be made with the dark sweet cherries of Limousin, even, some purists say, with *unpitted* cherries because their pits, used to make almond extract, add more flavor. That's the quickest way I know to break a tooth, so no pits in this recipe.

1 quart (4 cups) dark sweet cherries, halved and pitted

2 tablespoons granulated sugar

2 tablespoons all-purpose flour

BATTER:

½ cup granulated sugar

⅓ cup unsifted all-purpose flour

¼ teaspoon salt

4 large eggs, at room temperature

2 tablespoons unsalted butter, melted

1½ cups milk, at room temperature

1½ teaspoons vanilla extract

½ teaspoon almond extract

¼ cup sliced almonds

1 to 2 tablespoons confectioners' (10X) sugar (topping)

1. Preheat oven to 375°F. Lightly butter shallow 2-quart round or oval baking dish. Spread cherries over bottom of dish and sprinkle with granulated sugar, then with flour.

2. Batter: Combine granulated sugar, flour, and salt in large bowl. Beat eggs until frothy in second bowl, then whisk in butter, milk, vanilla, and almond extract. Whisking constantly, gradually add egg mixture to dry ingredients, and continue whisking until as smooth and thin as crêpe batter. Pour batter evenly over cherries and sprinkle with sliced almonds.

3. Slide clafoutis onto middle oven shelf and bake until billowing and brown—40 to 45 minutes.

4. Transfer clafoutis to wire baking rack and cool 30 to 40 minutes.

5. To serve, sift confectioners' sugar over clafoutis, spoon onto colorful dessert plates, then if you like, sift a little more confectioners' sugar over each portion.

Roasted Rhubarb Cobbler with Whole-Wheat Topping

Makes 6 to 8 Servings

To be honest, I've never been a fan of rhubarb. Then, one day recently, I discovered how to roast it, add a crumbly whole-wheat topping, and turn it into a first-rate cobbler. It can all be done in the same baking dish. Roast the rhubarb, then add a topping and bake.

Note: Because of the oxalic acid rhubarb contains (with toxic concentrations in the leaves), only the stalks are edible. And they must be cooked in a nonreactive baking dish, and their bitterness tamed with sugar or honey.

RHUBARB:

2 pounds rhubarb, trimmed and sliced ½ inch thick (about 7½ to 8 cups)

¾ cup superfine sugar

3 tablespoons water

WHOLE-WHEAT TOPPING:

1 cup sifted all-purpose flour

½ cup unsifted whole-wheat flour

¼ cup granulated or raw sugar

1 tablespoon baking powder

½ teaspoon ground cinnamon

¼ teaspoon ground ginger

¼ teaspoon salt

½ cup (1 stick) refrigerator-cold unsalted butter, diced

⅔ cup milk

OPTIONAL TOPPING:

1 cup heavy cream, whipped to soft peaks with 2 tablespoons confectioners' (10X) sugar and 1 teaspoon vanilla extract, or 1 recipe Mock Devonshire Cream (page 273) or Crème Fraîche (page 274)

1. Preheat oven to 400°F. Lightly butter 13 x 9 x 2-inch ovenproof glass baking dish.

2. Rhubarb: Place all three ingredients in baking dish, toss well, and let stand uncovered at room temperature until rhubarb juices begin to run—about 10 minutes.

3. Cover baking dish with foil, slide onto middle oven shelf, and bake until sugar has dissolved completely and juices begin to thicken—about 20 minutes. Remove foil, stir well, and bake uncovered until rhubarb is fork-tender and juices are syrupy—about 20 minutes longer. Remove from oven and set aside.

4. Whole-Wheat Topping: Place first seven ingredients (all-purpose flour through salt) in large mixing bowl and add butter. Using pastry blender, cut butter into flour mixture until texture of lentils. Forking briskly, add milk, and continue forking just until soft dough forms. Drop dough by rounded teaspoons on top of rhubarb, spacing evenly.

5. Slide cobbler onto middle oven shelf and bake uncovered until bubbling and nicely browned—20 to 25 minutes.

6. Transfer cobbler to wire baking rack and cool 20 to 30 minutes.

7. To serve, spoon warm cobbler onto bright dessert plates, then, if you like, drift with whipped cream, Mock Devonshire Cream, or Crème Fraîche.

R & R Crumble

R & R, as in raspberries and rhubarb. I'd hoped to use frozen rhubarb here, ditto frozen raspberries, but frozen rhubarb seems to be a thing of the past. Or, at best, seasonal. So I call for fresh rhubarb, fresh raspberries, too, but have simplified things by cooking the rhubarb in the casserole in which the crumble will bake. At least, it saves on dish-washing.

Tip: For 1 pound rhubarb, you'll need about 4 stalks approximately 14 inches long. When trimmed and cut into 1-inch lengths, you should have 4 cups.

1 pound rhubarb, trimmed and cut into 1-inch lengths (see Tip above)

1 cup granulated sugar

¼ cup water

½ cup fresh orange juice blended with 1 tablespoon cornstarch

2 cups red raspberries

TOPPING:

1 cup sifted all-purpose flour

¾ cup uncooked quick-cooking rolled oats

¾ cup firmly packed light brown sugar

¼ teaspoon salt

6 tablespoons (¾ stick) unsalted butter, melted with

¼ teaspoon finely grated orange or lemon zest

OPTIONAL ACCOMPANIMENT:

1 cup heavy cream, whipped to soft peaks, or 1 recipe Nutmeg Sauce (page 283)

1. Preheat oven to 400°F. Lightly butter shallow 1½-quart ovenproof glass or ceramic casserole at least 9 inches across or spritz with nonstick cooking spray.

2. Place rhubarb, granulated sugar, and water in casserole, mix well, and cover with sheet of baking parchment.

3. Slide onto middle oven shelf and bake until fork-tender—about 20 minutes, stirring at half time.

4. Topping: Meanwhile, place flour, rolled oats, brown sugar, and salt in large mixing bowl and toss well to mix. Drizzle in melted butter mixture and toss well again.

5. Remove casserole from oven and stir in orange juice mixture. Gently fold in raspberries, then scatter topping evenly over all.

6. Return to middle oven shelf and bake uncovered until bubbly and tipped with brown—20 to 25 minutes longer.

7. Remove crumble from oven, set on wire baking rack, and cool 10 minutes.

8. To serve, carry still-warm crumble to table and dish up. Accompany, if you like, with a bowl of softly whipped cream or pitcher of Nutmeg Sauce so that everyone can help himself.

Crisps & Cobblers

Green Tomato–Corn Bread Crisp

Makes 8 Servings

We make green tomato mincemeat, green tomato pies, so why not green tomato cobblers, crisps, and crumbles? Green tomatoes are tart and lemony and delicious when turned into desserts.

Note: True green tomatoes are completely green and hard, but unripe tomatoes showing only faint blushes of pink that are firm if not rock-hard can also be baked into puddings.

Tips: To give the topping a bit more crunch, I've used a mix of stone-ground cornmeal and the granular kind all supermarkets sell. Because it contains cornmeal only, the batter is as thin as pancake batter but emerges from the oven pie-crust crisp, which, to quote a friend, "is kind of nice." Certainly it's a welcome change of pace. The fastest way to grate fresh ginger? Peel, then whisk back and forth on a fine-toothed Microplane.

TOMATOES:

8 medium-size green tomatoes (about 3 pounds), cored and thinly sliced but not peeled

1 tablespoon fresh lemon juice

1 teaspoon finely grated fresh ginger (see Tips above)

¾ cup firmly packed light brown sugar

½ cup unsifted all-purpose flour

¼ cup granulated sugar

½ teaspoon ground cinnamon

¼ teaspoon freshly grated nutmeg

¼ teaspoon salt

¼ cup (½ stick) refrigerator-cold unsalted butter, diced

CORN BREAD TOPPING:

¾ cup unsifted yellow stone-ground cornmeal

¼ cup yellow cornmeal (not stone-ground; see Tips above)

¼ cup granulated sugar

¼ teaspoon baking soda

⅛ teaspoon salt

⅔ cup buttermilk (not fat-free)

1 large egg

3 tablespoons unsalted butter, melted

OPTIONAL ACCOMPANIMENT:

1 pint vanilla or dulce de leche ice cream

1. Preheat oven to 375°F. Lightly butter shallow 2½-quart casserole at least 9 inches across or spritz with nonstick cooking spray and set aside.

2. Tomatoes: Place tomatoes, lemon juice, and ginger in large nonreactive bowl, toss lightly, and set aside.

3. Place next six ingredients (brown sugar through salt) in medium bowl and whisk hard to mix. Add butter and use pastry blender to cut in until size of lentils.

4. Spread one-fourth crumbly sugar mixture over bottom of casserole, add one-fourth tomato mixture, then repeat three times, ending with tomato layer. Cover loosely with sheet of baking parchment or oiled aluminum foil, slide onto middle oven shelf, and bake until tomatoes bubble and soften slightly—about 30 minutes.

5. Corn Bread Topping: Whisk first five ingredients (stone-ground cornmeal through salt) together in medium bowl and make well in middle of dry ingredients. Whisk buttermilk, egg, and melted butter until frothy in small bowl. Pour into well in dry ingredients and mix only enough to combine—a few floury specks should be visible. Pour batter on top of tomatoes, distributing evenly.

6. Return crisp to oven and bake uncovered until topping is nicely browned and tomatoes bubble—about 30 minutes.

7. Remove crisp from oven, set on wire baking rack, and cool 20 minutes.

8. To serve, carry crisp to table and dish up on colorful plates, topping each portion with scoop of ice cream if you like.

Crisps & Cobblers

Green Tomato Crumble with Apples and Raisins

Makes 8 Servings

Even easier than the green tomato crisp that precedes but no less delicious.

Note: Best apples to use? Gala or Golden Delicious.

Tip: Unless you're Southern, you're not apt to have stale corn bread lying around. No problem. Simply buy corn muffins in the supermarket's bakery department. Once home, unwrap the muffins and let stand at room temperature for about a day until firm enough to break into ½-inch pieces. For 2½ cups muffin pieces, you'll need approximately ½ pound corn bread or two large muffins (about 3½ ounces each and 3 inches across the top).

TOMATOES:

6 medium-size green tomatoes (about 2 pounds), cored and cut in ¾-inch dice but not peeled

3 large (about 1½ pounds) apples (see Note above), cored, peeled, and cut in ¾-inch dice

⅓ cup firmly packed light brown sugar

⅓ cup granulated sugar blended with 3 tablespoons all-purpose flour

¼ cup dark seedless raisins

¼ cup golden seedless raisins (sultanas)

¼ cup water

½ teaspoon finely grated lemon zest

1 tablespoon fresh lemon juice

¼ teaspoon ground cinnamon

¼ teaspoon ground allspice

¼ teaspoon freshly grated nutmeg

TOPPING:

½ cup unsifted all-purpose flour

½ cup firmly packed light brown sugar

¼ teaspoon salt

¼ cup (½ stick) refrigerator-cold unsalted butter, diced

2½ cups stale corn bread or muffins, broken into ½-inch pieces (see Tip above)

OPTIONAL ACCOMPANIMENT:

1 pint vanilla ice cream or 1 recipe Mock Devonshire Cream (page 273)

1. Preheat oven to 375°F. Lightly butter 3-quart nonreactive casserole or soufflé dish or spritz with nonstick cooking spray and set aside.

2. Tomatoes: Place all ingredients (tomatoes through nutmeg) in large nonreactive bowl and toss well to mix. Transfer to casserole and cover loosely with sheet of baking parchment or oiled aluminum foil.

3. Slide onto middle oven shelf and bake, stirring occasionally, until fruits soften slightly and juices thicken — about 35 minutes. Remove casserole from oven, stir well, and set aside.

4. Topping: Place flour, brown sugar, and salt in medium bowl and toss well. Add butter, then using fingers, work in until uniformly crumbly. Gently fold in corn bread. Scatter topping over green tomato mixture, distributing evenly.

5. Return crumble to middle oven shelf and bake uncovered until fruits bubble and topping is tipped with brown — about 25 minutes.

6. Remove crumble from oven, set on wire baking rack, and cool 20 minutes.

7. To serve, carry crumble to table and dish up, topping each portion, if you like, with scoop of ice cream or generous ladling of Mock Devonshire Cream.

Cobbler of Wine-Poached Dried Fruits

Makes 6 Servings

Cobblers only when fresh fruits are in season? Nonsense. Dried fruits make superb off-season substitutes. In fact, their depth of flavor is exceptional.

Note: Choose dried fruits that take about the same time to cook, also those of similar hue lest dark ones—prunes or dates, to name two—muddy the mixture. How long dried fruits take to cook depends upon how recently they were dried, so reject any that have been hanging about in your pantry. When buying dried fruits, examine the package. Are the fruits shriveled? If so, avoid. Do they feel plump when you handle the package? If so, buy.

Tip: The best wine to use for poaching dried fruits? I favor a spritely German Riesling or, even better, a gingery Gewürztraminer.

FRUITS (SEE NOTE ABOVE):

¾ cup (about 4¾ ounces) dried apricots

¾ cup (about 3½ ounces) dried peaches, cut in 1- to 1½-inch chunks

¾ cup (about 2¼ ounces) dried apple slices, cut in 1- to 1½-inch chunks

¼ cup golden seedless raisins (sultanas)

1 (750-milliliter) bottle dry white wine (see Tip above)

2 tablespoons honey

1 (3-inch) strip orange zest

½ cinnamon stick

4 whole cardamom pods (preferably green cardamom)

TOPPING:

1½ cups Homemade Biscuit Mix (page 262)

¼ teaspoon ground cinnamon

¼ teaspoon ground cardamom

¾ cup milk

OPTIONAL ACCOMPANIMENT:

1 cup heavy cream, whipped to soft peaks, or 1 recipe Crème Fraîche (page 274)

1. Lightly butter shallow 2-quart casserole at least 8 inches across or spritz with non-stick cooking spray and set aside.

2. Fruits: Place all ingredients (apricots through cardamom pods) in medium nonreactive Dutch oven and bring to boil over moderate heat. Adjust so liquid simmers gently and cook uncovered, stirring occasionally, until fruits plump and

soften—about 30 minutes. Using slotted spoon, lift fruits to casserole; remove orange zest, cinnamon stick, and cardamom pods and discard. Set casserole aside.

3. Preheat oven to 400°F. Boil remaining poaching liquid uncovered over high heat, stirring often, until reduced to about ½ cup—about 2 minutes. Pour over fruits in casserole and set aside while you prepare topping.

4. Topping: Whisk biscuit mix, ground cinnamon, and cardamom together in medium mixing bowl. Forking briskly, drizzle in milk and continue forking just until soft dough forms. Drop dough by rounded tablespoons on top of fruit mixture, spacing evenly.

5. Slide cobbler onto middle oven shelf and bake just until biscuit topping is cooked through and dappled with brown—25 to 30 minutes.

6. To serve, remove cobbler from oven and dish up at table. And, if you like, put out a bowl of softly whipped cream or Crème Fraîche so that everyone can help himself.

Custards
&
Creams

Classic Baked Custard

Makes 8 Servings

Does anyone bake custard anymore? I wonder. It's quintessential "comfort food," something our grandmothers innately knew. My mother, too. Whenever my brother or I was feeling "poorly," Mama would bake custard—always in individual custard cups that made us feel special. This is her deliciously silky recipe.

Tip: To save time, heat the half-and-half and milk together. I do it in a spouted 2-quart ovenproof glass measuring cup in the microwave. It takes about 8 minutes on MEDIUM (50 percent power) in my 650-watt microwave. If yours has a higher wattage, the milk mixture will heat faster, maybe much faster.

5 large eggs

¾ cup sugar

1½ teaspoons vanilla extract

¼ teaspoon salt

2 cups steaming hot half-and-half (see Tip above)

2 cups steaming hot milk

Freshly grated nutmeg

1. Preheat oven to 325°F. Lightly butter eight 6-ounce custard cups or ramekins and set aside. Also fold damp tea towel to fit large shallow roasting pan and press flat over bottom of pan (this helps anchor custards as they bake).

2. Beat eggs, sugar, vanilla, and salt at high speed in large electric mixer bowl until thick and lemony—about 2 minutes. Reduce mixer speed to low, then slowly add steaming half-and-half and milk, and beat quickly to blend.

3. Ladle into custard cups, dividing amount evenly, then using Microplane, grate a little nutmeg on top of each custard.

4. Arrange custard cups, not touching, on folded dish towel in roasting pan. Pull out middle oven shelf, center roasting pan on shelf, then add enough boiling water to pan to come about one-fourth way up sides of custard cups.

5. Gently slide shelf back into oven and bake custards until cake tester, inserted in center of one, comes out clean—about 1 hour.

6. Remove custards from oven and from water bath and cool to room temperature. Place custards, not touching, on rimmed tray lined with damp tea towel. Lay baking sheet on top, and refrigerate 12 hours or overnight before serving.

7. To serve, set custard cups on bright dessert plates. I personally don't go to the trouble of unmolding each custard because I think they're more attractive served in the cups in which they baked. But if you'd like to unmold them, carefully loosen each around edge with thin-blade spatula dipped in hot water. Set dessert plate upside down on top of each custard and invert, giving a gentle shake, then carefully lift off custard cups.

Baked Vanilla Bean Custard

Makes 6 Servings

People often ask me if custard made with a vanilla bean tastes different from the same custard made with vanilla extract. Yes, which is why most chefs insist upon it. Vanilla beans impart a freshness, a depth of flavor that no extract can match. Now that vanilla beans are widely available, there's every reason to try this recipe.

Note: My mother always grated a little nutmeg on top of her custards, but I've made that optional for those who prefer a vanilla custard that tastes purely of vanilla.

1. Preheat oven to 325°F. Lightly butter 1½-quart baking dish or spritz with nonstick cooking spray and set aside.

2. Place milk and cream in medium saucepan. Split vanilla bean lengthwise, scrape seeds into milk mixture, then drop in split vanilla bean. Mix in ¼ cup sugar and the salt and set over moderate heat. Cook, stirring occasionally, just until bubbles begin to form around edge of pan—about 4 minutes.

3. Meanwhile, using hand electric mixer, beat remaining ¼ cup sugar with eggs and egg yolks at high speed until thick—about 2 minutes.

4. Remove steaming milk mixture from heat, then with mixer at low speed, pour slowly through large fine sieve into egg mixture and continue beating until all milk is incorporated. Discard vanilla bean pod.

5. Pour custard mixture into baking dish and set baking dish in medium roasting pan. Pull out middle oven shelf, center pan on shelf, then add enough boiling water to pan to come halfway up sides of baking dish.

6. Gently slide shelf back into oven and bake custard 35 to 40 minutes until cake tester, inserted midway between center and rim, comes out clean.

2 cups milk

⅓ cup light cream or half-and-half

1 vanilla bean

½ cup sugar

⅛ teaspoon salt

3 large eggs

2 large egg yolks

Freshly grated nutmeg (optional)

7. Remove custard from oven and from water bath, then if you like, top with light sprinkling of nutmeg. Cool custard 30 minutes before serving, or, if you prefer, cover with plastic food wrap and refrigerate 12 hours or overnight.

8. Serve cold—I do this at table in front of family and/or friends. If fresh peaches or strawberries are in season, I may slice into small serving bowl, sweeten as needed, then pass so everyone can spoon a little fresh fruit alongside their custard.

Variation:

Individual Vanilla Bean Custards: Preheat oven to 325°F. Dampen tea towel, then fold flat over bottom of medium roasting pan (this helps anchor custards as they bake) and set aside. Lightly butter six 6-ounce ramekins or custard cups or spritz with nonstick cooking spray and set aside. Prepare custard mixture as directed and pour into ramekins, dividing amount evenly. Arrange ramekins, not touching, on towel-lined roasting pan.

Pull out middle oven shelf, center pan on shelf, then add enough boiling water to pan to come halfway up sides of ramekins. Gently slide shelf into oven and bake custards until cake tester, inserted in center of one, comes out clean—about 35 minutes. Remove custards from oven and from water bath, grate a little nutmeg on top of each, if desired, then cool 30 minutes before serving. Or, if you prefer, arrange on rimmed tray, cover with plastic food wrap, and refrigerate 12 hours or overnight before serving.

I usually serve these in their ramekins, but you can loosen custard in each ramekin with small thin-blade spatula, dip bottoms of ramekins briefly in hot water, then invert on dessert plates. Makes 6 servings.

Custards & Creams

Floating Island

Makes 6 Servings

Called both Oeufs à la Neige (Eggs in Snow) and Ile Flottante (Floating Island) in France, this soft vanilla custard topped with clouds of poached meringue is believed to be French—or maybe Austrian, as it has long been a favorite in that country. So, was Floating Island introduced to France by Louis XVI's wife, Austrian Archduchess Marie Antoinette? No one can say for sure. I adored Floating Island as a little girl and my mother made it to reward me for a good piano lesson or report card.

1. Bring milk and half-and-half to simmer in deep 12-inch skillet (not iron) or Dutch oven over moderately low heat, stirring often—about 5 minutes.

2. Meanwhile, using hand electric mixer, beat the 3 egg whites, cream of tartar, and salt until frothy in large bowl. With mixer at low speed, add ½ cup sugar, tablespoon by tablespoon, and continue beating, still at low speed, until stiff peaks form—about 3 minutes.

3. Drop meringue by rounded tablespoons into simmering milk mixture, spacing equidistantly so meringues don't touch one another—you should have six large meringues. Poach 2 minutes, then using tablespoon dipped in hot water, gently turn meringues and poach until instant-read thermometer, inserted horizontally into center of largest meringue, registers 160°F—2 to 3 minutes.

4. Using wet slotted spoon, transfer meringues to large wet plate, spacing so they do not touch one another, and set aside while you prepare custard using the milk/half-and-half poaching liquid.

5. With hand electric mixer, beat the 4 egg yolks with the remaining ¼ cup sugar at high speed until well blended. With mixer at low speed, blend in about ½ cup hot milk mixture. Stir back into pan and set over moderately low heat. Cook, stirring constantly, just until custard thickens and coats metal spoon—45 seconds to 1 minute. Do not allow to boil or custard will curdle.

6. Remove from heat and stir in vanilla. Chill custard by setting pan in sink full of ice water. This takes about 25 minutes if you stir custard frequently.

7. To serve, pour chilled custard into large, broad glass or crystal bowl, then using slotted spoon dipped into cold water, ease meringues on top, distributing decoratively and evenly.

1½ cups milk

1½ cups half-and-half

3 large eggs, separated + 1 large egg yolk

¼ teaspoon cream of tartar

⅛ teaspoon salt

¾ cup sugar

1½ teaspoons vanilla extract

Coconut Custards

Makes 8 Servings

Some coconut custards contain shredded coconut, which in my opinion adds unpleasant texture to otherwise silken puddings. So I've substituted canned coconut milk for regular milk in this custard. Nearly every supermarket now carries canned coconut milk thanks to our ongoing love affair with Thai food (see Coconut Milk, page xxiv). Then, to boost this custard's delicate coconut flavor, I've added *pure* coconut extract. Most high-end groceries sell it, as do online suppliers (see Sources, page 291). Please, please, please do not settle for artificial coconut extract. You'll be sorry if you do because it tastes like cheap perfume.

1. Preheat oven to 325°F. Lightly butter eight 6-ounce ramekins or custard cups or spritz with nonstick cooking spray and set aside. Also fold damp tea towel to fit large shallow roasting pan and press flat over bottom of pan (this helps anchor custards as they bake).

2. Combine all ingredients in large mixing bowl, whisking until smooth, then pour into ramekins, dividing amount evenly. Arrange ramekins, not touching, on damp towel in pan. Pull out middle oven shelf, center pan on shelf, then add enough boiling water to pan to come about one-fourth way up sides of ramekins.

3. Gently slide shelf back into oven and bake custards until cake tester, inserted in center of one, comes out clean—about 50 minutes.

4. Remove custards from oven and from water bath and cool to room temperature—about 30 minutes. Arrange custards, not touching, on rimmed tray lined with damp tea towel. Lay baking sheet on top, and refrigerate 12 hours or overnight before serving.

5. To serve, center refrigerator-cold custards, still in their ramekins, on brightly colored dessert plates. Nothing more needed.

2 (13.5- or 13.66-ounce) cans unsweetened coconut milk (not low-fat or fat-free)

⅔ cup light cream

½ cup sugar

3 large eggs, beaten with 2 large egg yolks and ⅛ teaspoon salt

1½ teaspoons pure coconut extract (see headnote)

¼ teaspoon vanilla extract

Custards & Creams

Blue Ridge Jam Custards

Makes 6 Servings

This old recipe dates to the days when country women put up jars and jars of jams and jellies and, then unable to afford sugar, used their homemade jams and jellies to help sweeten desserts.

1. Lightly butter six 5- or 6-ounce custard cups or ramekins or spritz with nonstick cooking spray, and arrange, not touching, on rimmed baking sheet lined with damp tea towel (this anchors custards as they chill). Set aside.

2. Whisk milk and sugar mixture together in medium-size heavy saucepan. Set over moderate heat and cook, stirring occasionally, until mixture thickens slightly and bubbles around edge—5 to 6 minutes.

3. In medium bowl, whisk eggs and egg yolks together briskly, add about ½ cup hot milk mixture, then stir back into pan. Cook, stirring constantly, just until custard thickens lightly and instant-read thermometer inserted in middle of custard registers 160°F—45 seconds to 1 minute. Remove from heat and mix in vanilla.

4. Stirring often to prevent it from "skinning over," quick-chill custard in ice bath until slightly thicker than medium white sauce—about 20 minutes.

5. Add generous tablespoon cold jam to each custard cup, dividing amount evenly, then slowly spoon in cold custard, again dividing evenly and taking care not to disturb jam. Lay baking sheet on top, and refrigerate until custard has firmed up—3 to 4 hours.

6. Just before serving, preheat oven to 350°F. Swirl meringue into six 2-inch rounds on rimmed baking sheet lined with greased parchment, dividing total amount evenly.

7. Slide onto lower oven shelf and bake until meringues are nicely browned and instant-read thermometer inserted horizontally in middle of one registers 160°F—about 15 minutes.

8. To serve, center each custard cup on bright dessert plate, then using small spatula lightly spritzed with nonstick cooking spray, gently lift meringue swirls from parchment and ease on top of custards.

2 cups milk or 1 cup each milk and half-and-half

¼ cup granulated sugar mixed with 1 tablespoon all-purpose flour

2 large eggs

2 large egg yolks, well beaten with ¼ teaspoon salt

1 teaspoon vanilla extract

6 generous tablespoons refrigerator-cold berry jam (see headnote)

2 large egg whites, whipped to soft peaks with 1 tablespoon confectioners' (10X) sugar (meringue)

Molasses Custard

Makes 6 Servings

Long a Southern favorite, molasses custard doesn't seem to have made the voyage north of the Mason-Dixon or west of the Mississippi. Or perhaps I should say, it never became as popular elsewhere. Too bad, because this is an easy make-ahead dessert.
   Note: Use unsulfured molasses, a fairly light one, never blackstrap, which is too strong and too dark.

1. Preheat oven to 325°F. Lightly butter six 5-ounce ramekins or custard cups or spritz with nonstick cooking spray and set aside. Also fold damp tea towel to fit large shallow roasting pan and press flat over bottom of pan (this helps anchor custards as they bake).

2. Whisk all ingredients together until well combined in medium bowl, then pour into ramekins, dividing amount evenly. Arrange ramekins, not touching, on folded dish towel in roasting pan.

3. Pull out middle oven shelf, center pan on shelf, then add enough boiling water to pan to come halfway up sides of ramekins.

4. Gently slide shelf back into oven and bake custards until cake tester, inserted in center of one, comes out clean—about 50 minutes.

5. Remove custards from oven and from water bath and cool 30 minutes before serving. Or, if you prefer, arrange on rimmed tray, lay baking sheet on top, and refrigerate 12 hours or overnight before serving.

6. To serve, set custard cups on bright dessert plates. I personally don't unmold these little molasses custards. In my opinion, they're more attractive served in the cups in which they baked. Moreover, this eliminates any risk of the custards' cracking or collapsing as they're unmolded.

2½ cups light cream or half-and-half

3 large eggs, well beaten with 2 tablespoons raw sugar

¼ cup unsulfured molasses (not too dark; see Note above)

1½ teaspoons vanilla extract

⅛ teaspoon salt

Custards & Creams

Tea Custard

Makes 8 Servings

I first tasted this delicate custard in Portugal where it's called Pudim de Chá (*chá* being the Portuguese word for "tea"). Later, while traveling about England, I found any number of restaurants serving tea puddings, some of them cornstarch-thickened, some of them true egg-thickened custards. Given the fact that the English and the Portuguese have considered themselves old friends since the fourteenth century when Philippa of Lancaster married D. João I (King John I) of Portugal in 1387, I'm not sure whether tea pudding is a Portuguese recipe or an English one, though I'm inclined to think the former. The Portuguese, after all, discovered tea in China in the sixteenth century during its great Age of Discovery. Tea didn't become an English "institution" until a hundred years later.

Note: There's an even richer tea pudding recipe, an egg-yolk-thickened one, in my cookbook *The Food of Portugal,* still in print after nearly thirty years.

Tip: Choose a fragrant black (not green) tea for this recipe—Earl Grey, perhaps, Darjeeling, or English Breakfast.

1 quart (4 cups) half-and-half

3 tea bags (see Tip above)

1 cup sugar

4 large eggs

⅛ teaspoon salt

1. Preheat oven to 325°F. Lightly butter eight 5- or 6-ounce custard cups or ramekins or spritz with nonstick cooking spray and set aside. Also fold damp tea towel to fit large shallow roasting pan and press flat over bottom of pan (this helps anchor custards as they bake).

2. Place half-and-half, tea bags, and sugar in medium nonreactive saucepan, set over moderate heat, and bring to a simmer—about 7 minutes. Remove from heat and steep 5 minutes. Lift out tea bags, one by one, squeezing each over cream mixture to extract as much liquid as possible.

3. Whisk eggs and salt in medium bowl until smooth, then whisking hard, add hot cream mixture in slow steady stream and continue whisking until smooth. Pour into custard cups, dividing amount evenly.

4. Stand custard cups, not touching, in towel-lined roasting pan. Pull out middle oven shelf, center pan on shelf, then add enough boiling water to pan to come halfway up sides of custard cups.

5. Gently slide middle shelf into oven and bake custards until instant-read thermometer, inserted in center of one, comes out clean and registers 160°F—about 45 minutes.

Recipe continues

Custards & Creams

6. Remove custards from oven and from water bath and cool 30 minutes. Set custards on rimmed baking sheet lined with damp tea towel, lay baking sheet on top, and refrigerate 12 hours or overnight.

7. To serve, gently loosen custard in each cup with small thin-blade spatula, dip bottoms of cups briefly in hot water, then invert on decorative dessert plates.

River of Gold Flan

Makes 8 to 10 Servings

The Douro, Portugal's River of Gold, sweeps from the Atlantic across the mountainous north of Portugal into Spain, its slopes intricately terraced with vineyards. This is port wine country and port is what gives this flan its flavor. Choose a fine tawny or, if you should have a bottle open, a vintage port. What follows is a less rich variation of the flan that appears in my *Food of Portugal.*

Tip: Use a swivel-bladed vegetable peeler to strip the zest from an orange. You want the orange zest only, not the bitter white pith.

1. Caramel: Butter shallow, fluted 2-quart ring mold well and set in freezer. Place sugar and water in small heavy saucepan, set over moderately high heat, and cook—swirling pan occasionally but not stirring—until mixture is syrupy and color of caramel—8 to 10 minutes. Watch carefully lest caramel burn. Spoon 2 tablespoons caramel into small ramekin and reserve for flan. Pour balance of caramel into chilled mold, swirling bottom to coat, and set in freezer.

2. Flan: Preheat oven to 325°F. Combine half-and-half, cream, and sugar in large heavy saucepan and drop in orange zest. Set over moderately low heat and bring to a simmer; stir in reserved 2 tablespoons caramel.

3. Whisk egg yolks until frothy, then add 1 cup hot cream mixture, whisking briskly. Stir back into pan, reduce heat to low, and cook and stir 1 minute. Remove from heat and mix in port wine.

4. Pour flan mixture through large fine sieve set over large heatproof bowl and discard solids. Quick-chill flan mixture in ice bath 20 minutes, stirring often. Pour mixture into ring mold and set in middle of large roasting pan.

5. Pull middle oven shelf out, center roasting pan on shelf, then add enough boiling water to pan to come about halfway up sides of ring mold.

6. Slide shelf into oven and bake uncovered until cake tester, inserted between rim and center, comes out clean—about 1½ hours.

7. Remove flan from oven and from water bath, cool on wire baking rack 1 hour, then cover with foil and chill overnight.

8. To serve, dip ring mold briefly in hot water, then invert flan on large round platter with turned-up rim to catch liquid caramel. Cut into wedges at table and spoon a bit of caramel over each portion.

CARAMEL:

⅔ cup sugar

⅓ cup water

FLAN:

3 cups half-and-half

1 cup heavy cream

1 cup sugar

3 strips orange zest about 3 inches long (see Tip above)

2 tablespoons caramel (see above)

12 jumbo egg yolks (save whites for Pudim Molotov, page 252)

¼ cup port wine (see headnote)

Custards & Creams

Sericaia (Cinnamon-Dusted Baked Custard)

Makes 6 Servings

The recipe for this unusually light Portuguese dessert is adapted from one served at País das Uvas, an *adega* (restaurant/winery) in Vila de Frades (Village of Friars), where owner António Honrado's wife Jacinta and her mother Francisca dish up an impressive array of classics from the Alentejo Province, Portugal's breadbasket. Sericaia is often accompanied by the glacéed green plums of Elvas, a famous Alentejo delicacy. But I think sericaia superb as is—no sugarplums needed.

Note: If Portugal has a favorite spice, cinnamon wins hands down. Ever since Vasco da Gama found the water route to India's treasury of spices at the turn of the sixteenth century and brought cinnamon home to Portugal, Portuguese cooks have been using it to flavor both sweets and savories.

Tip: To approximate a true sericaia, bake it in an ungreased shallow round terracotta or ceramic baking dish, even an ovenproof glass pie plate that transmits heat slowly, not in a metal pan that may overheat—and curdle—the custard.

½ cup sugar

⅓ cup sifted all-purpose flour

¼ teaspoon salt

1 cup milk

Zest of ½ medium lemon removed in strips with a vegetable peeler

½ cinnamon stick

4 large eggs, separated

1½ teaspoons ground cinnamon

1. Preheat oven to 350°F. Combine ¼ cup sugar with flour and salt in small heavy nonreactive saucepan, then whisk in milk. Drop in lemon zest and cinnamon stick, set over moderate heat, and cook, stirring constantly, until mixture simmers and stiff batter forms—5 to 7 minutes. Remove from heat.

2. Whisk egg yolks until smooth in medium bowl. Remove cinnamon stick and lemon zest from hot milk mixture and discard. Add hot mixture slowly to beaten yolks and continue beating until smooth. Cool mixture 15 minutes, whisking occasionally to prevent skin from forming on top.

3. Using hand electric mixer, beat egg whites at high speed in second medium bowl until fluffy. Gradually add remaining ¼ cup sugar and continue beating until soft peaks form.

4. Gently fold one-third beaten whites into cooled yolk mixture, then scoop atop remaining beaten whites, and fold in until no streaks of yellow show.

Recipe continues

5. Spoon custard into ungreased shallow 9-inch pottery or ovenproof-glass pie plate, one heaping tablespoonful at a time and placing each addition at a right angle to the previous one. Sift cinnamon over all, till no custard shows.

6. Center pie plate on baking sheet, slide onto middle oven rack, and bake uncovered until sericaia seems set when you nudge pie plate and cracks are forming on surface—25 to 30 minutes.

7. Remove sericaia from oven, set on wire baking rack, and cool to room temperature.

    Note: Sericaia will fall slightly as it cools and the top will crack a bit more, but this is as it should be.

Rice Pudding

Makes 4 to 6 Servings

This mid-nineteenth-century recipe from Mary Ivey of Wayne County, southeast of Raleigh, appeared in a long out-of-print 1950s collection of family favorites printed by the North Carolina Federation of Home Demonstration Clubs. Attributing it to her great grandmother, Ivey said, "It was used by my grandmother, who helped operate the Seven Springs resort hotel when it was famous for its Saturday night square dances, which sometimes lasted all night, my grandfather playing the violin, and his sister the piano."

Note: This recipe would be equally delicious made with almond milk instead of cow's milk.

1 cup long-grain rice, cooked by package directions

1½ cups milk (see Note above)

½ cup dark seedless raisins

½ cup sugar

Finely grated zest of ½ medium lemon

½ teaspoon freshly grated nutmeg

⅛ teaspoon salt

1. Preheat oven to 325°F. Butter 1½-quart casserole or spritz with nonstick cooking spray.

2. Mix all ingredients well in medium bowl and pour into casserole.

3. Slide onto middle oven shelf and bake uncovered until rice has absorbed almost but not quite all milk and is golden-brown around edge—about 45 minutes.

4. To serve, carry casserole to table and dish pudding up while hot. Or, if you prefer, cool pudding about 20 minutes before serving.

Crème Brûlée

Makes 6 Servings

This late seventeenth-century French classic—rich vanilla custard glazed with a layer of caramelized sugar as thin as onion skin—is known in Britain as Burnt Cream and in Portugal as Leite Creme, where branding irons are used to "burn" sugar crystals into heart-shaped designs on top of the custard. Crème Brûlée, for years a dessert staple in nearly all high-end restaurants and for that reason considered the province of the chef, isn't difficult to make, especially now that little chef's butane torches are widely available. They caramelize the sugar so quickly, so easily, I suggest that you invest in one of these little torches, sometimes called "crème brûlée torches." They are inexpensive, ranging in price from about $25 to $60, and are sold by specialty kitchen shops as well as online (see Sources, page 291). But before you try this recipe, get the feel of your particular torch; each operates a bit differently.

Note: To use the chef's torch to caramelize the sugar, follow manufacturer's directions. Sugar can also be caramelized in the broiler (see Steps 8 and 9).

Tip: It's necessary to bake the custard in flameproof ramekins or custard cups attractive enough to serve at table. Flameproof is key here because the ramekins must be sturdy enough to withstand an intense blue flame.

1. Preheat oven to 350°F. Lightly butter six 6-ounce flameproof ramekins or custard cups and set aside. Also fold damp tea towel to fit large shallow roasting pan and press flat over bottom of pan (this helps anchor custards).

2. Using hand electric mixer, in a medium bowl, beat eggs and egg yolks at moderate speed until frothy—about 30 seconds, then with mixer at low speed, blend in cream, milk, sugar mixture, vanilla, and salt.

3. Pour custard mixture into ramekins, dividing amount evenly. Arrange ramekins, not touching, on folded dish towel in roasting pan.

4. Pull out middle oven shelf, center pan on shelf, then add enough boiling water to pan to come about one-fourth way up sides of ramekins.

5. Gently slide shelf back into oven and bake custards until cake tester, inserted in center of one, comes out clean—about 35 minutes.

Recipe continues

2 large eggs

2 large egg yolks

1½ cups light cream

1½ cups milk

½ cup sugar blended with 1 tablespoon all-purpose flour

1½ teaspoons vanilla extract

⅛ teaspoon salt

CARAMELIZED TOPPING:

3 tablespoons sugar

6. Remove custards from oven and from water bath and cool 30 minutes. Arrange on rimmed tray, lay baking sheet on top, and refrigerate until well chilled and fairly firm — at least 4 hours.

7. When ready to proceed, set chilled custards, still on rimmed tray, on kitchen counter and allow to "temper" for about half an hour. Gently blot up any drops of moisture that may have formed on custards taking care not to break skin on surface.

8. If using broiler to caramelize sugar on top of custards, position oven shelf so it's about 5 inches below the broiler unit and preheat electric broiler 15 full minutes. Most gas broilers do not need to be preheated.

9. Caramelized Topping: Sprinkle 1½ teaspoons sugar evenly on top of each chilled custard, then using butane chef's torch as manufacturer directs and working quickly, caramelize sugar on each custard just until it melts and turns the color of amber. This should only take a few seconds, so watch carefully. The idea is to caramelize the sugar without warming the chilled custard — not as difficult as it may sound.

Note: If using broiler to caramelize sugar, slide tray of custards onto repositioned oven shelf and broil 3 to 4 minutes, until sugar melts and browns nicely, watching constantly and turning tray around so all brown evenly.

10. To serve, center each custard on a bright dessert plate and carry to dinner table.

Mama's Tapioca Pudding

Makes 6 Servings

Whenever I'd been a good girl—had a better-than-usual piano lesson or made an A in arithmetic (rare!)—my mother would treat me to one of my favorite puddings. Though the simplest tapioca puddings are thickened with tapioca only, my mother enriched hers with eggs; and to add welcome airiness, she folded the beaten whites in at the end, which suited me just fine.

Note: Because beaten raw egg whites give this pudding its lift, I specify pasteurized eggs to eliminate the risk of salmonella food poisoning. If your supermarket does not carry them, buy eggs from a local source you trust.

Tip: For a faintly caramel flavor, I sometimes use a half-and-half mix of granulated sugar and light brown sugar instead of granulated sugar only.

1. Combine milk, half-and-half, sugar, tapioca, beaten yolks, and salt in medium-size heavy saucepan and let stand 5 minutes.

2. Set over moderate heat and bring to a simmer, stirring often. Remove from heat immediately and mix in vanilla. Cool 20 minutes, stirring occasionally to prevent top from "skinning over."

3. Using whisk or hand electric mixer, beat egg whites and confectioners' sugar to soft peaks. Fold about one-third beaten whites into tapioca mixture, then fold in balance until no streaks of yellow or white show.

4. Turn into colorful 1½-quart dessert bowl, cover, and refrigerate at least 4 hours before serving.

2 cups milk

1 cup half-and-half

½ cup granulated sugar, or ¼ cup each granulated sugar and firmly packed light brown sugar (see Tip above)

¼ cup quick-cooking tapioca

2 large pasteurized eggs (see Note above), separated and yolks well beaten

¼ teaspoon salt

1½ teaspoons vanilla extract

1 tablespoon confectioners' (10X) sugar

Variations:

Coconut Tapioca Pudding: Prepare basic recipe as directed using all granulated sugar, but substitute 1 (13.66-fluid-ounce) can unsweetened coconut milk (not low-fat or fat-free) plus 1½ cups half-and-half for the 2 cups milk and 1 cup half-and-half. Just before refrigerating, fold in ½ cup finely grated fresh (or packaged unsweetened flaked) coconut. Makes 6 servings.

Pecan Tapioca Pudding: Prepare basic recipe as directed using equal parts granulated and firmly packed light brown sugar and 1½ cups each milk and half-and-half. Just before refrigerating, fold in ½ cup coarsely chopped lightly toasted pecans (6 to 8 minutes in a 350°F oven). Makes 6 servings.

Custards & Creams

Zabaglione

Makes 6 Servings

I first tasted the ambrosial wine-laced egg yolk custard in a small sidewalk cafe in Venice and, from that day forward, ordered it every time it appeared on a dessert menu. During that trip, at least. The good news is that zabaglione (called *sabayon* in France) isn't difficult to make despite its billowing glory.

Note: So what do you do with the leftover egg whites? My choice? Meringue cookies or Pudim Molotov (page 252).

1. Place egg yolks in top of nonreactive 2-quart double boiler or heatproof bowl set on counter while water heats in double boiler bottom over moderately low burner heat. Then with hand electric mixer at low speed, beat until frothy. Raise mixer speed to moderate and add sugar in slow steady stream and continue beating until fluffy. Beat in wine and salt.

2. Set double boiler top or bowl over simmering water (bottom should not touch water), and beat at high speed until mixture balloons to three or four times original size—about 15 minutes of steady beating. Zabaglione should be color of mayonnaise and consistency of softly whipped cream.

3. To serve, mound at once into stemmed goblets or for even more glamour, layer into goblets with thinly sliced fresh peaches or strawberries.

Note: Like soufflé, zabaglione quickly deflates, so waste no time serving it.

7 large egg yolks (see Note above)

¾ cup superfine sugar

⅔ cup sweet Marsala or Madeira wine

⅛ teaspoon salt

Peaches or strawberries for serving (optional)

Old-Timey Tar Heel Banana Pudding

Makes 8 Servings

People still dispute what goes on top of a proper banana pudding: whipped cream or lightly browned meringue? I belong to the meringue school and think that this old North Carolina recipe exemplifies the best.

Note: To be on the safe side, I call for pasteurized eggs because they may not cook completely in the time it takes to brown the meringue. Most supermarkets sell pasteurized eggs, as well as nearly all high-end groceries. Davidson is the brand my supermarket sells. If pasteurized eggs are unavailable, buy from a local source you know and trust.

¾ cup granulated sugar

⅓ cup unsifted all-purpose flour

¼ teaspoon salt

4 cups milk

1 cup half-and-half

3 large pasteurized eggs (see Note above), separated

1½ teaspoons vanilla extract

75 vanilla wafers (most of an 11-ounce box)

6 small firm-ripe bananas

(about 2 pounds), peeled and thinly sliced

3 tablespoons confectioners' (10X) sugar

¼ teaspoon cream of tartar

1. Preheat oven to 350°F.

2. Combine granulated sugar, flour, and salt in medium-size heavy saucepan, add milk and half-and-half, and whisk until smooth. Set over moderate heat and cook, stirring constantly, until thickened, smooth, and no raw floury taste lingers—about 7 minutes.

3. Whisk egg yolks together in small bowl until smooth and stir in about ½ cup hot milk mixture. Stir back into pan, reduce heat to moderately low, and cook, whisking constantly, until thickened like custard—about 3 minutes. Do not allow to boil because custard may curdle. Remove from heat, mix in vanilla, and set aside, whisking often to prevent a skin from forming on top.

Recipe continues

4. Spread thin layer of custard (about ½ cup) over the bottom of ungreased 9 x 9 x 2-inch ovenproof glass baking dish. Arrange 25 vanilla wafers in single layer on top of custard, cover with one-third of bananas and one-third remaining custard. Repeat layers twice, ending with custard.

5. Using hand electric mixer in a medium bowl, beat egg whites, confectioners' sugar, and cream of tartar to soft peaks, then swirl on top of banana pudding, spreading so meringue touches baking dish all around.

6. Slide onto middle oven shelf and bake until meringue is nicely tipped with brown — 15 to 20 minutes.

7. Cool pudding 30 minutes, then cover with baking sheet (just lay on top of baking dish not touching meringue) and refrigerate several hours or overnight.

8. To serve, carry baking dish to table and dish up well-chilled pudding. Cover and refrigerate leftovers — not that there will be any.

Kheer (Indian Rice Pudding)

Makes 6 Servings

This rice pudding, which reminds me so much of those I enjoyed while traveling about India, comes from Sally Massengale via my good friend Moreton Neal, who appended this note: "After reading a book about India in our book group (*The White Tiger,* I think), Sally served an Indian meal with this dessert. It was such an enchanting flavor combination we all wanted the recipe. Later I made Kheer for a group I spoke to about edible flowers, and they loved it, too. It's prettier with some chopped pistachios sprinkled on top."

Notes: Many high-end or specialty groceries sell bottled rose water, ditto dry-roasted pistachio nuts — shelled or unshelled, salted or unsalted (my choice though many people like the sweet/salt combo). Rose water and dry-roasted pistachios can also be ordered online (see Sources, page 291). If the pistachios are not blanched (skinned), gently rub their skins off with a clean dish towel (salted nuts will be less salty once the skins are removed).

Tip: I prefer the seeds of green cardamom (look for green pods) for this rice pudding. The best way to crush them? With a mortar and pestle or, if you're lucky enough to have one, in a little electric spice grinder.

1. Soak rice in enough cold water to cover 15 minutes, then drain well.

2. Place rice in small heavy saucepan, add ¾ cup water, and bring to a boil. Reduce heat to low, cover, and simmer gently until all water is absorbed — about 10 minutes.

3. Combine half-and-half, sugar, and cardamom seeds in large heavy saucepan and mix in rice. Bring to a boil over moderately high heat, then reduce heat to low and simmer uncovered, stirring frequently to avoid sticking, until rice has absorbed almost all liquid and is consistency of soft pudding — 45 minutes to 1 hour.

4. Remove from heat and cool to room temperature. Mix in rose water, then cover and chill well — about 2 hours.

5. To serve, spoon into stemmed goblets and sprinkle each portion with chopped pistachios.

½ cup uncooked basmati rice

¾ cup water

1 quart (4 cups) half-and-half

½ cup sugar

½ teaspoon cardamom seeds (inner dark seeds), crushed (see Tip above)

1 teaspoon rose water (see Notes above)

¼ cup moderately finely chopped shelled and skinned dry-roasted pistachio nuts (see Notes above)

Rice à l'Impératrice

Makes 8 Servings

A showy rice pudding studded with diced candied fruits that's deceptively easy to make. Though usually made with dairy milk, it can also be made with almond or coconut milk; in fact I personally prefer unsweetened almond milk. Use your most decorative tube mold here, invert the chilled pudding onto a bright plate, then, if you like, garnish with puffs of whipped cream and glacéed red and green cherries (not maraschinos). I find Rice à l'Impératrice perfect for Christmas celebrations.

Note: You should make this dessert the day before you plan to serve it because it must chill long enough for the gelatin to firm up.

2½ cups milk, unsweetened almond milk, or coconut milk (not low-fat or fat-free)

½ cup uncooked long-grain rice

1½ (0.25-ounce) envelopes unflavored gelatin (about 3¾ level teaspoons)

½ cup granulated sugar

4 large egg yolks, lightly beaten

1½ teaspoons vanilla extract

⅓ cup diced mixed candied fruits soaked in 1 tablespoon Grand Marnier or other orange liqueur

1 cup heavy cream, whipped to soft peaks

OPTIONAL GARNISH:

½ cup heavy cream, whipped to stiff peaks with 2 tablespoons confectioners' (10X) sugar

4 glacéed red cherries, halved

4 glacéed green cherries, halved

1. Bring 1½ cups milk to gentle boil in medium-size saucepan over moderate heat. Add rice, stirring vigorously, then reduce heat to lowest point. Cover pan and cook, stirring now and then, until rice is tender and has absorbed all milk—about 15 minutes. Scoop rice into large heatproof bowl, fluff with fork, and set aside.

2. Meanwhile, pour remaining 1 cup milk into small pan, sprinkle gelatin over surface, and allow to soften 3 minutes. Add sugar and stir well. Set over moderate heat and cook, stirring often, until mixture steams—about 5 minutes.

3. Whisking briskly, pour about ½ cup hot milk mixture into beaten egg yolks, then stir back into pan. Reduce heat to lowest point and cook, stirring constantly, until consistency of stirred custard—about 30 seconds to 1 minute. Do not allow custard to boil because it may curdle. Remove from heat and stir in vanilla.

4. Fold custard into rice along with diced candied fruits and cool to room temperature—20 to 30 minutes. Finally, fold in whipped cream.

5. Scoop mixture into ungreased decorative 1½-quart ring mold, cover with plastic food wrap, and refrigerate overnight.

6. To serve, gently loosen pudding around edge of mold and central tube with small thin-blade spatula, dip mold briefly in hot water, then invert onto bright dessert plate. Finally, garnish, if you like, with fluffs or pipings of whipped cream and artfully placed glacéed red and green cherries.

Kiss Pudding

Makes 6 Servings

Why do so many of our grandmothers' puddings contain beaten egg whites, often raw or at best only partially cooked? Because eggs were plentiful, eggs were cheap, and eggs, mostly from local farms or maybe our grandmothers' own hens, were safe. Moreover, they were a quick and effective way to create desserts as light and airy as an angel's kiss. Today, however, the mass-produced eggs sold at supermarkets may not be as reliable as Grandma's. So whenever a recipe of mine calls for raw eggs or those not cooked long enough to reach 160°F, the internal temperature the American Egg Board and U.S. Department of Agriculture deem safe, I urge you to use pasteurized eggs (now sold at many supermarkets) to minimize the risk of salmonella food poisoning. And if pasteurized eggs are unavailable? Follow Grandma's lead and buy from a local source you know and trust.

3 large pasteurized eggs (see headnote), separated

1 cup sugar

⅓ cup cold milk blended with 3 tablespoons cornstarch and ¼ teaspoon salt

3 cups steaming hot milk

1½ teaspoons vanilla extract

1 recipe Thin Chocolate Sauce (page 269)

1. Using hand electric mixer, beat egg yolks and ¾ cup sugar in small heavy saucepan until light and thick, then blend in cold milk–cornstarch mixture.

2. Whisking hard, add hot milk slowly and, when incorporated, set over moderately low heat. Cook, stirring constantly, until consistency of medium white sauce—3 to 5 minutes. Do not allow to boil because custard will curdle. Remove from heat and stir in vanilla.

3. Using clean bowl and beaters, whip egg whites until foamy. Raise mixer speed to high and gradually add remaining ¼ cup sugar. Continue beating until billowing and soft peaks form—no longer.

4. Fold about ½ cup beaten whites into hot custard mixture to lighten it, then carefully fold in remaining beaten whites until no streaks of white or yellow show.

5. Spoon into medium bowl, cover, and chill several hours.

6. To serve, spoon pudding into dessert dishes or stemmed goblets. Top each portion with a trickle of chocolate sauce, and pass the rest.

Chocolate Pots de Crème

Makes 6 Servings

Back when I worked in *The Ladies' Home Journal* test kitchen in New York, one of our jobs was to cook for the VIPs our editors-in-chief often invited in to lunch. The executive dining room adjoined the test kitchen and more than once I peeked through the swinging door to catch a glimpse of Isak Dinesen or Daphne du Maurier or the Duke and Duchess of Windsor. Before long the *Journal's* executive dining room became known as "the best restaurant in town." A favorite always, an easy make-ahead, was this rich chocolate pudding served in fine Herend china demitasse cups, Queen Victoria pattern. What follows is my slightly less rich spin on that *LHJ* dessert.

Note: Choose a top-quality chocolate for this recipe, one that melts easily and smoothly.

1. Combine cream, ¼ cup milk, the sugar, and salt in heavy medium saucepan. Cook over medium heat, stirring constantly, until sugar dissolves and bubbles appear at edge of pan—about 2 minutes. Add chocolate and cook and stir until chocolate melts—about 1 minute.

2. Whisk egg yolks and remaining ¼ cup milk until blended not frothy—about 30 seconds. Blend about ½ cup chocolate mixture into yolk mixture, then stir back into pan. Cook, stirring constantly, until mixture thickens and an instant read thermometer inserted in center registers 160°F—about 2 minutes. Do not boil or mixture may curdle.

3. Remove from heat and mix in vanilla. Pour into 6 ungreased 3- to 4-ounce porcelain pots de crème or demitasse cups, dividing amount evenly. Arrange, not touching, on rimmed tray lined with damp tea towel. Set baking sheet on top and refrigerate 3 to 4 hours before serving.

4. When ready to serve, top each pot de crème, if you like, with dollop of whipped cream. Good, too, with Mock Devonshire Cream (page 273) or Crème Fraîche (page 274).

1½ cups heavy cream

½ cup milk

½ cup sugar

¼ teaspoon salt

4 ounces unsweetened chocolate (see Note above), coarsely chopped

4 large egg yolks

2 teaspoons vanilla extract

OPTIONAL TOPPING:

½ cup heavy cream softly whipped with 1 tablespoon confectioners' (10X) sugar and ¼ teaspoon vanilla extract

Variation:

Mocha Pots de Crème: Prepare as directed, adding 1 tablespoon instant espresso powder or crystals to cream mixture in Step 1. Makes 6 servings.

Custards & Creams

Feliciana Parish
Sweet Potato Crème Caramel

Makes 6 Servings

Some years ago while on article assignment for *Gourmet* magazine, I traveled about deepest Louisiana well north of New Orleans and discovered small-town restaurants, plantation-house B & Bs, and home cooks using local ingredients to best advantage and to the hilt, among them sugar and sweet potatoes. Louisiana is a major producer of sweet potatoes and in particular of the vermillion-fleshed Beauregards developed at Louisiana State University in 1987. They now account for 90 percent of the sweet potatoes grown in Louisiana. This recipe was adapted from *Plantation Country,* a first-rate fund-raiser published in 1981 by the Women's Service League of St. Francisville, Louisiana. It has been reprinted many times over the years, not only because of its distinct sense of time and place but also because its recipes are unusual (exotic even), local, and cherished by club members.

1. Preheat oven to 325°F. Lightly butter six 5- or 6-ounce heatproof ramekins or custard cups and set aside. Also fold damp tea towel to fit large shallow roasting pan and press flat over bottom of pan (this helps anchor custards as they bake).

2. Caramel: Melt sugar in medium (9-inch) heavy skillet over moderately low heat, stirring constantly, until syrupy and the color of amber—about 5 minutes. Pour into ramekins, dividing amount evenly and rotating so caramel coats bottoms nicely. Arrange ramekins, not touching, on folded dish towel in roasting pan and set aside while you proceed with recipe. This gives caramel time to firm up—takes about 10 minutes at room temperature.

3. Custard: Heat milk in small heavy saucepan over moderate heat, stirring frequently, until bubbles begin to form around edge of pan—about 4 minutes.

4. Meanwhile, using hand electric mixer, beat sweet potato, sugar, rum, vanilla, and salt at high speed in large bowl until smooth. With mixer at low speed, beat in eggs one at a time, then with mixer still at low speed, add hot milk in slow steady stream.

Recipe continues

CARAMEL:

¾ cup sugar

CUSTARD:

2 cups milk

¾ cup firmly packed unseasoned puréed baked sweet potato (from about 1 large, 10½ ounces)

¼ cup sugar

2 tablespoons dark rum or good bourbon

2 teaspoons vanilla extract

¼ teaspoon salt

4 large eggs

5. With slow, steady hand, pour custard into caramel-coated ramekins in roasting pan, dividing amount evenly. Pull out middle oven shelf, center pan on shelf, then add enough boiling water to pan to come one-fourth way up sides of ramekins.

6. Gently slide middle shelf back into oven and bake custards until cake tester, inserted in center of one, comes out clean — 45 to 50 minutes.

7. Remove custards from oven and from water bath and cool 30 minutes. Set custards on small rimmed baking sheet lined with clean dish towel, lay baking sheet on top, and refrigerate 12 hours or overnight.

8. To serve, gently loosen custard in each ramekin with small thin-blade spatula, dip bottoms of ramekins briefly in hot water, then invert on dessert plates, letting caramel run down sides of custards and pool around them on plates.

Pudim Abade de Priscos
(Pudding of the Abbot of Priscos)

Makes 6 Servings

This unusual golden custard is one of Portugal's classic "egg sweets," created, it's said, by convent nuns to impress visiting VIPs, which explains such amusing recipe names as Angel's Cheeks and Nun's Tummies. What makes this particular pudding from the northerly Minho Province unique is that it contains bacon. Yes, bacon, proving that bacon and eggs do indeed go together—even in desserts. Trend-conscious young American pastry chefs are now discovering what Portuguese cooks have known for hundreds of years.

Note: Be sure to use fresh (unsmoked, uncured) slab bacon for this recipe.

Tip: So what do you do with all those orphaned egg whites? Make Pudim Molotov (page 252) or your favorite angel food cake.

1. Preheat oven to 350°F.

2. Caramel: Combine sugar and boiling water in very small heavy saucepan, stirring until sugar dissolves. Bring to a boil over moderate heat, adjust so mixture bubbles gently, then cook without stirring until pale amber in color—about 25 minutes.

   Note: Top the pan with spatter-shield to keep sugary mist from coating everything in sight.

3. Remove from heat and pour into ungreased fluted 1½-quart metal ring mold. Cool about 5 minutes, then tilt mold this way and that until side and bottom are evenly coated. Allow to cool while you proceed with recipe.

4. Pudding: Bring sugar, water, bacon, lemon zest, and cinnamon stick to a boil in medium nonreactive saucepan over moderate heat, adjust heat so mixture bubbles gently, then cook until syrupy—about 10 minutes. Remove from heat and strain into 2-quart heatproof measuring cup or bowl.

5. Whisking egg mixture vigorously, add strained syrup slowly and continue beating until smooth.

Recipe continues

CARAMEL:

¾ cup sugar

½ cup boiling water

PUDDING:

2 cups sugar

1½ cups water

2 ounces fresh slab bacon (see Note above), diced

Zest of 1 large lemon, removed in strips with a vegetable peeler

1 cinnamon stick, about 3 inches long

10 large egg yolks, well beaten with 1 large whole egg and ¼ cup tawny or vintage port

Custards & Creams

6. Pour into caramel-coated mold, set in medium baking pan, and place on pulled-out middle oven shelf. Pour enough boiling water into baking pan to come halfway up sides of pudding mold.

7. Gently slide middle shelf back into oven and bake pudding uncovered until cake tester, inserted midway between center and edge of pudding, comes out clean — 50 to 60 minutes.

8. Remove pudding from oven and from water bath, set on wire baking rack, and cool until only slightly warmer than room temperature — about 1 hour. Cover with foil and refrigerate overnight.

9. To serve, dip pudding mold briefly in hot water to soften caramel, then invert pudding on decorative round dessert plate. Cut into wedges — this pudding is rich, rich, rich.

Chocolate-Hazelnut Panna Cotta

Makes 8 Servings

Instead of chilling this panna cotta in ramekins and unmolding before serving, I decided to use one large bowl, then layer the chilled panna cotta into stemmed goblets with barely whipped cream. This finished panna cotta tastes more of chocolate than of hazelnuts, so I've added hazelnut extract—*pure* hazelnut extract, not some perfume-y imitation.

Note: A few fancy high-end groceries sell pure hazelnut extract, but if you can't find it, order it online (see Sources, page 291). This will take time, so I've made the hazelnut extract optional though I'm so fond of hazelnut flavor I'm willing to wait for it to arrive.

Tip: Because chocolate-hazelnut spread is stickier than toffee, scoop it from the jar onto a flat plate before you begin the recipe, mounding it up in the center and scraping what you can from the jar with a small thin-blade spatula and/or small rubber scraper. This way you can quickly push the spread into the hot cream mixture instead of pausing mid-recipe to pry the stuff from the jar. Forget about any recalcitrant bits clinging to the jar—the amounts are too small to affect the recipe.

1. Soften gelatin in cold water in small ramekin and set aside while you proceed with the recipe.

2. Bring half-and-half, 1½ cups heavy cream, the sugar, and salt to boil in large heavy saucepan over moderate heat. Add chocolate-hazelnut spread, reduce heat to low, and simmer, stirring frequently, until smooth—3 to 5 minutes. Add softened gelatin and simmer, stirring constantly, until gelatin dissolves completely—about 3 minutes more.

3. Remove from heat and mix in hazelnut extract, if using, and vanilla. Cool 30 minutes, stirring occasionally to keep mixture from "skinning over." Finally, pour all through large fine sieve set over deep 2-quart bowl.

4. Set in refrigerator—do not cover—and chill overnight.

5. When ready to serve, whip remaining 1 cup heavy cream until it peaks very softly. Beginning with panna cotta and topping off with softly whipped cream, layer decoratively into 8 balloon goblets.

1½ (0.25-ounce) envelopes unflavored gelatin (about 3¾ level teaspoons)

½ cup cold water

3 cups half-and-half

2½ cups heavy cream

¼ cup raw sugar

¼ teaspoon salt

1 (13-ounce) jar chocolate-hazelnut spread (see Tip above)

1½ teaspoons pure hazelnut extract (optional; see Note above)

½ teaspoon vanilla extract

Custards & Creams

Dulce de Leche Pots de Crème

Makes 4 Servings

Simply translated, *dulce de leche* means "milk candy" and though long a favorite in South America and Mexico, it has only recently begun rivaling the popularity of chocolate in this country (there are now Girl Scout Dulce de Leche Cookies). Usually, dulce de leche is made by caramelizing sweetened condensed milk (slow, not so easy, and dangerous if boiled or baked in unopened cans). This recipe takes a bit of standing and stirring, it's true, but the rich caramel flavor of these little custards is reward enough.

Note: I personally prefer the supreme silkiness of yolks-only pots de crème, but if you have no immediate use for the whites, use two whole eggs instead.

1. Place sweetened condensed milk, evaporated milk, and raw sugar in medium-size heavy saucepan, set over moderate heat, and bring to rolling boil. Reduce heat to low and cook, stirring frequently, until the color of caramel and the consistency of stirred custard—20 to 25 minutes.

2. Whisk egg yolks and salt in medium heatproof bowl until smooth, then whisking briskly, add about ½ cup hot milk mixture and continue whisking until smooth. Stir back into pan, set over moderate heat, and cook and stir just until mixture begins to simmer—do not bring to rolling boil because mixture may curdle.

3. Remove from heat and blend in vanilla. Pour into four ungreased 5- or 6-ounce ramekins or custard cups, dividing amount evenly.

4. Serve warm or, if you prefer, cover and chill several hours before serving. The pudding will never set like custard or gelatin desserts, but it will thicken. Whether you choose to serve these little pots de crème "straight up" or topped with whipped cream "to cut the richness," as they say Down South, is up to you. For a dinner party I may go "continental" and top with Mock Devonshire Cream (page 273) or Crème Fraîche (page 274).

1 (14-ounce) can sweetened condensed milk (not low-fat or fat-free)

1 (12-ounce) can evaporated milk (not low-fat or fat-free)

¼ cup raw sugar

4 large egg yolks or 2 large whole eggs (see Note above)

¼ teaspoon salt

1½ teaspoons vanilla extract

OPTIONAL TOPPING:

1 cup heavy cream beaten to soft peaks with 1 tablespoon confectioners' 10X sugar

Custards & Creams

Chocolate Soufflé

Makes 6 Servings

Soufflés keep getting a bad rap. They're fragile, yes, and must be rushed to the table before they collapse, and sometimes they never rise at all. No wonder soufflés spook so many cooks. In truth, soufflés aren't very temperamental once you learn that the fastest road to ruin is overbeating the egg whites. In other words, don't beat to stiff peaks. As my Cornell food chemistry professor preached day after day, "The secret of a high-rising soufflé is to beat the egg whites *only until they billow and flow, not run, from the bowl*." Once you learn that lesson, your soufflés should be as puffy as a summer cloud.

Note: I was taught that soufflé dishes should not be buttered because the soufflés would fall flat. Later, spending time in Paris, I discovered that French chefs butter, then sugar their dessert soufflé molds, and their soufflés climb sky-high.

Tip: It's best, I find, to make the chocolate base ahead of time, cover, and refrigerate. About 2 hours before you're ready to proceed, remove the chocolate base from refrigerator and bring to room temperature.

TO PREPARE SOUFFLÉ DISH (SEE NOTE ABOVE):

1 teaspoon unsalted butter, at room temperature

2 tablespoons granulated sugar

SOUFFLÉ:

¼ cup (½ stick) unsalted butter, cut into pats

5 tablespoons all-purpose flour

5 tablespoons unsweetened cocoa powder

2 cups scalding hot milk

4 large eggs, separated

¾ cup granulated sugar

1½ teaspoons vanilla extract

¼ teaspoon salt

1 tablespoon confectioners' (10X) sugar (to dust top of soufflé; optional)

1. Preheat oven to 375°F. To prepare soufflé dish: Lightly butter 1½-quart soufflé dish, add sugar, then tilt dish from side to side until bottom and sides are evenly coated with sugar. Tap out excess sugar and set soufflé dish aside.

2. Soufflé: Melt butter in medium-size heavy saucepan over moderately low heat. Add flour and cocoa and blend into thick paste. Add milk and cook, stirring constantly, until thickened and smooth—3 to 5 minutes. Remove from heat.

3. Beat egg yolks with ½ cup sugar in small bowl until frothy, blend in about ½ cup hot chocolate mixture, then stir back into pan. Set over low heat and cook, stirring constantly, 2 minutes. Do not allow to boil or mixture may curdle.

4. Remove from heat, mix in vanilla, and transfer to large bowl. Cool to room temperature, stirring often to hasten cooling and prevent mixture from "skinning over."
    Note: You can prepare chocolate base ahead of time, cover, and refrigerate until 2 hours before proceeding (see headnote and Tip); 20 minutes before beginning Step 5, preheat oven.

5. Beat egg whites with salt and 1 tablespoon of remaining ¼ cup sugar in large electric mixer bowl at moderate speed until frothy—about 1 minute. Scatter another tablespoon remaining sugar over whites and continue beating until beginning to turn silvery—about 1 minute more. Add a third tablespoon remaining sugar, raise mixer speed to high, and beat 30 seconds.

6. With machine off, scatter final tablespoon sugar over whites, then beat at high speed just until egg whites billow and peak ever so softly—about 1 minute. Stop machine the instant egg whites reach this point; if you continue beating whites to stiff peaks, you may ruin your soufflé. This is key.

7. By hand, gently fold about 1 cup beaten whites into chocolate mixture to lighten it, then add remaining whites and fold in with lightest of touches until no streaks of brown or white remain. This is also key.

8. Pour soufflé batter into prepared soufflé dish, center on baking sheet, and set on pulled-out middle oven shelf. Slide shelf back into oven and bake until soufflé quivers slightly when you nudge dish and is puffed and lightly browned—40 to 45 minutes.

9. To serve, remove soufflé from oven, quickly sift confectioners' sugar evenly on top, if desired, then rush soufflé to table. Serve as is or accompany, if you like, with Crème Anglaise (page 270).

Fresh Peach Soufflé

Makes 6 Servings

Unlike most soufflés, this one contains no butter and is thickened with cornstarch instead of flour, so it's unusually delicate and soars to the top of the baking dish. Still, if you master the technique described in the Chocolate Soufflé headnote (which precedes), you should have no trouble.

TO PREPARE SOUFFLÉ DISH:

1 teaspoon unsalted butter, at room temperature

2 tablespoons granulated sugar

SOUFFLÉ:

1 cup puréed peeled pitted dead-ripe full-of-flavor peaches (about 3 medium)

⅓ cup granulated sugar blended with 3 tablespoons cornstarch

2 tablespoons fresh lemon or lime juice

4 large egg yolks

¼ cup heavy cream

1 tablespoon dark rum

6 large egg whites, at room temperature

¼ teaspoon salt

3 tablespoons granulated sugar

2 teaspoons confectioners' (10X) sugar (to dust top of soufflé)

1. Preheat oven to 375°F. To prepare soufflé dish: Lightly butter 2-quart soufflé dish, add sugar, then tilt dish from side to side until bottom and sides are evenly coated with sugar. Tap out excess sugar and set soufflé dish aside.

2. Soufflé: Combine peach purée, sugar-cornstarch mixture, and lemon juice in medium nonreactive saucepan. Set over moderate heat and cook, stirring constantly, just until mixture thickens and clears—2 to 3 minutes. Remove from heat.

3. Beat egg yolks and cream in small bowl until smooth, whisk in about ½ cup hot peach mixture, then stir back into pan. Reduce heat to low and cook, stirring constantly, 2 minutes. Do not allow to boil or mixture may curdle.

4. Remove from heat and mix in rum, then transfer to large bowl. Cool to room temperature, stirring often to hasten cooling and prevent mixture from "skinning over."

5. Beat egg whites with salt and 1 tablespoon sugar in large electric mixer bowl at moderate speed until frothy—about 1 minute. Scatter another tablespoon sugar over whites and continue beating until beginning to turn silvery—about 1 minute more.

6. Add third and final tablespoon sugar, raise mixer speed to high, and beat just until egg whites billow and peak ever so softly—about 1 minute. Stop machine the instant egg whites reach this point; if you continue beating whites to stiff peaks, you may ruin your soufflé. This is key.

7. By hand, gently fold about 1 cup beaten whites into peach mixture, then add remaining whites and fold in with lightest of touches until no streaks of orange or white remain. This is also key.

8. Pour soufflé batter into prepared soufflé dish, center on baking sheet, and set on pulled-out middle oven shelf. Slide shelf back into oven and bake until soufflé quivers slightly when you nudge dish and is puffed and lightly browned—about 35 minutes.

9. To serve, remove soufflé from oven, quickly sift confectioners' sugar evenly on top, then rush soufflé to table. Serve as is or accompany, if you like, with Quick Cardinal Sauce (page 284).

Variation:

Fresh Strawberry Soufflé: Prepare Peach Soufflé as directed, but substitute 1 cup puréed red-ripe strawberries (about 6 ounces) for peaches. Also use 1 tablespoon each fresh orange and lemon juice in place of 2 tablespoons lemon juice, and 1 tablespoon Grand Marnier or other orange liqueur instead of rum. Delicious with or without Quick Raspberry Sauce (page 278). Makes 6 servings.

Orange Soufflé

Makes 6 Servings

Quicker than the two previous soufflés—easier, too, because the orange base does not need to be cooked and cooled. Equally delicious is the Grand Marnier variation that follows. Either is perfect for a small dinner party *if* you bake the soufflé in six buttered-and-sugared 1-cup ramekins, which can go into the oven on a rimmed baking sheet—no water bath needed. Baking time: 20 to 25 minutes, and yes, your guests will be willing to wait. The trick is to get a jump on things by making the orange base ahead of time and having everything else at-the-ready. I do recommend, however, that you do a trial run first—just for the family.

1. Preheat oven to 350°F. To prepare soufflé dish: Lightly butter 1½-quart soufflé dish, add sugar, then tilt dish from side to side until bottom and sides are evenly coated with sugar. Tap out excess sugar and set soufflé dish aside.

2. Soufflé: Using hand electric mixer, beat egg yolks in medium bowl at high speed until thick and lemony—about 3 minutes. Add ½ cup sugar and next four ingredients (marmalade through orange juice), then beat at low speed just enough to combine.

3. With pristine beaters, beat egg whites and salt in large electric mixer bowl at moderate speed until frothy. Add 1 tablespoon remaining sugar and beat at moderate speed about 1 minute. Add another tablespoon remaining sugar and continue beating until whites begin to turn silvery—about 1 minute more. Add a third tablespoon remaining sugar, and beat at high speed 10 to 15 seconds.

4. With machine off, scatter final tablespoon remaining sugar over whites, then beat at high speed just until whites billow and peak softly—about 1 minute. Stop machine as soon as whites reach this point; further beating may ruin your soufflé. This is key.

5. By hand, gently fold about 1 cup beaten whites into orange mixture to lighten it, then add remaining whites and fold in with lightest of touches—no streaks of orange or white should show. This is also key.

TO PREPARE SOUFFLÉ DISH:

1 teaspoon unsalted butter, at room temperature

2 tablespoons granulated sugar

SOUFFLÉ:

6 large eggs, separated

¾ cup granulated sugar

¼ cup firmly packed orange marmalade

2 tablespoons fresh lemon juice

1 teaspoon finely grated orange zest

1 tablespoon fresh orange juice

¼ teaspoon salt

2 teaspoons confectioners' (10X) sugar (to dust top of soufflé; optional)

6. Scoop soufflé batter into prepared soufflé dish and set in medium roasting pan. Pull middle oven shelf out, center roasting pan on shelf, then add enough boiling water to pan to come about halfway up sides of soufflé dish.

Note: If you prefer to bake six individual soufflés, see recipe headnote for directions.

7. Gently slide shelf back into oven and bake until soufflé quivers slightly when you nudge dish and is puffed and touched with brown — 40 to 45 minutes.

8. To serve, remove soufflé from oven and from water bath, quickly sift confectioners' sugar evenly on top, if desired, then rush soufflé to table.

Variation:

Grand Marnier Soufflé: Prepare as directed, but substitute 3 tablespoons Grand Marnier for the lemon and orange juices and increase orange zest to 1½ teaspoons. Makes 6 servings.

Custards & Creams

Raspberry Bavarian Cream

Makes 6 Servings

Because fresh raspberry season is so short, I make this rosy Bavarian cream with frozen unsweetened raspberries.

Note: Frozen strawberries can be substituted, if you like.

1. Place milk in small heavy nonreactive saucepan, add sugar and gelatin, and stir to combine. Set aside 1 minute for gelatin to soften. Set over low heat and cook, stirring constantly, until sugar and gelatin are completely dissolved—about 3 minutes.

2. Whisking hard, slowly add hot milk mixture to beaten egg yolk, stir back into pan, and cook, stirring constantly, over low heat 2 to 3 minutes. Do not allow to boil or mixture will curdle.

3. Remove from heat and fold in raspberry purée. Quick-chill mixture by setting pan in large bowl of crushed ice and letting stand, stirring occasionally, until consistency of unbeaten egg whites—about 20 minutes.

4. Transfer gelatin mixture to large mixing bowl. Fold in about half the whipped cream, then fold in balance and continue folding until no streaks of white or red remain.

5. Cover and refrigerate several hours.

6. To serve, scoop into dessert dishes or stemmed goblets and, if you like, top with Quick Raspberry Sauce or Crème Anglaise.

¾ cup milk

½ cup granulated sugar

1 (0.25-ounce) envelope unflavored gelatin

1 large egg yolk, lightly beaten

1 (10-ounce) package frozen raspberries (see Note above), thawed, puréed, and sieved to remove seeds

1½ cups heavy cream, whipped to soft peaks with 1 tablespoon confectioners' (10X) sugar

OPTIONAL TOPPING:

1 recipe Quick Raspberry Sauce (page 278) or Crème Anglaise (page 270)

Vanilla Bavarian Cream

Makes 6 Servings

Thickened both with gelatin and egg yolks and enriched with whipped cream, the dessert that was so popular in our grandmother's day deserves to be rediscovered. Serve with fresh strawberries or peaches at their peak of flavor.

1. Place milk in small heavy saucepan, add sugar and gelatin, and stir to combine. Set aside 1 minute to allow gelatin to soften. Drop in vanilla bean, set over low heat, and cook, stirring constantly, until sugar and gelatin are completely dissolved—about 5 minutes. Remove vanilla bean. Scrape any black seeds clinging to bean into milk mixture, then discard vanilla bean.

2. Whisking hard, add about ½ cup hot milk mixture to beaten egg yolks, stir back into pan, and cook over low heat, stirring constantly, until lightly thickened—3 to 4 minutes. Do not allow to boil or mixture will curdle.

3. Quick-chill gelatin mixture by setting pan in large bowl of crushed ice and letting stand, stirring occasionally, until consistency of unbeaten egg whites—about 25 minutes.

4. Transfer gelatin mixture to large mixing bowl. Fold in about half the whipped cream, then fold in balance and continue folding until no streaks of white or yellow remain.

5. Cover and refrigerate several hours.

6. To serve, scoop into dessert dishes or stemmed goblets, layering or topping with fresh strawberries or peaches.

2 cups milk

½ cup sugar

1 (0.25-ounce) envelope unflavored gelatin

1 large vanilla bean, split lengthwise

4 large egg yolks, lightly beaten

1½ cups heavy cream, whipped to soft peaks

1½ cups hulled dead-ripe fresh strawberries or peeled and pitted peaches (about ½ pound), either thinly sliced and sweetened to taste

Showstopper Bavarian Cream

Makes 12 Servings

If you're planning a special dinner party and want a showstopping dessert, this is the one to serve. It's a variation on the Badische Cream I enjoyed at Brenners Park-Hotel in the German spa town of Baden-Baden that's equally famous for its luxurious casino. This dessert takes time to make, I'll admit, but it can be done in stages well ahead of time, even assembled hours in advance. All you have to do at the last minute is add the garnishes. Get ready for "oohs" and "aahs" and recipe requests.

1. Several hours or day before, prepare both sauces as directed as well as raspberry purée for Raspberry Bavarian Cream and store in separate covered containers in refrigerator.

2. When ready to proceed, prepare Raspberry and Vanilla Bavarian Cream but each only through Step 4 (no refrigeration needed at this point).

3. Spoon one-third Quick Raspberry Sauce into 3-quart glass or crystal bowl (I use a tall stemmed bowl shaped like a giant brandy snifter to showcase the layers). Carefully spoon one-half raspberry cream on top, then spoon another one-third raspberry sauce around edge.

4. Scoop half vanilla cream on top, taking care not to squash it or raspberry cream below. Top with remaining raspberry cream and raspberry sauce, again spooning sauce around edge so layers show clearly. Finally, top with remaining vanilla cream (handle gently) and spoon thin layer of Crème Anglaise evenly over all.

5. Cover bowl and refrigerate 3 to 4 hours before serving. Also cover and refrigerate remaining Crème Anglaise.

6. To serve, remove dessert from refrigerator, cluster fresh raspberries artfully on top, and sprig with lemon verbena. Pass remaining Crème Anglaise separately.

1 recipe Crème Anglaise (page 270)

1 recipe Quick Raspberry Sauce (page 278)

1 recipe Raspberry Bavarian Cream (page 114)

1 recipe Vanilla Bavarian Cream (page 115)

GARNISH:

20 to 25 perfect large raspberries

3 to 4 small sprigs lemon verbena, lemon geranium, or mint

Sweet Potato Panna Cotta with Clementines in Lemongrass Syrup

Makes 8 Servings

Panna cotta (Italian for "cooked cream") is one of the loveliest desserts imaginable, an easy make-ahead with no end of variations. Sweet potatoes, it seemed to me, would make a stellar panna cotta. And so they do, sauced with clementines in Lemongrass Syrup. All are party-perfect, all can be made several days in advance.

Notes: Lemongrass Syrup is unusually aromatic and superb drizzled over fresh sliced peaches and strawberries as well as clementines. And what a wonderful way to sweeten tea—iced or hot. I like to keep a snugly capped jar of Lemongrass Syrup at-the-ready in the fridge—it lasts for weeks.

Tip: For more about lemongrass and clementines, see Ingredients (pages xxviii and xxiv).

LEMONGRASS SYRUP (SEE NOTES AND TIP ABOVE):

3 large stalks fresh lemongrass (about ½ pound)

2 cups granulated sugar

1 cup raw sugar

1¾ cups cold water

CLEMENTINES:

8 clementines (about 1 pound), peeled and divided into segments

Rind of 3 clementines (in largish pieces)

2½ cups Lemongrass Syrup (recipe left)

¼ cup fresh lemon juice

PANNA COTTA:

2 tablespoons cold water

2 teaspoons unflavored gelatin

2½ cups heavy cream or a 50/50 mix of heavy cream and half-and-half

½ cup Lemongrass Syrup (recipe left)

¼ teaspoon salt

1 cup firmly packed puréed unseasoned baked sweet potato, at room temperature

1. Lemongrass Syrup: Trim coarse tops and roots from lemongrass, then with cutlet bat or broad side of cleaver, smash each stalk. Cut into 2-inch lengths.

2. Bring all syrup ingredients to rolling boil in large nonreactive pan over moderate heat—this takes 8 to 10 minutes. Set pan off heat, cover, and cool syrup 1 hour.

Recipe continues

Custards & Creams

3. Pour cooled syrup through large fine sieve into large nonreactive bowl, pressing solids to extract as much syrup as possible. Makes about 3 cups.

4. Pour strained syrup into 1-quart preserving jar, screw lid down tight, and refrigerate until needed.

5. Clementines: Drop one-third of segments into 1-quart preserving jar and top with one-third rind. Repeat twice. Combine Lemongrass Syrup and lemon juice, pour into jar, screw lid down tight, and refrigerate until ready to serve.

6. Panna Cotta: Place water in small ramekin, scatter gelatin on top, and soften 15 minutes. Do not stir.

7. Meanwhile, combine cream, Lemongrass Syrup, and salt in a medium-size heavy nonreactive saucepan, set over moderately low heat, and cook, stirring now and then, just until sugar dissolves and mixture steams—6 to 8 minutes. Do not boil.

8. Remove from heat, add softened gelatin, and stir until it dissolves completely. Add sweet potato purée and whisk until smooth.

9. Ladle panna cotta mixture into eight ungreased 6-ounce ramekins or molds, dividing amount evenly. Set on large rimmed baking sheet (or two small ones), lay baking sheet on top, and refrigerate at least 8 hours or overnight.

10. To unmold, dip bottom of each ramekin briefly, one by one, in hot water and loosen around edge with small thin-blade spatula dipped in hot water. Place colorful dessert plate upside down on top of ramekin, then invert, shaking gently to unmold. Easy does it.

11. To serve, arrange clementines decoratively around each unmolded panna cotta, then spoon Lemongrass Syrup alongside. Don't be stingy.

Dulce de Leche Panna Cotta

Makes 8 Servings

A friend who tasted my test of this recipe urged me to call it Oh-My-God (or OMG) Dulce de Leche Panna Cotta because it is "killer"—achingly sweet and smoother than silk. Though softly set, this panna cotta does not collapse when unmolded, *if* chilled for at least 24 hours.

Note: You can shortcut prep time significantly by using store-bought dulce de leche. There are many brands, among them Nestlé. High-end groceries sell dulce de leche, ditto Latino markets, and it's available online (see Sources, page 291). Commercial dulce de leches vary from brand to brand—in color and flavor as well as in consistency, which can affect the final result of this dessert. I developed this panna cotta using dulce de leche I'd made, myself—slowly caramelizing sweetened condensed milk (not to be confused with evaporated milk) as directed on page 122 until reduced to 1 cup, exactly the amount of dulce de leche you need for this panna cotta. I urge you to follow my lead. Making dulce de leche does take time, but it requires little "babysitting" as my good friend Sara Moulton would say.

Tips: This panna cotta must chill for 24 hours, so prepare it a day or two in advance. Use this time to make the Crème Anglaise; pour into a pitcher, cover, and refrigerate till ready to serve.

DULCE DE LECHE (SEE NOTE ABOVE):

1 (14-ounce) can sweetened condensed milk (not low-fat or fat-free)

PANNA COTTA (SEE TIPS ABOVE):

1½ (0.25-ounce) envelopes unflavored gelatin (about 3¾ level teaspoons)

⅓ cup cold water

2½ cups heavy cream

1 (12-ounce) can evaporated milk (not low-fat or fat-free)

¼ cup raw sugar

¼ teaspoon salt

1 cup Dulce de Leche (see Note above)

1½ teaspoons vanilla extract

SAUCE:

1 recipe Crème Anglaise (page 270; see Tips above)

Recipe continues

Custards & Creams

1. Dulce de Leche: Scoop sweetened condensed milk into 6-cup double boiler top or heatproof bowl, set over simmering water (double boiler top should never touch water below), and cook uncovered, whisking briskly and scraping pan sides down every 20 minutes, until color of creamy peanut butter and almost, but not quite, as thick—about 2 hours. Toward end of cooking, check level of water in double boiler bottom and top off if needed to keep depth at about an inch. Makes 1 cup dulce de leche.

2. Panna Cotta: About 30 minutes before dulce de leche is done, soften gelatin in cold water in small ramekin and set aside while you proceed with recipe.

3. Bring cream, evaporated milk, sugar, and salt to boil in large heavy saucepan over moderate heat. Add dulce de leche and simmer, stirring frequently, until silky-smooth—3 to 5 minutes. Add softened gelatin and simmer, stirring constantly, until gelatin dissolves completely—3 to 5 minutes more.

4. Remove from heat, mix in vanilla, and cool 30 minutes, stirring occasionally to keep mixture from "skinning over." Finally, pour all through large fine sieve set over large bowl.

5. Ladle panna cotta mixture into eight ungreased 6-ounce ramekins, dividing amount evenly. Set on large rimmed baking sheet (or two small ones) and refrigerate at least 24 hours. Do not cover.

6. To unmold, dip bottom of each ramekin briefly, one by one, in hot water and loosen around edge with small thin-blade spatula dipped in hot water. Place colorful dessert plate upside down on top of ramekin, then invert, shaking gently to unmold. If panna cotta sticks, place dish towel wrung out in hot water on top of inverted ramekin, and shake gently once more. Persist and recalcitrant puddings *will* unmold. Easy does it.

7. Sauce: To serve, pour a little chilled Crème Anglaise over each panna cotta and pass the rest.

Lemon Verbena Panna Cotta

Makes 6 Servings

Lemon verbena, also called lemon beebrush, is one of the loveliest lemony herbs and deserves to be better known. The best place to find it? At a local nursery that specializes in herbs or your farmers' market. I tried growing it on a sunny windowsill, but was forever battling aphids and white flies, so now, I buy lemon verbena whenever I need a few sprigs.

This panna cotta infused with lemon verbena is one I've tried to re-create from memory. Years ago when I lived on New York's Gramercy Park, it was a signature dessert at Chef Diane Forley's Verbena, a fine little garden restaurant on the ground floor of a Victorian townhouse on Irving Place, a few blocks south of the park. That townhouse and the one next door have morphed into the luxurious Inn at Irving Place, but Verbena, the garden restaurant where I spent so many happy lunches is gone.

Tip: Bruising lemon verbena leaves heightens their delicate flavor and the best way to do it is to crumple them, then rub the leaves firmly between your fingers as you add them to the pan in Step 1.

1. Bring water and lemon verbena to boil in small nonreactive saucepan over high heat. Reduce heat to low and simmer uncovered—no need to stir—until reduced to about ½ cup—approximately 5 minutes.

2. Add sugar and cook, stirring constantly, until sugar dissolves and syrup is clear—about 1 minute. Add lemon zest, cool mixture 30 minutes, then cover and refrigerate 8 hours or overnight.

3. When ready to proceed, sprinkle gelatin over lemon juice in small heatproof bowl and allow to soften 15 minutes. Set bowl in pan of simmering water and stir until gelatin has completely dissolved—about 2 minutes.

4. Remove bowl of gelatin from water, then strain lemon verbena syrup into gelatin and stir to combine.

5. Whisk half-and-half with heavy cream in medium bowl until smooth, then slowly whisk in gelatin mixture.

Recipe continues

¾ cup cold water

25 fresh lemon verbena leaves (about 2 inches long), cut in half lengthwise and bruised (see Tip above)

½ cup sugar

5 (¼ x 2-inch) strips lemon zest

1½ (0.25 g) envelopes unflavored gelatin (about 3¾ level teaspoons)

¼ cup fresh lemon juice

1 cup half-and-half

1 cup heavy cream

GARNISH:

12 fresh lemon verbena leaves

6. Place six ungreased 5- or 6-ounce ramekins on large rimmed baking sheet (or two small ones). Moisten 6 of the lemon verbena leaf garnishes and smooth one, right side down, over bottom of each ramekin. Dividing panna cotta mixture evenly, pour directly on leaves in bottoms of ramekins and continue adding until ramekins are nearly full.

7. Cover and refrigerate 8 to 10 hours or overnight.

8. When ready to serve, dip bottom of each ramekin briefly, one by one, in hot water and loosen around edge with small thin-blade spatula dipped in hot water. Place colorful dessert plate upside down on top of ramekin, then invert, shaking gently to unmold panna cotta. Garnish each portion with one of the remaining lemon verbena leaves.

Classic Cornstarch Pudding

Makes 4 Servings

I guess you might call this a beginner's recipe. Certainly it was for me. Cornstarch pudding is quick, it's easy, but it's a learning experience, too. Did you know, for example, that cornstarch has twice the thickening power of flour? Or that unlike flour, it begins to thin out as soon as it has thickened? That's why you must get your cornstarch pudding off the heat ASAP. If you follow my directions exactly, your pudding should be properly thick and silky. And the same goes for the caramel and chocolate variations that follow.

1. Combine sugar and cornstarch in medium-size heavy saucepan, then gradually whisk in half-and-half.

2. Set over moderate heat and cook, stirring constantly, just until bubbles appear around edge of pan. Reduce heat at once to low.

3. Whisk about ½ cup hot cornstarch mixture into beaten egg, stir back into pan, and cook, stirring constantly, just until thickened and instant-read thermometer, inserted in middle of pudding, registers 160°F—about 3 minutes.

4. Remove pudding from heat, add butter and vanilla, and whisk until butter melts. Then, stirring often to prevent skin from forming on top of pudding, cool 15 minutes.

5. To serve, spoon warm pudding into dessert dishes and top each portion with whipped cream or Crème Anglaise. Of, if you prefer, scoop pudding into large bowl, press plastic food wrap flat on top, and refrigerate several hours before serving.

½ cup sugar

2 tablespoons cornstarch

2 cups half-and-half or milk, or 1 cup each half-and-half and milk

1 large egg, lightly beaten

1 tablespoon unsalted butter, at room temperature

1½ teaspoons vanilla extract

1 cup heavy cream, softly whipped, or 1 recipe Crème Anglaise (page 270)

Variations:

Caramel Cornstarch Pudding: Prepare as directed, but substitute ⅔ cup firmly packed light brown sugar for the ½ cup granulated sugar. Makes 4 servings.

Chocolate Cornstarch Pudding: Prepare as directed, but add one finely grated (1-ounce) square semisweet or bittersweet chocolate to hot cornstarch mixture along with egg in Step 3. Makes 4 servings.

Custards & Creams

Bill Smith's Butterscotch Pudding

Makes 6 Servings

For many years now, my good friend Bill Smith has been the chef at Crook's Corner in Chapel Hill, NC, to which lovers of Southern cooking make daily pilgrimages. When I told Bill I was writing a pudding cookbook, he graciously sent this recipe—in restaurant portions, which begin with 16 cups half-and-half, 18 egg yolks, and 3 pounds light brown sugar. I've quartered those portions here. Bill also appended these comments: "I've never made a small batch of this recipe. Also, because butterscotch extract isn't always available, I switched to molasses and people here love it. On occasion I do have the butterscotch extract so I add just a little to bump things up. I remember trying this recipe with raw sugar and with demerara sugar, but it came out too runny, so just stick with regular old light brown."

Note: I usually pack brown sugar firmly into the measuring cup but for this recipe just spoon it into a dry cup measure and level off the top with the edge of a small thin-blade spatula.

Tip: The only butterscotch extract to use here is pure butterscotch extract. Some supermarkets and many high-end groceries sell it, but if it's unavailable where you live, either order it online (see Sources, page 291), or omit it. The pudding is plenty butterscotch-y without it.

1 quart (4 cups) half-and-half

½ vanilla bean, split lengthwise

8 tablespoons (½ cup) unsifted cornstarch

¼ teaspoon salt

4 large egg yolks

2 tablespoons refrigerator-cold unsalted butter, diced

1½ cups light brown sugar (see Note above)

1½ tablespoons unsulfured molasses (not too dark)

½ teaspoon pure butterscotch extract (optional; see Tip above)

OPTIONAL TOPPING:

1 cup heavy cream, whipped to soft peaks

1. Place 2 cups half-and-half and vanilla bean in medium-size heavy saucepan, set over moderate heat, and cook, stirring occasionally, just until bubbles begin to form around edge of pan—about 4 minutes.

2. Meanwhile, combine remaining half-and-half with cornstarch and salt in small bowl, whisking hard until smooth. Add egg yolks and again whisk until smooth.

3. Ladle about 1 cup hot half-and-half into egg mixture and stir back into saucepan. Reduce heat to low and cook, stirring constantly, until beginning to thicken—about 3 minutes.

4. Over lowest heat, add butter bit by bit, stirring until completely melted. Add sugar the same way, whisking to incorporate, then molasses, and butterscotch extract, if using.

5. Remove from heat and cool 20 minutes, whisking often to prevent a skin from forming on surface. Discard vanilla bean.

6. Transfer pudding to large bowl, press parchment paper flat on surface, and refrigerate several hours or overnight.

7. To serve, mound pudding in stemmed parfait glasses and top, if you like, with drifts of whipped cream. Equally delicious with Mock Devonshire Cream (page 273) or Crème Fraîche (page 274).

Chocolate Mousse

Makes 8 Servings

There are chocolate mousses and then there are those "quick-and-easies" swirled up out of marshmallow fluff, faux whipped cream, and melted chocolate chips. Not my idea of a first-class chocolate mousse. The one below measures up and isn't difficult to make but, make a note, you must use a quality dark chocolate (bittersweet or semisweet) that melts easily and smoothly — like Ghirardelli's Extra Bittersweet Chocolate baking bar. Many supermarkets carry it and nearly all specialty groceries do. Moreover, premium baking chocolates can be ordered online (see Sources, page 291).

Note: Because the egg whites are merely beaten, not cooked, I call for pasteurized eggs, which many supermarkets now sell. If unavailable, use eggs from a local source you trust.

Tip: When melting as much as 6 ounces of chocolate, "slowly" in the top of a double boiler is the way to go. The water below should never boil, only tremble, and the top of the double boiler should never touch that water because if it does, the chocolate will not melt smoothly.

6 ounces bittersweet or semisweet baking chocolate (see headnote, also Tip above), coarsely chopped

2 tablespoons steaming hot freshly brewed espresso or strong coffee

5 large pasteurized eggs (see Note above), separated

1½ cups heavy cream, whipped to soft peaks with 2 tablespoons confectioners' (10X) sugar, 1½ teaspoons vanilla extract, and ⅛ teaspoon salt

2 tablespoons granulated sugar

OPTIONAL TOPPING:

1 recipe Mock Devonshire Cream (page 273) or Crème Fraîche (page 274)

1. Place chocolate and espresso in double boiler top and set over barely simmering water. Reduce burner heat to lowest point and cook, stirring constantly, until chocolate melts — 8 to 10 minutes. If chocolate seems to be melting too fast, remove from heat and continue melting on retained heat, stirring until absolutely smooth.

2. Whisk egg yolks until frothy, blend in a little melted chocolate, then stir back into pan and cook over simmering water, whisking constantly, until no raw eggy taste lingers — 2 to 3 minutes. Scoop into large bowl and fold in whipped cream mixture.

3. Using hand electric mixer, beat egg whites at medium speed a minute or so until silvery. Add 1 tablespoon granulated sugar and beat at medium speed a few seconds, then add final tablespoon sugar. Raise mixer speed to high and beat until whites peak softly—about 1 minute more.

4. Fold about 1 cup beaten whites into chocolate mixture to lighten it, then with gentlest of touches, fold in remaining whites making sure no streaks of brown or white show.

5. Cover mousse and refrigerate at least 12 hours or overnight.

6. To serve, spoon into balloon goblets or decorative dessert dishes, then, if you like, drift with Mock Devonshire Cream or Crème Fraîche.

Variations:

Mocha Mousse: Prepare as directed, but in Step 1, blend 2 tablespoons instant espresso powder or crystals into melted chocolate. Makes 8 servings.

Mexican Chocolate Mousse: Prepare as directed, but at end of Step 2, fold ½ teaspoon ground cinnamon into thickened egg yolks and chocolate along with whipped cream mixture. Makes 8 servings.

Custards & Creams

Perfectly Silky Chocolate Pudding

Makes 6 Servings

I've always wondered why people settle for pudding mixes when making them from scratch is so quick and easy. And, oh my, the difference in flavor. The proof's in this chocolate pudding.

Note: Choose top-quality unsweetened chocolate for this recipe.

1. Combine granulated sugar, cornstarch, and salt in medium-size heavy saucepan, then gradually blend in 2½ cups milk. Set over moderate heat and cook, stirring constantly, until mixture bubbles gently for 1 minute—no longer or mixture may thin.

2. Whisk egg with remaining ½ cup milk in small heatproof bowl until smooth.

3. Whisking briskly, blend about 1 cup hot milk mixture into egg mixture, stir back into pan, and mix in chocolate. Reduce heat to moderately low and cook, stirring constantly, until chocolate melts and mixture is smooth—2 to 3 minutes. Do not boil or pudding may curdle. Remove from heat, add vanilla, and whisk until satiny.

4. Spoon into six ungreased 5- or 6-ounce ramekins, dividing amount evenly. Arrange on rimmed baking sheet, top with second baking sheet, set in refrigerator, and chill at least 3 hours.

5. Serve cold and, if you like, crown each portion with dollop of whipped cream. Also good with Mock Devonshire Cream (page 273) or Crème Fraîche (page 274).

1 cup granulated sugar

3 tablespoons cornstarch

¼ teaspoon salt

3 cups milk

1 large egg

3 ounces unsweetened chocolate, moderately finely chopped

2 teaspoons vanilla extract

OPTIONAL TOPPING:

1 cup heavy cream, whipped to soft peaks with 2 tablespoons confectioners' (10X) sugar and ½ teaspoon vanilla extract

Spanish Cream

Makes 6 to 8 Servings

Southerners have always doted on creamy puddings and this one was a particular favorite among our grandmothers. I like Spanish Cream straight up, but for dinner parties top it with dead-ripe peaches, blueberries, raspberries, or strawberries, sweetening as needed to taste. If I've chosen peaches, I slice them thin and spike with a little dark rum or Kentucky's best bourbon.

Note: Because beaten raw egg whites are integral to this pudding, I use pasteurized eggs to eliminate the risk of salmonella food poisoning. If your supermarket does not sell pasteurized eggs, buy eggs from a local source you trust.

1. Place half-and-half and milk in medium-size heavy saucepan and sprinkle gelatin evenly over surface. Let stand 5 minutes.

2. Mix in granulated sugar and salt, set over moderate heat, and cook, stirring frequently, until mixture steams—about 10 minutes.

3. Whisking egg yolks vigorously, blend in about ½ cup hot gelatin mixture, then stir back into pan. Set over moderately low heat and cook, stirring constantly, until the consistency of custard sauce—about 2 minutes. Do not boil or mixture may curdle. Remove from heat, mix in vanilla, then transfer to large bowl and cool 20 minutes, stirring frequently.

4. Using whisk or hand electric mixer, beat egg whites and confectioners' sugar to soft peaks in second large bowl. Fold about one-third beaten whites into custard, then fold in balance until no streaks of yellow or white show.

5. Cover and refrigerate about 2 hours until gelatin begins to thicken. Remove from refrigerator and with hand electric mixer at high speed, beat until fluffy. Finally, fold in whipped cream. Cover and refrigerate overnight.

6. To serve, mound pudding in colorful dessert dishes. Or to dress it up for a party, top with fresh fruit (see headnote for suggestions).

2 cups half-and-half

1 cup milk

1 (0.25-ounce) envelope unflavored gelatin

⅔ cup granulated sugar

¼ teaspoon salt

3 large pasteurized eggs (see Note above), separated and yolks well beaten

1½ teaspoons vanilla extract or rum extract

2 tablespoons confectioners' (10X) sugar

1 cup heavy cream, whipped to soft peaks

Custards & Creams

Sandra Gutierrez's Manjar de Leche y Canela (Cinnamon and Milk Pudding)

Makes 8 Servings

My friend Sandra Gutierrez had barely received my SOS for old family puddings when she e-mailed this recipe. Though born in the U.S., Sandra has deep Guatemalan roots and spent some of her growing-up years there. The author of *The New Southern-Latino Table* and *Latin American Street Food,* Sandra is a pro who tests each recipe carefully. "This," she says, "is one of the simplest puddings found in Latin America. In my family, we'd eat it with a side of sliced fruit—usually mangoes or berries." Sandra adds that this milk pudding is sometimes used as a filling for sweet empanadas or in lieu of pastry cream in tarts. "But I love it alone and have a hard time waiting for it to cool."

Notes: Mexican cinnamon is brittle, so to keep it from breaking into the pudding, tie in cheesecloth. Sandra likes this pudding on the thick side, but tells how to thin it.

1. Whisk 4 cups milk, cornstarch, sugar, and salt until smooth in large non-stick saucepan and drop in cinnamon stick.

2. Set over moderately high heat and cook, stirring constantly with wooden spoon, until mixture comes to soft boil and thickens to consistency of soft pudding—8 to 10 minutes.

3. Remove from heat and if you prefer thinner pudding, add as much of remaining 1 cup milk as needed, stirring vigorously until smooth. Discard cinnamon stick and mix in vanilla.

4. Transfer pudding to clean serving bowl, smooth plastic food wrap or parchment paper flat on top of pudding to prevent it from "skinning over," and refrigerate at least 2 hours or overnight.

5. To serve, remove pudding from refrigerator and peel off plastic food wrap. Sift ground cinnamon evenly on top of pudding and dish up at table, accompanying, if you like, with sliced mangoes or strawberries.

4 to 5 cups milk, depending on how thick you like your pudding

½ cup unsifted cornstarch

1½ cups sugar

Pinch salt

1 (3-inch) stick Mexican cinnamon, tied in cheesecloth (see Notes above)

½ teaspoon vanilla extract

GARNISH:

½ teaspoon ground cinnamon

OPTIONAL ACCOMPANIMENT:

2 medium mangoes (about 1 pound), peeled, pitted, and thinly sliced, or 1 pound ripe strawberries, hulled and thinly sliced

Chocolate Pudding Cake

Makes 8 Servings

Also called Brownie Pudding, this dessert has been around since the 1930s, perhaps even longer. Like the Lemon Pudding Cake (see page 138), this one separates as it bakes, emerging from the oven with a layer of cake on top and a creamy pudding underneath. The method of mixing, however, is altogether different. No need to separate eggs—key for Lemon Pudding Cake. In fact this recipe has no eggs. To deepen the flavor of the Chocolate Pudding Cake I grew up eating, I substitute raw sugar for some of the granulated and add a little instant espresso powder.

PART ONE:

1 cup sifted all-purpose flour

½ cup granulated sugar

¼ cup unsifted unsweetened cocoa powder

3 tablespoons raw sugar

2 teaspoons baking powder

½ teaspoon salt

½ cup coarsely chopped pecans or walnuts

½ cup milk

¼ cup (½ stick) unsalted butter, melted, or ¼ cup vegetable oil

1½ teaspoons vanilla extract

PART TWO:

⅔ cup granulated sugar combined with 2 tablespoons unsweetened cocoa powder

1 cup boiling water blended with 2 teaspoons instant espresso powder

TOPPING:

1 cup heavy cream, whipped to soft peaks with 2 tablespoons confectioners' (10X) sugar and ½ teaspoon vanilla extract, or 1 pint vanilla or dulce de leche ice cream

1. Preheat oven to 350°F. Lightly butter 9 x 9 x 2-inch baking pan or spritz with nonstick cooking spray and set aside.

2. Part One: Combine first six ingredients (flour through salt) in large bowl, add pecans, and toss well to mix.

3. Whisk milk, butter, and vanilla together in small bowl until frothy, add to dry ingredients, and mix well. Scoop batter into pan, spreading to corners.

4. Part Two: Sprinkle sugar mixture evenly over batter in pan, then pour hot water mixture evenly over all. Do not mix.

5. Slide onto middle oven shelf and bake until pudding bubbles along sides of pan and top feels springy when touched—40 to 45 minutes.

6. Remove pudding cake from oven, set pan on wire baking rack, and cool 30 minutes.

7. To serve, spoon pudding cake onto dessert plates and top each portion with whipped cream or, if you prefer, scoops of vanilla or dulce de leche ice cream.

Grandma Anna Weigl's Rum Pudding with Fruits and Nuts

Makes 12 Servings

This recipe comes from my friend Andrea Weigl, Assistant Features Editor at the Raleigh *News & Observer,* who grew up in a German family in Pittsburgh. Her father's mother (née Anna Pfennig) was born in a small Bavarian town in 1907 and attended a Catholic vocational school as a teenager to learn the skills needed to be a nanny, cook, and/or maid. At 21, she emigrated to Pittsburgh where an uncle lived and became the cook and nanny for a well-to-do family in nearby Braddock. There, through the local German community, she met her husband-to-be, a tailor named Leo Weigl. "My grandmother was a force," Andrea told me. "She canned a bushel of peaches the day she gave birth to her fourth child . . . her energy didn't wane until she was in her 70s."

There are plenty of family stories about Grandma Weigl, Andrea continued, "and many are about cooking. My brother talks longingly about her nut rolls. My cousins and aunt talk about the care packages she sent at Christmas, filled with nut horns, snicker-doodles, and iced walnut drop cookies. My father remembers that she would go through 25-pound bags of flour and sugar while baking for the church's annual sale." Grandma Weigl's rum pudding made with glacéed (candied) red and green cherries is a festive holiday dessert, though some like it even better in strawberry season when fresh berries replace the candied fruit.

Note: The ladyfingers to use for this recipe are the soft sponge-cake-like ones our grandmothers counted on for so many quick desserts, not the crisp Italian ones now proliferating on supermarket shelves.

12 ladyfingers (3-ounce package; see Note above), split horizontally, or 1 (10.75-ounce) frozen pound cake, crusts trimmed if desired, cut into 12 slices, and each slice halved lengthwise to make 24 strips

¼ cup dark rum

1½ tablespoons cornstarch

1 cup sugar

2 cups milk

2 large egg yolks, well beaten

½ cup coarsely chopped lightly toasted hazelnuts (see How to Toast Hazelnuts, page xxviii), or untoasted walnuts

⅓ cup well-drained canned pineapple chunks, coarsely

diced and patted dry on paper toweling

⅓ cup coarsely chopped glacéed cherries (about equal parts red and green), or hulled firm-ripe strawberries if in season

TOPPING:

1 cup heavy cream, whipped to soft peaks (add 2 tablespoons confectioners'

(10X) sugar if using fresh strawberries)

OPTIONAL GARNISH:

2 tablespoons coarsely

chopped lightly toasted hazelnuts

2 tablespoons each coarsely chopped red and green glacéed cherries

or 12 perfect medium strawberries (leave hulls on for additional color)

1. Arrange split ladyfingers side-by-side on large rectangular platter and sprinkle with rum. Let stand while you proceed with recipe.

2. Combine cornstarch and sugar in small heavy saucepan and blend in milk, pressing out lumps. Set over moderate heat and cook, stirring constantly, just until mixture begins to thicken—about 5 minutes. Do not boil or sauce will thin out.

3. Whisk about ½ cup hot sauce into beaten egg yolks, stir back into pan, and cook over low heat, stirring constantly, until custard-like—about 2 minutes. Remove from heat and cool pudding 20 minutes, stirring often to prevent skin from forming on surface.

4. Spread pudding evenly over rum-soaked ladyfingers, then sprinkle evenly first with hazelnuts, then pineapple, then glacéed cherries.

5. Cover pudding with plastic food wrap and refrigerate several hours or overnight.

6. Just before serving, swirl whipped cream into peaks and valleys on top of pudding, and if desired, garnish decoratively with chopped hazelnuts and candied cherries or, if it's strawberry season, with perfect whole berries.

7. Serve on colorful dessert plates with freshly made coffee.

Lemon Pudding Cake

Makes 6 to 8 Servings

Children adore this dessert because the batter magically separates as it bakes, leaving a soft yellow cake on top and a creamy lemon pudding underneath—two desserts in one. My mother made pudding cakes often and they barely lasted a day. This version is a little tarter than my mother's, still it's plenty sweet.

1. Preheat oven to 350°F. Lightly butter 8 x 8 x 2-inch nonreactive baking pan or spritz with nonstick cooking spray and set aside.

2. Whisk granulated sugar, flour, and salt together in medium bowl, then beat in melted butter, lemon zest and juice. Using hand electric mixer, beat egg yolks in large bowl until light and lemony—1 to 2 minutes at high speed, then add milk and beat just enough to incorporate. Combine lemon mixture with milk mixture in large bowl.

3. With pristine egg beaters and bowl, whip egg whites to soft peaks. Fold about ½ cup beaten whites into lemon mixture to lighten it, then fold in balance, making sure no streaks of white or yellow remain. Easy does it.

4. Scoop batter into baking pan, spreading to corners, then center pan in medium roasting pan. Center roasting pan on pulled-out middle oven shelf, then add enough boiling water to pan to come about halfway up sides of baking pan.

5. Gently slide shelf back into oven and bake until pudding jiggles slightly when nudged and top is lightly browned and feels springy when touched—35 to 40 minutes.

6. Remove pudding cake from oven and from water bath, set on wire baking rack, and cool to room temperature. Sift confectioners' sugar evenly on top.

7. To serve, carry baking pan to table and dish up. Nothing more needed.

¾ cup granulated sugar

¼ cup sifted all-purpose flour

⅛ teaspoon salt

3 tablespoons unsalted butter, melted

1 teaspoon finely grated lemon zest

⅓ cup fresh lemon juice

3 large eggs, separated

1½ cups milk

1 tablespoon confectioners' (10X) sugar

Strawberry Cream

Makes 6 to 8 Servings

This recipe, adapted from a 1977 Wisconsin fund-raiser titled *Muskego Morsels,* was originally written in bewilderingly vague terms. We tested the Strawberry Cream and lest there be any confusion, I've rewritten it here, including every detail. In fact, I've modernized the technique for what is essentially an old-fashioned cornstarch pudding.

Note: The minute the cornstarch mixture thickens and clears, remove it from the heat. If you continue cooking beyond this point, the mixture will thin out. This is a good rule for all cornstarch-thickened sauces and puddings.

Tip: To make a strawberry fan, lay berry on cutting board, then with sharp paring knife, beginning at pointed end of berry, make a series of slices about ⅛ inch apart cutting to—but not through—the green cap at the top of the berry. Then gently spread the cuts out so they resemble a miniature fan.

1. Bring water to a boil in medium-size heavy nonreactive saucepan over moderate heat. Whisking briskly, add cornstarch mixture slowly, then sugar, and cook, whisking constantly, just until mixture thickens and clears—about 3 minutes (see Note above).

2. Remove from heat and mix in lemon zest and juice. Set aside and cool to room temperature, about 45 minutes, whisking often to prevent a skin from forming on surface.

3. Fold in strawberries and finally whipped cream; continue to fold until no streaks of red or white remain.

4. Turn into large nonreactive bowl, cover, and chill 2 to 3 hours.

5. To serve, spoon into stemmed goblets and top each portion, if you like, with a strawberry fan.

1⅔ cups water

5 tablespoons cornstarch blended with 6 tablespoons cold water

½ cup sugar

½ teaspoon finely grated lemon zest

3 tablespoons fresh lemon juice

1 pint (2 cups) diced, hulled firm-ripe fresh strawberries (about 10 ounces)

1 cup heavy cream, whipped to soft peaks with 2 tablespoons sugar

OPTIONAL GARNISH:

8 large whole firm-ripe strawberries with hulls (green caps) intact, cut into fans (see Tip above)

Variation:

Small whole blueberries or raspberries can be substituted for strawberries in this recipe, but you will have to adjust the amount of sugar because some berries are tarter than others. Garnish? Omit the strawberry fan and sprig each portion with fresh mint, lemon verbena, or lemon geranium. Makes 6 to 8 servings.

Swedish Cream

Makes 6 Servings

I first tasted this glorious dessert with the consistency of semi-soft gelato as a young assistant food editor at *The Ladies' Home Journal* in New York. One of our editors had brought the recipe home from one of her out-of-town jaunts, waving the piece of paper on which she'd typed it and urging us to test it straight away. We did and became instant fans. We published the recipe for Swedish Cream in the early '60s and soon cooks from one coast to the other were serving it at fancy dinner parties. What follows is my own version.

Note: If the strawberries seem overly tart, sweeten as needed to taste.

1. Combine sugar and gelatin in medium-size heavy saucepan, pressing out all lumps. Blend in heavy cream, set over moderately low heat, and cook, stirring frequently, until sugar and gelatin dissolve completely—about 5 minutes.

2. Remove from heat and pour into large heatproof bowl. Blend in sour cream and vanilla, stirring until absolutely smooth.

3. Cover with foil or plastic food wrap and refrigerate at least 12 hours or overnight.

4. To serve, layer Swedish cream and strawberries into tall stemmed goblets as decoratively as you can, then sprig, if you like, with fresh mint.

1 cup sugar

1 (0.25-ounce) envelope unflavored gelatin

2¼ cups heavy cream

2 cups firmly packed sour cream (not low-fat or fat-free)

1½ teaspoons vanilla extract

1 quart (4 cups) red-ripe strawberries, hulled and moderately thinly sliced (see Note above)

OPTIONAL GARNISH:

4 to 6 small sprigs fresh mint, lemon verbena, or lemon geranium

Custards & Creams

Rum Cream with Sliced Peaches

Makes 6 Servings

This is a spin on my all-time favorite pudding—Swedish Cream, which precedes. I now serve this rum variation more often because so few people have tasted it.

Note: Frozen sliced peaches tend to be tart so sweeten them, if you like, to taste. I don't because that bit of tartness helps tame the sweetness of the pudding.

1. Combine sugar and gelatin in medium-size heavy saucepan, pressing out all lumps. Blend in heavy cream, set over moderately low heat, and cook, stirring frequently, until sugar and gelatin dissolve completely—about 5 minutes.

2. Remove from heat and pour into large heatproof bowl. Blend in sour cream, rum, rum extract, and vanilla, stirring until no streaks of brown or white show.

3. Cover with foil or plastic food wrap and refrigerate at least 12 hours or overnight.

4. To serve, layer rum cream and peaches into tall stemmed goblets as decoratively as you can.

1 cup firmly packed light brown sugar

1 (0.25-ounce) envelope unflavored gelatin

2 cups heavy cream

2 cups firmly packed sour cream (not low-fat or fat-free)

2 tablespoons dark rum

1½ teaspoons pure rum extract

1 teaspoon vanilla extract

4 cups (about 2 pounds) thinly sliced fresh or thawed frozen peaches (see Note above)

Blackberry Trifle

Makes 6 to 8 Servings

This old Appalachian recipe dates back to the days when nearly everyone—even city folk—kept a few hens for eggs and for eating. My own family did back during World War II, and it was my job to feed the hens and gather their eggs.

Note: I call for pasteurized eggs here because the meringue isn't likely to reach the 160°F internal temperature deemed necessary to avoid the risk of salmonella food poisoning by both the U.S. Department of Agriculture and the American Egg Board. Many supermarkets now sell pasteurized eggs, but if they're unavailable in your area, buy eggs from a local source you know and trust.

1. If using fresh berries, rinse well. Purée berries with ½ cup granulated sugar in electric blender at high speed. Press purée through coarse sieve and set aside; you should have about 1½ cups purée.

2. Combine remaining ½ cup granulated sugar, the cornstarch, and salt in medium-size heavy saucepan, add milk and cream, and whisk until smooth. Set over moderate heat and cook, whisking constantly, until thickened, smooth, and no raw starch taste lingers—about 3 minutes.

3. Whisk egg yolks in small bowl until smooth, add about ½ cup hot milk mixture, and stir back into pan. Reduce heat to moderately low and cook, whisking constantly, until thickened like custard—5 to 7 minutes. Remove from heat, mix in vanilla, and cool to room temperature, about 30 minutes, whisking often to prevent a skin from forming on top.

4. Meanwhile, preheat oven to 350°F. Butter deep 2-quart baking dish. Spoon one-third cooled custard into baking dish. Top with half the diced pound cake and half the blackberry purée. Repeat layers using another one-third custard, remaining diced cake and blackberry purée. Top with remaining custard.

5. Using hand electric mixer, beat egg whites, confectioners' sugar, and cream of tartar to soft peaks, then swirl on top of trifle, spreading so meringue touches baking dish all around. Slide trifle onto middle oven shelf and bake until meringue is nicely tipped with brown—15 to 20 minutes.

6. To serve, remove trifle from oven and scoop onto bright dessert plates either in kitchen or at table. Or, if you prefer, cool trifle about 20 minutes before serving—this makes it a bit easier to serve.

3 cups fresh or thawed frozen blackberries (do not drain)

1 cup granulated sugar

1½ tablespoons cornstarch

¼ teaspoon salt

2 cups milk

1 cup heavy cream

3 large pasteurized eggs (see Note above), separated

1½ teaspoons vanilla extract

½ family-size (16-ounce) frozen pound cake, cut into ½-inch dice (about 5 cups)

3 tablespoons confectioners' (10X) sugar

¼ teaspoon cream of tartar

Custards & Creams

Ina Lieb's Pumpkin Pudding

Makes 8 Servings

My long-time friend Barbara Fairchild, for many years *Bon Appétit* editor-in-chief, sent me this recipe of her mother's. Barbara explained that it was the filling Ina baked into Thanksgiving pies—the family favorite—then suggested that I skip the crust and bake the filling as individual puddings. A terrific idea.

⅔ cup firmly packed light brown sugar

1 tablespoon all-purpose flour

1 teaspoon ground ginger

1 teaspoon ground cinnamon

1 teaspoon ground allspice

½ teaspoon freshly grated nutmeg

½ teaspoon salt

¼ teaspoon ground cloves

3 large eggs, well beaten

⅓ cup unsulfured molasses (not too dark)

1 (15-ounce) can solid-pack pumpkin (not pumpkin pie filling)

1 (12-ounce) can evaporated milk (not low-fat or fat-free)

TOPPING:

1 cup heavy cream, whipped to soft peaks

1. Preheat oven to 350°F. Very lightly butter eight 5- or 6-ounce ramekins or custard cups and set aside. Also fold damp tea towel to fit large shallow roasting pan and press flat over bottom of pan (this helps anchor the puddings as they bake).

2. Combine first eight ingredients (brown sugar through cloves) in large mixing bowl, pressing out sugar lumps with fingers and mixing until well blended.

3. Mix in eggs, then molasses, then pumpkin, whisking each time until smooth. Add milk in slow, steady stream, whisking all the while until no streaks of white or brown remain.

4. Ladle into ramekins, dividing amount evenly, and arrange not touching on folded dish towel in roasting pan. Pull out middle oven shelf, center roasting pan on shelf, then add enough boiling water to pan to come about one-fourth way up sides of ramekins.

5. Gently slide shelf back into oven and bake until puddings jiggle when nudged and a cake tester inserted in center comes out clean—45 to 50 minutes.

6. Remove puddings from oven and from water bath and cool about 30 minutes. At this point you can serve the puddings. Or you can cover them and refrigerate overnight.

7. Serve puddings in their ramekins topped with generous billows of whipped cream.

Gooseberry Fool

Makes 6 Servings

My mother was in love with gooseberries and whenever they were in season (late spring until summer's end), we could expect a gooseberry fool every week or so. As a child, I found gooseberries way too tart but have outgrown my dislike for them. For centuries an English favorite, gooseberry fool has never been very popular here, though I suspect that this recipe may win a few fans. What, exactly, is a fool? Puréed berries folded into custard, then topped with sweetened whipped cream.

Note: If fresh gooseberries are unavailable, is it OK to substitute canned gooseberries? In my opinion, no. The fresh are so far superior.

1 quart (4 cups) fresh gooseberries (see Note above), washed, stemmed, and blossom ends removed

¼ cup water (about)

2 cups granulated sugar

CUSTARD:

1 cup half-and-half or light cream

3 tablespoons granulated sugar

2 large eggs, lightly beaten with ¼ teaspoon freshly grated nutmeg

TOPPING:

1 cup heavy cream, softly whipped with 3 tablespoons confectioners' (10X) sugar and ½ teaspoon vanilla extract

1. Place berries in large heavy nonreactive saucepan and crush with potato masher. Add water and sugar, set over moderate heat, and cook, stirring often, until berries are soft—about 10 to 12 minutes. Put all through food mill set over large nonreactive bowl, then press pulp through fine sieve—tedious but essential to remove all seeds and bits of skin. Set purée aside.

2. Custard: Combine all ingredients in small heavy saucepan, set over moderately low heat, and cook, stirring constantly, just until consistency of medium white sauce—3 to 5 minutes. Do not allow to boil because custard will curdle.

3. Stirring often to prevent skin from forming on top, quick-chill custard in ice bath about 20 minutes, then fold into gooseberry purée.

4. To serve, mound gooseberry mixture into glass or crystal bowl, then add topping and swirl into peaks and valleys.

Irish Potato Pudding

Makes 6 Servings

A frugal old-timey recipe from the North Carolina Piedmont that was particularly popular at threshing time. It's both unusual and easy, what one friend called "a very sweet, soft vanilla pudding with a little mashed potato texture." If you refrigerate the leftovers—and you should—they can be cut into cheesecake-like wedges the next day and served cold.

1. Preheat oven to 350°F. Lightly butter 1½-quart casserole or spritz with nonstick cooking spray and set aside.

2. Boil potatoes in unsalted water to cover until tender—15 to 20 minutes. Drain well and mash. You should have about 2 cups mashed potatoes.

3. Place potatoes in large mixing bowl, then with hand electric mixer, beat in remaining ingredients in order listed and scoop into casserole.

4. Slide onto middle oven shelf and bake pudding until lightly browned and instant-read thermometer inserted midway between center and rim reads 160°F—50 to 60 minutes.

5. Serve hot—as is or accompanied by fresh or thawed frozen sliced peaches or whole berries, sweetened as needed to taste.

1½ pounds (about 4 medium) all-purpose Maine or Eastern potatoes, peeled and quartered

1 cup sugar

½ cup (1 stick) unsalted butter, softened

2 large eggs beaten with 2 teaspoons vanilla extract and ½ teaspoon salt

1 cup milk

Peaches or berries, for serving (optional)

Enca Mello Lameiro's Pudim de Laranja (Orange Pudding)

Makes 10 to 12 Servings

My long-time friend Enca, a petite strawberry blonde from Lisbon who was based for years at the Portuguese National Tourist Office in New York, is a gifted Portuguese cook. I featured her Creamed Salt Cod in my award-winning *Food of Portugal*—nearly 30 years in print and still going strong. This silken orange pudding is an old family recipe, a specialty of Enca's Great Aunt Berta. "Whenever someone asked her for a recipe," Enca told me, "she would never reveal the right version—only to my mother, one of her favorite nieces, and then on the condition that she would never pass the recipe on to anyone else." Enca's mother agreed and only after Aunt Berta passed on did she share this recipe with her daughter. "As you know," Enca continued, "no Portuguese meal is a meal without dessert." So Aunt Berta's Pudim de Laranja might be served after any everyday meal. No special occasion needed. It's been a family favorite for more than 100 years. Though Enca doesn't consider this a "special occasion pudding," I definitely do. One taste and I think you'll agree.

Note: The best oranges to use for this recipe are fairly tart ones. "I use Valencias," Enca said, "the big ones." She grates the zest of four oranges and juices three to give the pudding its intense orange flavor. Enca bakes this pudding very slowly in an oven-proof ring mold that measures about 10 inches across and 3 inches deep. She also bakes it in a hot water bath, which accounts for the pudding's extraordinary texture.

TO PREPARE RING MOLD:

1 teaspoon unsalted butter, softened

1 tablespoon sugar

PUDDING:

2 cups (1 pound) sugar

12 large eggs

4 large Valencia oranges (about 2¼ pounds), zest of all 4 finely grated and 3 oranges juiced (save the fourth for garnish)

GARNISH:

1 cup heavy cream, stiffly whipped

2 large Valencia oranges (the one left after zest is grated + 1 more), both sectioned

4 sprigs fresh mint, lemon verbena, or lemon geranium

1. Preheat oven to 250°F.

2. To Prepare Ring Mold: Butter 2-quart ovenproof glass or nonreactive metal ring mold, add sugar, and tilt mold from side to side until evenly coated with sugar. Tap out excess sugar and set mold aside.

3. Pudding: Place sugar, eggs, orange zest, and juice in large electric mixer bowl and beat at low speed just long enough to combine. Raise speed to high and beat until frothy — about 1 minute.

4. Pour mixture into ring mold and set in middle of large roasting pan. Pull middle oven shelf out, center roasting pan on shelf, then add enough boiling water to pan to come about halfway up sides of ring mold. Set piece of buttered parchment or foil, buttered side down, lightly on top of mold.

5. Gently slide shelf back into oven and bake pudding 1½ hours. Remove parchment and continue baking pudding uncovered until cake tester, inserted halfway between rim and central tube, comes out clean — 1 to 1½ hours longer.

6. Remove pudding from oven and cool in upright mold on wire baking rack about 30 minutes.

7. Carefully loosen pudding around edge and central tube with small thin-blade spatula, then invert on colorful round platter. Cover with turned-upside-down large mixing bowl and refrigerate for at least 4 hours — "longer is even better," Enca says.

8. Garnish: Remove pudding from refrigerator, decorate with dollops of whipped cream (piped rosettes if you want to be fancy), orange sections, and mint sprigs. Carry to the dinner table and get ready for "oohs" and "aahs."

Mummy's Orange Charlotte

Makes 10 Servings

This recipe comes from my good friend Moreton Neal, who once had her own restaurant in Chapel Hill, North Carolina. She e-mailed it to me with this back story: "During my Mississippi childhood in the '50s and '60s, we ate a whole lot of gelatin desserts: pumpkin chiffon pie, black bottom pie, snow pudding, Bavarian cream—and then there were aspics and molds of all flavors. The cook went through gelatin at about the rate that I use olive oil today.

"This Charlotte Russe was a specialty of my grandmother, Eola Moreton, whom we called 'Mummy.' Most Sundays after church we gathered at her house for dinner, and this refreshing orange Charlotte was the perfect dessert after a heavy midday meal.

"I haven't made Orange Charlotte in a while (in fact, I haven't bought a package of gelatin in years). Last time I did, I got creative and sprinkled Cointreau on the ladyfingers, which ruined the fresh orange taste."

Note: Because the egg whites used in this recipe are merely beaten, not cooked, either use pasteurized eggs, which many supermarkets now sell, or eggs from a local source that you trust to minimize the risk of salmonella food poisoning.

Tip: Grate the orange zest before peeling and sectioning the oranges. Also section the oranges over a bowl to catch the juice, then use that juice as part of the 1 cup fresh orange juice below.

1½ (0.25-ounce) envelopes unflavored gelatin (about 3¾ level teaspoons)

1 cup fresh orange juice (from 2 to 3 medium oranges, about 1 pound; see Tip above)

½ cup granulated sugar

½ cup water

1 tablespoon finely grated orange zest (see Tip above)

10 ladyfingers (soft sponge-cake-like ones), split lengthwise

Sections from 3 medium oranges, peeled and seeded (see Tip above)

2 large pasteurized egg whites (see Note above)

1 cup heavy cream, whipped to soft peaks

OPTIONAL GARNISH:

½ cup heavy cream, whipped to stiff peaks with 1 tablespoon confectioners' (10X) sugar

3 to 5 small sprigs fresh mint, lemon verbena, or lemon geranium

1. Sprinkle gelatin over orange juice in measuring cup and let soften 5 minutes. Meanwhile, heat sugar and water in small heavy nonreactive saucepan over moderate heat, stirring until sugar dissolves and the syrup comes to a boil—about 3 minutes.

2. Remove from heat, add gelatin and orange zest, and stir until gelatin dissolves. Transfer to medium nonreactive bowl, cover, and chill mixture until consistency of unbeaten egg whites—45 to 60 minutes.

3. Meanwhile, grease 8-inch springform pan or spritz with nonstick cooking spray, then stand split ladyfingers on end around side of pan with cut sides facing inward. Finally, arrange orange sections in pinwheel pattern on bottom of pan and set aside.

4. Remove gelatin mixture from refrigerator and using hand electric mixer at high speed, beat until thick and frothy—about 2 minutes.

5. With clean beaters, beat egg whites until stiff. Fold about ½ cup beaten whites into gelatin mixture, then fold in balance followed by whipped cream—no streaks of orange or white should show.

6. Spoon mixture into springform pan, taking care not to disturb ladyfingers or orange sections. Cover, set in refrigerator, and chill overnight.

7. Before serving, trim off any ladyfinger ends that extend above surface of charlotte. Release and remove springform pan side, invert charlotte on colorful round platter, then carefully remove springform pan bottom. If you like, pipe decorative rosettes of sweetened whipped cream around edge of charlotte and sprig with fresh mint.

8. To serve, carry charlotte to table and cut into wedges—a dessert as showy as this deserves an audience.

Slight Pudding

Makes 6 Servings

A 150-year-old Southern pudding — "slight" because it's easy and inexpensive — maybe the precursor of the pudding cakes we're so fond of today. It's best, I find, when cooled, covered, and refrigerated several hours before being served because the custard layer on the bottom has time to thicken.

1. Preheat oven to 350°F. Butter 2-quart ovenproof glass baking dish and set aside.

2. Place flour in medium saucepan, then whisking hard, add milk slowly and continue whisking until well blended; drop in butter. Set over moderate heat and cook, stirring constantly, until thickened and smooth — about 3 minutes. Remove from heat.

3. Beat egg yolks with ½ cup sugar and lemon zest in medium bowl until smooth, then whisking briskly, add hot milk mixture in slow steady stream and continue whisking until smooth.

4. With clean beaters, whip egg whites to soft peaks with remaining 2 tablespoons sugar in second medium bowl. Fold about one-fourth beaten whites into yolk mixture to lighten it, then fold in remaining whites until no streaks of white or yellow remain. Easy does it.

5. Pour batter into baking dish and set in medium roasting pan. Pull middle oven shelf out, center roasting pan on shelf, then add enough boiling water to pan to come about halfway up sides of baking dish.

6. Gently slide shelf back into oven and bake pudding uncovered until cake tester inserted midway between middle and rim comes out clean — about 45 minutes.

7. Remove pudding from oven and cool at least 30 minutes before serving. Even better, cool to room temperature, cover, and refrigerate several hours before serving.

⅓ cup sifted all-purpose flour

3 cups milk

1 tablespoon unsalted butter

3 large eggs, separated

½ cup + 2 tablespoons sugar

½ teaspoon finely grated lemon zest

Tiramisu

Makes 12 Servings

This layered Italian dessert (its name means "pick-me-up") is said to have been created in or around Venice in the 1960s, but exactly where no one seems to know. It became the trendy new dessert in New York and other big metropolitan areas sometime in the '80s thanks to a *New York Times* article. Suddenly every restaurant—and not just Italian ones—was serving its own version. Though New Yorkers soon tired of tiramisu, it remained popular elsewhere and now, thanks to the Food Network, is once again *the* show-off dessert. Fortunately, it's a deceptively easy make-ahead.

Note: Most specialty groceries and many supermarkets sell crisp Italian ladyfingers; they can also be ordered online (see Sources, page 291).

1. Spritz 13 x 9 x 2-inch ceramic or pottery baking dish with nonstick cooking spray and set aside.

2. Prepare zabaglione as directed and remove from heat. In large bowl, beat ricotta with hand electric mixer at moderate speed until smooth and light—about 2 minutes. Add zabaglione and beat only enough to combine.

3. Brush each ladyfinger with espresso mixture making sure each side is moistened but not soggy. Arrange 18 ladyfingers (three rows of six) side-by-side in bottom of baking dish, trimming ends slightly as needed to make fit. Spread half ricotta mixture on top, then half whipped cream, and half grated chocolate. Repeat layers, adding any ladyfinger trimmings to top layer.

4. Cover baking dish with plastic food wrap and refrigerate tiramisu several hours or better yet, overnight.

5. To serve, cut tiramisu into large squares and center each on a brightly colored dessert plate.

1 recipe Zabaglione (page 90)

1 (15-ounce) container ricotta cheese (not low-fat or fat-free)

36 crisp Italian ladyfingers (see Note above)

1 cup strong espresso mixed with ¼ cup sweet Marsala or Madeira (Malmsey) wine

2 cups heavy cream, whipped to soft peaks with 1 tablespoon confectioners' (10X) sugar

4 ounces bittersweet chocolate, coarsely grated

Custards & Creams

Honeyed Lemon Sponge

Makes 12 Servings

If My Mother's Date-Nut Pudding (page 214) was my cold weather favorite, this cool gelatin dessert was what I begged for right through the South's long hot summer. Mother was happy to oblige because it is such a simple dessert. By the time I was six, I was in the kitchen helping — grating the lemon zest, juicing the lemons, and softening the gelatin in a little ramekin of tap water.

Note: Chill the evaporated milk overnight before you begin this recipe or set in freezer until partially frozen — this may take 1½ to 2 hours. Just be sure there's plenty of liquid in the can when you take it from the freezer because you are going to whip this to soft peaks just as you would heavy cream.

Tip: If neither strawberries nor peaches are in season, I substitute thawed frozen sliced peaches — sometimes even thawed frozen blueberries.

1½ (0.25-ounce) envelopes unflavored gelatin (about 3¾ level teaspoons), softened in ¼ cup cold water

1¼ cups boiling water

½ cup honey (a light golden one)

2 tablespoons sugar

Finely grated zest of 1 medium lemon

⅓ cup fresh lemon juice

¼ teaspoon salt

1½ cups fine vanilla wafer or graham cracker crumbs

1 (12-ounce) can ice-cold (see Note above) evaporated milk (not low-fat or fat-free)

OPTIONAL TOPPING:

1 pint (2 cups) fresh strawberries, hulled and thinly sliced, or 4 tree-ripened peaches (about 1 pound), peeled, pitted, and thinly sliced — either fruit sweetened to taste (see Tip above)

1. Place softened gelatin in large heatproof nonreactive bowl, add boiling water, and stir until dissolved. Add honey, sugar, lemon zest and juice, and salt and stir until gelatin dissolves completely.

2. Cover and refrigerate until consistency of unbeaten egg white — about 45 minutes. Also set small mixing bowl in freezer to chill for same length of time. I even chill the beaters of my hand electric mixer.

3. Toward end of chilling period, spritz nonreactive 13 x 9 x 2-inch baking dish (preferably glass or ceramic) with nonstick cooking spray. Spread half vanilla wafer crumbs evenly over bottom of baking dish and set aside.

4. Scoop partially set gelatin mixture into large electric mixer bowl and beat at high speed until smooth and stiff enough to mound softly.

5. Using hand electric mixer at high speed, whip evaporated milk in chilled mixing bowl to soft peaks. By hand, fold about 1 cup whipped milk into gelatin mixture, then fold in remainder until no streaks of white or yellow remain. Easy does it.

6. Scoop whipped mixture into baking dish on top of crumbs, carefully spreading to corners so crumbs aren't disturbed, then smooth top with rubber spatula. Taking equal care, cover gelatin mixture with remaining crumbs.

7. Set uncovered baking dish in refrigerator and chill until set—about 3 hours.

8. To serve, remove from refrigerator, cut into squares, place on bright dessert plates and, if you like, top each portion with fresh strawberries or peaches.

Apricot Fluff

Makes 6 Servings

Hugely popular when I was little, these cool desserts are no longer *cool* in today's definition of the word. Too bad, because this quintessential comfort food couldn't be easier to make.

1. Dissolve gelatin in 1 cup boiling water in medium-size heatproof nonreactive bowl and mix in lemon zest. Cover and refrigerate until consistency of unbeaten egg white—about 30 minutes.

2. Meanwhile, soak apricots in remaining 1 cup boiling water until soft—about 20 minutes. Drain apricots well, reserving liquid (you should have about ⅔ cup). Purée apricots in mini food processor or electric blender, adding just enough reserved soaking liquid, 1 tablespoon at a time, to thin purée to the consistency of medium white sauce—about 6 tablespoons in all.

3. With hand electric mixer set at high speed, whip gelatin mixture until fluffy. Fold in apricot purée, then whipped cream—no streaks of white or orange should show.

4. Cover bowl and refrigerate pudding until softly set—about 1 hour.

5. To serve, spoon into dessert dishes or stemmed goblets and sprig with fresh mint or lemon geranium.

1 (3-ounce) package lemon-flavored gelatin

2 cups boiling water

½ teaspoon finely grated lemon zest

½ cup firmly packed dried apricots (about 3 ounces)

1 cup heavy cream, whipped to soft peaks

6 sprigs fresh mint or lemon geranium

Variation:

Peach Fluff: Prepare as directed, substituting dried peaches for the apricots and adding ¼ teaspoon almond extract to the whipped cream. Makes 6 servings.

Syllabub

Makes 6 Servings

According to Alan Davidson *(The Oxford Companion to Food),* this "sweet, frothy confection which was popular in Britain from the 16th through the 19th centuries, has since been revived in a small way as a dessert." Originally, it's said, syllabub was made by milking a cow into a pitcher of spiced white wine. Today a fine port or Madeira wine is substituted, whipped cream replaces the milk, and to heighten the froth, beaten egg whites are often added. This particular recipe comes from Tidewater Virginia.

Note: Because raw egg whites are used in this syllabub, choose pasteurized eggs, which many supermarkets routinely sell. If unavailable, buy local eggs from a source you trust to minimize the risk of salmonella food poisoning.

1. Whip cream to soft peaks with ¼ cup confectioners' sugar and ¼ cup port or Madeira, then gently fold in remaining 2 tablespoons wine.

2. With clean bowl and beaters, whip egg whites with remaining ¼ cup confectioners' sugar to soft peaks. Fold in whipped cream mixture with a light touch, taking care not to deflate beaten egg whites.

3. To serve, arrange chilled orange sections in six large stemmed goblets and mound syllabub on top. That's all there is to it.

2 cups heavy cream

½ cup sifted confectioners' (10X) sugar

¼ cup + 2 tablespoons vintage port or Madeira (a sweet Malmsey or Bual)

2 large pasteurized egg whites (see Note above)

6 medium navel oranges, peeled, sectioned, seeded, and chilled well

Custards & Creams

Sara's Snow Pudding

Makes 6 to 8 Servings

Sara Moulton and I have been friends since the late '70s when I bought an apartment in the Gramercy Park co-op where she had grown up. I had barely arrived when the staff went on strike leaving us, the owners, in charge. I drew elevator duty as did a petite blonde named Betsy Moulton. Her shift preceded mine and being an old hand at building strikes, she taught me, the newbie, how to operate our antiquated lift (circa 1910).

When Betsy learned that I was a food writer, she said, "You must meet my daughter-the-chef. She's working in Boston but will be here this weekend, so why don't you come up for drinks?" Sara and I hit it off immediately. She soon relocated to New York with future husband Bill Adler and until they could find a flat of their own, they lived five floors up in the Moultons' large duplex. Looking for work, Sara asked if she could help me test recipes or something. And how! Turns out we worked well together, also that Sara loved to travel, so I asked if she'd like to join me on three overseas assignments as photo assistant/girl Friday.

We spent nearly a month in Holland, two weeks in Rio, ten days in Port Wine Country. I taught Sara how to rig lights for food shots, how to prep and style food and, my, what a quick study! She was also the perfect traveling companion—eager to see, help, and learn.

Sara often talked about her grandmother Ruth Moulton who'd graduated from Fannie Farmer's Boston Cooking School and whose recipe this is. Sara adored this snow pudding as a little girl. And still does. "There's just something magical about it," she says.

Note: Because the egg whites are merely whipped, not cooked, I call for pasteurized eggs, now a staple at many supermarkets. If unavailable, use eggs from a local source you trust.

1¼ cups cold water

1 (0.25-ounce) envelope unflavored gelatin

⅔ cup sugar

1 tablespoon finely grated lemon zest

⅓ cup fresh lemon juice

3 large pasteurized egg whites (see Note above), at room temperature

¼ teaspoon salt

TOPPING:

1 pint (2 cups) fresh strawberries, hulled and thinly sliced; or 4 medium-size tree-ripened peaches (about 1 pound), peeled, pitted, and thinly sliced—either fruit mixed with 1 tablespoon sugar, 2 teaspoons finely grated orange zest, and, if you like, 2 teaspoons Grand Marnier or other orange liqueur

1. Place ¼ cup water in small heavy nonreactive saucepan, sprinkle gelatin evenly on top, and soften 5 minutes. Mix in sugar and remaining 1 cup water and set over moderately high heat. Cook, stirring constantly, until the sugar and gelatin dissolve completely—about 2 minutes.

2. Stir in lemon zest and juice, then set pan in bowl of ice and water, and chill, stirring often, until consistency of unbeaten egg whites—about 45 minutes.

3. Beat egg whites and salt in large electric mixer bowl at high speed just until they peak softly—about 1 minute. Ease whites into second bowl and set aside.

4. Transfer chilled gelatin mixture to mixer bowl (no need to rinse) and beat at high speed until frothy—1 to 2 minutes. Scoop beaten whites on top of gelatin mixture and beat at high speed until tripled in volume and thick enough to form a ribbon when beater is withdrawn—8 to 10 minutes.

5. Divide pudding among 6 to 8 large balloon goblets, cover, and chill until set—about 3 hours. Also cover and refrigerate topping.

6. To serve, spoon topping over each portion of snow pudding, dividing amount evenly.

Note: Off-season, I like to top snow pudding with either Quick Cardinal Sauce (page 284) or Quick Raspberry Sauce (page 278).

Custards & Creams

Bread Puddings
&
Steamed Puddings

Days-of-Yore Bread Pudding

Makes 6 Servings

Whenever our grandmothers had bread going stale, they'd crumble it or cube it and make this frugal pudding—one of the easiest ever. It's an old, old North Carolina recipe I picked up years ago as an extension worker. If memory serves, it was served at a church luncheon and I managed to "crack" the recipe—with an assist from a few local fund-raiser cookbooks.

Note: I sometimes now substitute raw sugar for granulated because I'm keen for anything remotely caramel.

Tip: Freshly grated nutmeg is so much more delicate and fragrant than ground nutmeg, in fact it's light and lemony. I urge you to follow our grandmothers' lead: buy whole nutmegs and grate them whenever a recipe calls for nutmeg. Our grandmothers used little nutmeg graters—not as quick or easy as today's Microplanes.

1. Preheat oven to 350°F. Generously butter 2-quart casserole and set aside.

2. Whisk or beat first seven ingredients (milk through salt) until frothy in large mixing bowl. Add bread cubes and toss well to mix. Scoop into casserole, spreading to edge.

3. Slide onto middle oven shelf and bake pudding until lightly browned and cake tester inserted into pudding halfway between rim and center comes out clean—55 to 60 minutes.

4. To serve, rush pudding to table just as you would a soufflé, and waste no time spooning onto dessert plates. Accompany, if you like, with pitcher of Nutmeg Sauce or Butterscotch Sauce.

1⅓ cups milk

2 large eggs

½ cup sugar (see Note above)

2 tablespoons unsalted butter, melted

1½ teaspoons vanilla extract

½ teaspoon freshly grated nutmeg (See Tip above)

¼ teaspoon salt

4 cups ¼-inch cubes day-old bread (about 8 slices firm-textured white bread, crusts on)

1 recipe Nutmeg Sauce (page 283) or Butterscotch Sauce (page 268) (optional)

Martha Washington Pudding

Makes 6 to 8 Servings

Whether our first First Lady ever made this meringue-frosted bread pudding strewn with Madeira-plumped raisins is debatable. There's no denying, however, that the pudding named for her has been popular for at least a hundred years and won pride of place all across the South.

1. Place raisins and wine in small nonreactive bowl, cover, and let stand overnight — no need to refrigerate.

2. When ready to proceed, preheat oven to 350°F. Butter 2½-quart casserole or spritz with nonstick cooking spray and set aside.

3. Soak bread cubes 10 minutes in cream in medium bowl.

4. Whisk granulated sugar, egg yolks, and salt in large bowl until smooth. Fold in bread cubes along with unabsorbed cream, plumped raisins, and unabsorbed wine. Scoop into casserole.

5. Slide onto middle oven shelf and bake uncovered until pudding barely quivers when you nudge casserole — 40 to 45 minutes.

6. When pudding has baked 35 minutes, beat egg whites with cream of tartar in large electric mixer bowl a minute or so at moderately high speed until silvery. With machine at low speed, add confectioners' sugar gradually. Raise mixer speed to high and continue beating until egg whites peak softly — about 1 minute longer.

7. Remove pudding from oven and carefully swirl meringue on top. Slide pudding back into oven and bake until meringue is set and tipped with brown — about 15 minutes longer.

8. To serve, remove pudding from oven and dish up at table. Or, if you prefer, cool about 20 minutes before serving. If there should be any leftovers — not likely — cover and refrigerate.

1 cup dark seedless raisins or sultanas (golden seedless raisins)

1 cup sweet Madeira wine (Malmsey)

3 cups ¼-inch cubes day-old bread (about 6 slices firm-textured white bread, crusts on)

1 cup heavy cream

½ cup granulated sugar

3 large eggs, separated

¼ teaspoon salt

¼ teaspoon cream of tartar

⅓ cup unsifted confectioners' (10X) sugar

Bread Puddings & Steamed Puddings

The Best Chocolate Bread Pudding

Makes 4 to 6 Servings

With its deep chocolate flavor and mousse-like texture, this chocolate bread pudding is the best I have ever eaten. And that's a lot of chocolate bread puddings. The recipe was given to me years ago by Ruth Buchan, who edited the massive *Doubleday Cookbook* co-authored by me and my good friend and *Ladies' Home Journal* test kitchen colleague Elaine Hanna. We were so immersed in the project we both quit good jobs to devote full time to it, then spent ten long years researching, writing, and testing the more than five thousand recipes that appear in the book (this bread pudding is not among them because I got the recipe after the book was published). Though Elaine and I sometimes complained during those ten years of stress and toil, we were rewarded in the end. *The Doubleday Cookbook* swept the 1975 Tastemaker Awards, being named not only Best Basic Cookbook but also Cookbook of the Year — the coveted top honor. Even more rewarding, the hundreds of thousands of copies sold not to mention the reader praise that still comes our way.

Tip: For 1 cup solidly packed bread crumbs, you'll need about 3 slices firm-textured white bread, crusts and all.

2 (1-ounce) squares unsweetened chocolate, coarsely chopped

1½ cups milk

½ cup half-and-half

1 cup solidly packed moderately coarse soft white bread crumbs (see Tip above)

2 large eggs

¾ cup sugar

⅛ teaspoon salt

ACCOMPANIMENT:

1 recipe Crème Anglaise (page 270), Frothy Egg Sauce (page 277), Mock Devonshire Cream (page 273), or whipped cream

1. Place chocolate, milk, and half-and-half in medium-size heavy saucepan, set over moderately low heat, and cook, stirring constantly, until chocolate melts and mixture is smooth — 3 to 5 minutes.

2. Remove chocolate mixture from heat, stir in bread crumbs, cover, and let stand at room temperature 1 hour.

3. After 45 minutes, preheat oven to 350°F. Lightly butter 1½-quart baking dish or spritz with nonstick cooking spray.

Recipe continues

4. Break eggs into small mixing bowl, add sugar and salt, and whisk until frothy. Mix into chocolate–bread crumb mixture, then scoop into baking dish.

5. Center dish in small roasting pan, pull out middle oven shelf, and center roasting pan on shelf. Add enough boiling water to pan to come about halfway up sides of baking dish. Gently slide shelf back into oven and bake pudding until set like custard and cake tester inserted midway between center and rim of baking dish comes out clean—about 1 hour.

6. Remove pudding from oven and from water bath and cool about 30 minutes.

7. Serve warm. Or, if you prefer, cover pudding, refrigerate overnight, and serve cold. Whether warm or cold, accompany with Crème Anglaise, Frothy Egg Sauce, Mock Devonshire Cream, or whipped cream.

Rum-Raisin Bread Pudding

Makes 6 Servings

Always a popular flavor combination, raisins and rum go together zip-quick in this easy bread pudding. To shortcut prep time even further, I've used a firm-textured raisin bread swirled with cinnamon. You'll find several brands at your supermarket.

1. Preheat oven to 350°F. Lightly butter 8 x 8 x 2-inch baking dish or spritz with nonstick cooking spray and set aside.

2. Place raisins in small nonreactive bowl, add rum, and let stand while you proceed with recipe.

3. Generously spread one side of each slice of bread with butter, then cut slices into 1-inch cubes. Place in large mixing bowl and set aside.

4. Beat eggs and ⅓ cup sugar in small electric mixer bowl at high speed until color and consistency of mayonnaise—about 1 minute. Reduce mixer speed to medium and beat in remaining sugar. With mixer at low speed, drizzle in hot milk and continue beating until smooth—about 1 minute.

5. Add raisins and rum to bread cubes and toss well to mix. Then add egg mixture and using rubber spatula, fold in until well combined.

6. Scoop bread mixture into baking dish, spreading to corners, then set baking dish in middle of large roasting pan. Pull middle oven shelf out, center roasting pan on shelf, then add enough boiling water to pan to come about halfway up sides of baking dish.

7. Gently slide shelf back into oven and bake pudding until tipped with brown and cake tester, inserted midway between rim and middle of pudding, comes out clean—45 to 50 minutes.

8. Remove pudding from oven and from water bath and cool on wire baking rack 20 minutes.

9. To serve, spoon pudding onto bright dessert plates and top each portion with whipped cream or ice cream.

⅓ cup dark seedless raisins

¼ cup dark rum

6 slices firm-textured cinnamon-swirled raisin bread, crusts on (from a 1-pound loaf)

¼ cup (½ stick) unsalted butter, softened

2 large eggs

⅔ cup sugar

1½ cups steaming hot milk

TOPPING:

1 cup heavy cream, whipped to soft peaks, or 1 pint vanilla ice cream

Bread Puddings & Steamed Puddings

Lemon Meringue Bread Pudding

Makes 4 to 6 Servings

This is my riff on a dessert we test kitchen girls at *The Ladies' Home Journal* in New York often made for VIP luncheons. The Executive Dining Room adjoined the test kitchen and I sometimes sneaked a peek through the swinging door to catch a glimpse of a favorite author whose work appeared in the *Journal* — James Michener, maybe, Rebecca West, or Isak Dinesen. I cooked for all three. A tiny figure swathed in black in her declining years, Dinesen ate little — three Blue Points (oysters) on the half shell and three peeled green Thompson seedless grapes accompanied by Dom Perignon champagne. Still, I did once see her spooning up a bit of this bread pudding.

Tip: Use stale bread for this recipe, actually bread that's several days old.

2½ cups ½-inch cubes crustless stale bread (about 5 slices firm-textured white bread)

½ cup cold water

1½ teaspoons finely grated lemon zest

¼ cup fresh lemon juice

6 tablespoons unsalted butter, softened

½ cup granulated sugar

2 large eggs, separated

1 tablespoon confectioners' (10X) sugar

1. Preheat oven to 350°F. Butter 1-quart baking dish or spritz with nonstick cooking spray and set aside.

2. Place bread cubes, ¼ cup water, the lemon zest, and juice in medium nonreactive bowl, mix well, and let stand while you proceed with recipe.

3. Using hand electric mixer at high speed, cream butter and granulated sugar until fluffy — about 2 minutes. Beat in egg yolks one by one, then remaining ¼ cup water and continue beating until smooth — about 1 minute.

4. Gently fold yolk mixture into bread cube mixture. Scoop mixture into baking dish and set dish in medium roasting pan. Pull out middle oven shelf, center pan on shelf, then add enough boiling water to pan to come halfway up sides of baking dish.

5. Gently slide middle shelf into oven and bake 35 minutes. Remove from oven but not from water bath. Reduce oven temperature to 325°F.

Recipe continues

Bread Puddings & Steamed Puddings

6. With clean beaters and bowl, beat egg whites at medium speed until frothy. Reduce mixer speed to low, add confectioners' sugar, and continue beating to soft peaks—about 1 minute.

7. Swirl meringue on top of hot bread pudding, still in water bath. Return to middle oven shelf and slide back into oven. Bake just long enough for meringue to brown lightly and reach an interior temperature of 160°F—about 15 minutes (test by inserting instant-read thermometer horizontally just as you do to determine doneness of burgers).

8. Remove pudding from oven and from water bath and serve, making sure that everyone gets both plenty of bread pudding and meringue topping.

French Canadian Blueberry Pudding

Makes 6 to 8 Servings

I picked up this recipe years ago while traveling about the north of Maine on article assignment. It was called a *fungi,* which, I was told, means "thing." In truth, this is a type of bread pudding, a ridiculously easy one that's even easier to eat.

1. Preheat oven to 350°F. Butter 9 x 9 x 2-inch ovenproof glass baking dish well or spritz with nonstick cooking spray.

2. Butter one side of each slice of bread, then arrange four slices shoulder-to-shoulder and buttered sides up in baking dish. Spoon half of blueberries on top of bread, distributing evenly, and sprinkle with ½ cup granulated sugar. Top with remaining bread, again buttered sides up, then remaining blueberries and sugar. Using potato masher, mash firmly, crushing berries on top.

3. Slide onto middle oven shelf and bake uncovered 40 minutes. Remove from oven, crush berries again with potato masher. Return to oven and bake uncovered just until pudding is bubbly and juices are syrupy—10 to 20 minutes longer.

4. Remove pudding from oven, set on wire baking rack, and cool 30 minutes.

5. To serve, scoop pudding into dessert dishes and top each portion with generous spoonful of whipped cream or Mock Devonshire Cream.

¼ cup (½ stick) unsalted butter, at room temperature

8 slices firm-textured white bread, crusts on

1 quart (4 cups) fresh blueberries

1 cup granulated sugar

TOPPING:

1 cup heavy cream, whipped to soft peaks with 2 tablespoons confectioners' (10X) sugar and 1 teaspoon vanilla extract, or 1 recipe Mock Devonshire Cream (page 273)

Summer Pudding

Makes 6 to 8 Servings

This old English classic is such an easy recipe, such a delicious recipe, I'm surprised so few people know it. You can use almost any combination of summer berries, though the red ones make the prettiest pudding. And if you should hunger for Summer Pudding in the dead of winter? No problem. Simply substitute thawed frozen berries and their juices for the fresh.

Note: If this pudding is to unmold neatly, it must be heavily weighted during its twelve-hour stay in the refrigerator, so you must find something to hold the weights that exactly fits in the top of the bowl you're using—a flat saucer or dessert plate, perhaps, even a cut-to-fit circle of heavy-duty cardboard wrapped in aluminum foil.

1. Spritz deep, round-bottomed, nonreactive 1-quart bowl with nonstick cooking spray and set aside.

2. Bring sugar and water to boil in large heavy nonreactive saucepan over moderate heat, then cook and stir 1 minute. Add berries and simmer gently, stirring now and then, until fruit softens slightly—2 to 3 minutes. Taste for sugar and adjust as needed.

3. Pour berries into large sieve set over large nonreactive bowl and let juice drip through, taking care not to crush berries. Reserve berries and berry juice.

4. Dip one slice bread into berry juice, then center in bottom of spritzed bowl. Now line sides of bowl with bread, cutting remaining slices as needed for tight fit and dipping each piece into berry juice before pressing against side of bowl.

5. Pour half of berries into bread-lined bowl, top with juice-dipped slice of bread, then add remaining berries. Pour ¼ cup remaining berry juice evenly over all. Dip final slice of bread in berry juice and center on top so berries are largely covered. If any bread lining sides of bowl extends above level of bread-topped berries, fold in as needed to fit. Pour remaining berry juice into a one-pint preserving jar, screw lid down tight, and set in refrigerator.

6. Spread double thickness plastic food wrap across bread covering berries in bowl, lay flat saucer or aluminum-wrapped cut-to-fit cardboard circle on top (see Note above), then weight with several heavy unopened cans of food.

¾ cup sugar, or to taste (essential if you use cranberries)

¼ cup water

2 quarts (8 cups) ripe berries (about 2¾ pounds), any mixture you fancy (quartered strawberries, whole raspberries, blackberries, blueberries, red currants, or cranberries; see headnote)

7 to 8 slices day-old firm-textured white bread, crusts removed

5 sprigs fresh lemon verbena, lemon geranium, or mint

1 recipe Mock Devonshire Cream (page 273)

7. Set pudding in refrigerator and chill at least 12 hours before serving.

8. When ready to serve, remove pudding from refrigerator, lift off cans, then saucer or cardboard circle, and carefully peel off plastic food wrap. Gently loosen pudding around edge with small thin-blade spatula, then invert on large round dessert plate.

9. Slowly spoon about ¼ cup reserved berry juice over pudding and sprig with lemon verbena. Pour remaining berry juice into small pitcher and spoon Mock Devonshire Cream into small bowl, then serve as accompaniments to summer pudding, giving people the option of one or the other—or both.

Bread-and-Butter Blackberry Pudding

Makes 6 to 8 Servings

Though just-picked blackberries are my choice for this easy pudding, I must admit that fresh or frozen blueberries are almost as good. As for the bread, I used a 50/50 mix of firm-textured white bread and whole-wheat bread, though all white bread is equally delicious — in fact, some people prefer it.

1. Preheat oven to 350°F. Butter 9 x 9 x 2-inch baking dish well or spritz with nonstick cooking spray and set aside.

2. Combine first five ingredients (granulated sugar through salt) in small bowl and set aside.

3. Butter all eight slices of bread on one side, then arrange four slices whole-wheat bread buttered side up in pan. Scoop one-half berries on top, sprinkle one-half sugar mixture evenly over all, then mash well with potato masher so juices trickle down into bread. Repeat layers using white bread this time and mash well again.

4. Slide pan onto middle oven shelf and bake pudding uncovered for 45 minutes. Remove from oven and mash well again. Return to oven and bake uncovered until bubbling and syrupy — 20 to 25 minutes longer.

5. Remove from oven, set on wire baking rack, and cool 30 minutes.

6. Serve warm with whipped cream, vanilla ice cream, or Frothy Egg Sauce.

¾ cup granulated sugar

¼ cup raw sugar

¼ teaspoon ground cinnamon

¼ teaspoon freshly grated nutmeg

⅛ teaspoon salt

5 tablespoons unsalted butter, at room temperature

4 slices whole-wheat bread and 4 slices firm-textured white bread (see headnote), crusts on

1 quart (4 cups) dead-ripe blackberries, or fresh blueberries or thawed frozen blueberries (do not drain)

ACCOMPANIMENT:

Softly whipped cream, vanilla ice cream, or Frothy Egg Sauce (page 277)

Buttermilk-Biscuit Pudding

Makes 8 Servings

My good friend Mike Moore, a popular radio host at 1490 WLOE and 1420 WMYN in North Carolina's densely populated High Point/Greensboro/Winston-Salem/Reidsville area, sent me this recipe when he heard that I was writing a new cookbook devoted to puddings. The accompanying note said he didn't know the original source of the recipe, only that it was an old one and "especially good." What makes it unusual is that it's made with buttermilk instead of what Southerners call "sweet milk."

Note: Use leftover biscuits—if you should have as many as eight. Or simply bake a batch of biscuits a day ahead of time and let them stand at room temperature overnight before beginning this recipe. It's OK, by the way, to use a favorite brand of refrigerated ready-to-bake biscuits. I do so whenever I'm in a hurry.

1. Place crumbled biscuits in large nonreactive mixing bowl, add buttermilk, and set aside for 2 hours (no need to refrigerate).

2. Preheat oven to 375°F. Use a little of melted butter to butter 1½-quart casserole.

3. Quickly mash biscuits with buttermilk, then mix in remaining butter and all other remaining ingredients (sugar through lemon zest). Scoop into casserole, spreading to edge.

4. Slide pudding onto middle oven shelf and bake until tipped with brown and cake tester, inserted halfway between center and rim, comes out clean—50 to 60 minutes.

5. Serve warm topped, if you like, with whipped cream. Delicious, too, with Blueberry Maple Sauce (page 281).

5¾ cups coarsely crumbled day-old baking powder biscuits (you'll need about 8; see Note above)

2 cups buttermilk (not fat-free)

¼ cup (½ stick) unsalted butter, melted

1¾ cups sugar

2 large eggs, well beaten

½ teaspoon baking powder

¼ teaspoon baking soda

½ teaspoon finely grated lemon zest

Whipped cream, for topping (optional)

Mother's Bread Crumb–Date-Nut Pudding

Makes 8 Servings

The first date-nut pudding my mother made as a bride contained bread crumbs and precious little flour. Not satisfied, she experimented with the recipe over the years and her final improv, the one we all liked best, contained no bread crumbs at all (see page 214). This one has an altogether different texture, one, you might say, that's more pudding-like.

1. Preheat oven to 350°F. Butter 9-inch round layer cake pan well or spritz with nonstick cooking spray and set aside.

2. Soak bread crumbs in milk in large mixing bowl 20 minutes, stirring occasionally.

3. Mix in remaining ingredients (brown sugar to walnuts) in order listed and scoop into pan, spreading to edge.

4. Slide onto middle oven shelf and bake until pudding begins to pull from side of pan and cake tester, inserted midway between rim and middle of pan, comes out clean — about 30 minutes.

5. Remove pudding from oven and cool 20 minutes on wire baking rack.

6. To serve, cut into wedges and top each portion with whipped cream. Good, too, with Mock Devonshire Cream (page 273).

1 cup moderately fine soft white bread crumbs (about 2 slices firm-textured white bread, crusts on)

1 cup milk

½ cup firmly packed light brown sugar

⅓ cup granulated sugar

2 tablespoons all-purpose flour whisked with 1 teaspoon baking powder

½ teaspoon salt

1 large egg, lightly beaten

2 tablespoons unsalted butter, melted

1 cup coarsely chopped pitted dates

1 cup coarsely chopped walnuts

TOPPING:

1 cup heavy cream, whipped to soft peaks

Capirotada (New Mexican Bread Pudding)

Makes 4 to 6 Servings

I first visited Santa Fe as a young editor at *Venture: The Traveler's World,* a high-end travel magazine launched by *Look* magazine. My job was to edit each issue's 18-page travel guide. For our New Mexico issue, instead of flying to Albuquerque and driving up to Santa Fe, I opted for a day and a night in a stateroom aboard the Super Chief. It deposited me at dawn at a whistle stop called Lamy. At 7,000 feet, Santa Fe itself was a climb too steep for the Atchison, Topeka, and Santa Fe. A vintage school bus met me and before long, we were rattling to New Mexico's capital city 18 miles north, a low-rise sprawl of mud-brown buildings more exotic than anything I'd seen on any overseas assignment. In no time I was in love, not only with this adobe town but also with its food — to me as intriguing as its architecture. The explosive chilies, often taken with a side of pineapple sherbet, the adobe breads and fry breads, and not least, the desserts, among them this spicy bread pudding made with leftovers. New Mexico cooks use adobe bread for Capirotada, round yeast-leavened loaves baked in outdoor adobe ovens called *hornos.* But any stale, dry firm-textured white bread, crisply toasted and lightly buttered, works equally well.

1 cup sugar

2½ cups boiling water

1 teaspoon ground cinnamon

¼ teaspoon ground cloves or allspice

¼ teaspoon salt

1½ tablespoons (about) unsalted butter, at room temperature

8 slices stale firm-textured white bread (see headnote), crusts on, toasted

1 cup dark seedless raisins

1½ cups coarsely shredded Monterey Jack or sharp Cheddar cheese

Light or heavy cream, for serving (optional)

1. Preheat oven to 350°F. Lightly butter 2-quart baking dish or spritz with nonstick cooking spray and set aside.

2. Melt sugar in medium-size heavy saucepan over moderate heat, shaking pan often, until color of caramel — 3 to 4 minutes. Watch carefully as sugar melts because it turns color fast and is apt to burn.

Recipe continues

3. Remove from heat and add boiling water in slow steady stream — sugar will sputter and harden. No problem. Return sugar mixture to moderate heat and cook, stirring often, until sugar dissolves, forming a thin caramel syrup — 3 to 5 minutes. Again, watch carefully. Turn heat to lowest point, stir in cinnamon, cloves, and salt, and keep warm.

4. Lightly butter each toast slice on one side, then cut into 1-inch dice. Layer one-fourth toast in bottom of baking dish, add one-fourth raisins, then one-fourth cheese. Repeat layers three times. Pour hot caramelized sugar syrup evenly over all, then toss lightly to mix.

5. Slide onto middle oven shelf and bake until toast has absorbed all liquid and pudding is tipped with brown — 20 to 25 minutes.

6. Serve hot and, if you like, put out a pitcher of light or heavy cream to trickle over each portion. Not traditional but delicious.

Queen of Puddings

Makes 6 Servings

"This is my great aunt Alice Moreton Johnson's famous pudding," writes my Chapel Hill friend, Moreton Neal, who was generous enough to share the recipe for this old Mississippi family favorite. "My cousins (her grandchildren)," Moreton continued, "had this often for Sunday dinner dessert after church. They loved it and bragged about how wonderful it was. I was envious that they had the Queen of Puddings, though my own grandmother served some great desserts, herself, at our own family's Sunday dinner—notably her Orange Charlotte." See page 150 for recipe.

1. Preheat oven to 325°F. Butter deep 1½-quart casserole or spritz with non-stick cooking spray and set aside.

2. Bring milk to simmer in medium-size heavy saucepan over moderate heat. Remove from heat, mix in bread crumbs and butter, and cool slightly—about 10 minutes.

3. Separate 2 eggs, setting whites aside. Whisk egg yolks, remaining whole egg, ½ cup sugar, and lemon zest in medium bowl just until combined, then fold in bread crumb mixture.

4. Pour into casserole, set in medium baking pan, and center on pulled-out middle oven shelf. Pour enough hot water into baking pan to come halfway up sides of casserole.

5. Gently slide shelf back into oven and bake pudding uncovered until cake tester, inserted midway between center and edge of pudding, comes out clean—about 1 hour and 20 minutes.

6. Remove pudding from oven. Whisk currant jelly in small bowl until consistency of applesauce, then spread carefully over top of pudding. Set aside while you prepare meringue. Raise oven temperature to 350°F.

7. Using hand electric mixer, beat egg whites with salt at high speed in medium bowl until silvery. Gradually add remaining ¼ cup sugar and continue beating at high speed until soft peaks form. Swirl meringue into peaks and valleys on top of currant jelly on warm pudding.

Recipe continues

2 cups milk

1 cup moderately coarse day-old bread crumbs (about 2 slices firm-textured white bread, crusts on)

1 teaspoon unsalted butter

3 large eggs

¾ cup sugar

Finely grated zest of 1 medium lemon

¾ cup currant jelly

⅛ teaspoon salt

Bread Puddings & Steamed Puddings

8. Return pudding to middle oven shelf (no water bath needed) and bake until meringue is lightly browned and instant-read thermometer inserted horizontally into meringue registers 160°F—about 15 minutes. Remove pudding from oven and cool 15 to 20 minutes on wire baking rack.

9. Serve pudding directly from casserole, making sure each person gets plenty of meringue as well as pudding underneath.

French Bread Pudding with Whiskey Sauce

Makes 8 Servings

French bread isn't necessarily synonymous with the baguette, that long skinny heavily crusted loaf, which, in my opinion, doesn't make good bread pudding. I use buttery croissants—about a day old.

Note: If real croissants aren't available, simply bake four to six refrigerated crescent rolls as directed, then let them age at room temperature for about a day—but only if the weather's dry and humidity low.

Tip: Make Whiskey Sauce while pudding cools.

1. Preheat oven to 350°F. Butter 2-quart casserole or spritz with nonstick cooking spray and set aside.

2. Place all but last two ingredients (diced croissants and Whiskey Sauce) in large mixing bowl and whisk or beat until smooth. Add diced croissants and mix until well coated with egg mixture.

3. Scoop into casserole, spreading to edge, then set in middle of small roasting pan. Pull middle oven shelf out, center roasting pan on shelf, then add enough boiling water to pan to come about halfway up sides of casserole.

4. Gently slide shelf back into oven and bake pudding until it browns lightly and instant-read thermometer inserted midway between rim and center not only comes out clean but also registers 160°F—45 to 50 minutes.

5. Remove pudding from oven and cool in upright casserole on wire baking rack about 30 minutes.

6. To serve, spoon pudding onto bright dessert plates and pass Whiskey Sauce in small pitcher so everyone can have as much or as little as they like.

2½ cups milk

1 cup heavy cream

4 large eggs

½ cup sugar

1½ teaspoons vanilla extract

1 teaspoon ground cinnamon

½ teaspoon freshly grated nutmeg

½ teaspoon finely grated lemon zest

3 cups diced day-old croissants (from 2 to 3 large croissants or 4 to 6 made from refrigerated crescent dough)

1 recipe Whiskey Sauce (page 282; see Tip above)

Bread Puddings & Steamed Puddings

Maple Bread Pudding

Makes 8 Servings

This recipe comes from Judy Berek, a New Yorker who's been cooking and baking ever since she was a little girl. "I could get the meal on the table on time so I didn't have to do any other chores," she explained. Always a devout hobby cook, Judy began working on a cookbook after retiring ("I went from the Labor Movement to working for the government," is how she describes her career). Her first recipes were maple-syrup based because a friend owns a sugar house in Upstate New York. Her cookbook-in-progress, however, focuses not only on local foods but also on the Hudson Valley farmers who produce them whom she interviewed with an assist from her friend Betsy Wade, a 45-year *New York Times* veteran. The area where Judy has a country house "is a mixture of old family farms and young college-educated farmers who decided to leave the city or suburbia and become farmers." With Betsy Wade now on board, the cookbook will be written, Judy says.

Notes: Though Judy makes this bread pudding with challah, she suggests brioche as a substitute. Or any other rich bread—and the richer the better. She trims the crusts off the challah but when I asked if this wasn't a colossal waste of good bread, Judy explained that she buzzes the trimmings to crumbs that can be frozen and used in any recipe that calls for bread crumbs. Judy also insists upon extra-dark maple syrup (grade B) for cooking because of its rich maple flavor (see Sources, page 291).

Tip: Like many puddings popular in the Northeast, this one isn't very sweet. So Southerners, indeed anyone afflicted with a sweet tooth, may want to serve the pudding with Judy's superb Blueberry Maple Sauce.

1. Preheat oven to 250°F. Butter 2½-quart casserole and set aside.

2. Cut challah in ¾-inch cubes (you should have about 7½ cups) and spread on ungreased rimmed baking sheet. Slide onto middle oven shelf and allow to dry 10 to 15 minutes; remove from oven and set aside. Raise oven temperature to 350°F.

3. Whisk 1 cup milk with egg yolks until frothy in large mixing bowl. Bring remaining 2 cups milk and cream to a simmer in medium-size heavy saucepan over moderate heat, stirring occasionally—6 to 8 minutes.

Recipe continues

¾ **pound challah or brioche (see Notes above), crusts removed**

3 cups milk

4 large egg yolks

2 cups heavy cream

½ cup pure maple syrup (see Notes above)

Whole nutmeg (to grate on top)

1 tablespoon granulated maple sugar (to sprinkle on top—optional)

4. Whisking yolk mixture briskly, add hot milk mixture in slow, steady stream and continue whisking until smooth. Mix in maple syrup, then add bread cubes and stir well. Allow to stand at room temperature until nicely moistened—about 20 minutes.

5. Pour bread mixture into casserole and set in medium roasting pan. Grate nutmeg lightly on top. Pull middle oven shelf out, center roasting pan on shelf, then add enough boiling water to pan to come about halfway up sides of casserole.

6. Gently slide shelf back into oven and bake pudding uncovered 20 minutes. If you like a browner crust, sprinkle maple sugar on top of pudding. Continue baking until instant-read thermometer inserted midway between rim and center registers 160°F—50 to 60 minutes longer.

7. Remove pudding from oven and allow to stand for 20 minutes on wire baking rack.

8. Serve pudding hot with or without Blueberry Maple Sauce (page 281) or put out a pitcher of pure maple syrup so everyone can drizzle as much as they like over their portions.

Variations:

Maple Bread Pudding with Dried Fruits: Soak ½ cup each sultanas (golden seedless raisins), dried currants, and coarsely chopped dried apricots 10 minutes in enough boiling water to cover. Drain well. Prepare pudding as directed, adding dried fruits along with the bread cubes in Step 4. Makes 8 generous servings.

Maple Bread Pudding with Fresh Apples: Peel, core, and cut 1 large Cortland apple (about 8 ounces) into ¾-inch cubes. (Note: Cortlands, developed in 1898 at New York's Agricultural Experiment Station, are the apples to use not only because their snowy flesh, once cut, is slow to brown, but also because their flavor is both tart and sweet.) Prepare pudding as directed, adding apples along with bread cubes in Step 4 and, if you like, sprinkling ½ teaspoon ground cinnamon on top instead of the nutmeg. Makes 8 generous servings.

Upside-Down Peach Cups
with Spicy Peach Sauce

Makes 6 Servings

This is one of the most effective ways I know to jazz up bread pudding. If fresh peaches are in season, use them, but canned peach halves work equally well.

Note: If you use fresh peaches, choose yellow-fleshed free-stones (the pits slip right out) and brush each half well with a little fresh lemon or lime juice to reduce the risk of browning. Varieties I like: Elberta and Redhaven. For this recipe, you'll need 3 large peaches plus ½ peach for the sauce, about 1¼ pounds in all.

PEACH CUPS:

6 large peach halves, either fresh or well-drained peach halves canned in heavy syrup (see Note above)

1 large egg

½ cup sugar

½ teaspoon ground cinnamon

¼ teaspoon ground ginger

2 cups moderately coarse soft bread crumbs (about 4 slices firm-textured white bread, crusts on) tossed with 2 tablespoons melted unsalted butter

PEACH SAUCE:

½ cup sugar combined with 1⅓ cups water (if using canned peaches, use heavy syrup from can, + enough water to total 1⅓ cups)

½ peeled and pitted fresh large peach or 1 well-drained canned peach half, coarsely chopped

1½ tablespoons cornstarch

½ teaspoon ground cinnamon

1 tablespoon unsalted butter

1. Peach Cups: Preheat oven to 400°F. Butter six 5- or 6-ounce custard cups well, then place peach half in each, cut-side up. Place on rimmed baking sheet.

2. Beat egg, sugar, cinnamon, and ginger in small bowl until frothy, then mix in buttered bread crumbs. Spoon onto peaches, dividing amount evenly and flattening tops.

3. Slide onto middle oven shelf and bake until lightly browned and toothpick inserted in center of filling comes out clean—about 25 minutes.

Recipe continues

Bread Puddings & Steamed Puddings

4. Peach Sauce: About 10 minutes before peach cups are done, combine sugar mixture (or peach syrup), chopped peach half, cornstarch, and cinnamon in blender. Blend until puréed and transfer to small nonreactive saucepan. Set over moderate heat and cook, stirring constantly, until sauce thickens and clears—about 3 minutes. Do not cook longer or sauce will begin to thin. Remove from heat, add butter, and stir until butter melts. Strain into small pitcher or 2-cup spouted glass measuring cup.

5. To serve, loosen edges of oven-hot peach cups with the tip of a knife and invert on bright dessert plates, then top each peach cup with sauce, dividing total amount evenly.

Graham Cracker Pudding

Make 6 Servings

What few people know today is that in the beginning, graham crackers were health food, a crisp wafer made of finely ground whole-wheat flour created nearly a hundred years ago by, of all people, a Presbyterian minister in Bound Brook, New Jersey. His name? Sylvester Graham. Whole-wheat flour, which contains both bran and wheat germ, is still sometimes called Graham flour. So does that mean that graham cracker pudding qualifies as health food? Sadly, no. Today's graham crackers, sweetened with honey or sugar, bear little resemblance to Graham's original. But don't let that put you off. Graham cracker pudding has been an American classic for at least half a century. And it's delicious.

Tip: For 1⅓ cups crumbs, you'll need one-third of a 14.4-ounce box of graham crackers; one box has three packages inside, each of which contains nine double crackers—two square cookies forming one rectangle. When buzzed to crumbs, nine double graham crackers = 1⅓ cups crumbs. Exactly what you need for this recipe. Best way to crumb the crackers? I break crackers in two, then pulse in a food processor until the texture of coarse meal. A few seconds is all it takes. You can also crumb the crackers by sealing in a plastic zipper bag and whacking with a rolling pin.

1⅓ cups graham cracker crumbs (see Tip above)

1 cup moderately finely chopped pecans or walnuts

1 teaspoon baking powder

¼ teaspoon salt

3 large eggs, separated

½ cup milk

1 cup granulated sugar

½ teaspoon vanilla extract

TOPPING:

1 cup heavy cream, whipped to soft peaks with 2 tablespoons confectioners'

(10X) sugar and 1 teaspoon vanilla extract, or 1 recipe Mock Devonshire Cream (page 273) or Crème Fraîche (page 274)

1. Preheat oven to 350°F. Generously butter 9 x 9 x 2-inch baking pan, spritz well with nonstick cooking spray, or line with baking parchment and set aside.

2. Place graham cracker crumbs, pecans, baking powder, and salt in large bowl, toss well to mix, and set aside.

Recipe continues

Bread Puddings & Steamed Puddings

3. Beat egg yolks, milk, ¾ cup granulated sugar, and vanilla in large electric mixer bowl at high speed until light—about 1 minute. Add to crumb mixture and fold in—gently but thoroughly.

4. Beat egg whites at low mixer speed in large pristine bowl with pristine beaters until silvery—about 1 minute. With machine still at low speed, add remaining ¼ cup granulated sugar gradually, then raise mixer speed to high and beat until whites peak softly—about 2 minutes.

5. Fold about ½ cup beaten whites into crumb mixture to lighten it, then fold in remaining whites until no streaks of brown or white show. Easy does it. Scoop mixture into pan, spreading to corners.

6. Slide onto middle oven shelf and bake until lightly browned and cake tester, inserted halfway between center and rim, comes out clean—about 35 minutes.

7. Transfer pudding to wire baking rack and cool 10 minutes.

8. To serve, cut into squares, rectangles, or triangles, then drift each portion with topping of your choice.

Noodle Pudding

Makes 10 to 12 Servings

My new New York electronic pen pal Judy Berek sent me this recipe along with the following note: "This is the perfect noodle pudding for anyone raised by or fed by Ida Berek, my mother. Each Jewish Mother has her own recipe and this was the version my mother made, plus some extra heavy cream added, because I like it. There are versions that are not sweet and there are even versions with no dairy. To me those are wrong. People whose mothers made noodle pudding either of those ways think this one is wrong. I would hope those people would give it a try. If you have never had noodle pudding, think of it as rice pudding or bread pudding but with noodles as the starch." Judy's recipe has apples in it because "in fall in the Northeast apples are fabulous and essential." She prefers Cortlands—"a great cooking apple that holds its shape when cooked. It's firm not hard, a bit tart." If Cortlands are unavailable, substitute any apple that holds its shape. Judy adds that dried apricots can be substituted when the apple season's over, also that "in spring fresh peaches or apricots would be terrific." She even suggests using fresh blueberries in place of the raisins or currants. Judy admits that this pudding is not very sweet and says it's OK to add a little more sugar. I've given that option below. Also see Judy's Maple Bread Pudding (page 184) and her Blueberry Maple Sauce (page 281).

Note: To toast walnuts, spread in a pie pan, slide onto the middle shelf of a preheated 350°F oven, and toast for 8 to 10 minutes.

⅓ cup dark seedless raisins or dried currants (see headnote)

1 cup boiling water

5 large eggs, lightly beaten

¾ cup small-curd cottage cheese (not low-fat or fat-free)

⅓ to ⅔ cup sugar (depending on how sweet you like things)

1½ cups heavy cream

1½ teaspoons vanilla extract

1 package (12 ounces) wide or extra-wide noodles, cooked by package directions (they should be al dente—a bit firm because they'll continue to cook as they bake), then drained well

½ cup toasted walnuts (see Note above), broken into large pieces

2 medium (about ¾ pound) Cortland apples (see headnote), peeled, cored, and each cut into 8 wedges

2 tablespoons sugar mixed with ¼ teaspoon ground cinnamon (cinnamon sugar)

1½ tablespoons refrigerator-cold unsalted butter, diced

Recipe continues

Bread Puddings & Steamed Puddings

1. Preheat oven to 350°F. Butter deep 10-inch (2½- to 3-quart) ceramic or ovenproof glass casserole or spritz with nonstick cooking spray and set aside.

2. Place raisins in small heatproof bowl, add boiling water, and let stand until softened—about 10 minutes. Drain well.

3. Combine next five ingredients (eggs through vanilla) in large mixing bowl, beating or whisking until smooth. By hand, fold in drained raisins along with noodles, walnuts, and apples.

4. Scoop into casserole, spreading to edge, then sprinkle with cinnamon sugar and dot with butter.

5. Cover with foil, slide onto middle oven shelf, and bake 40 minutes. Remove foil and continue baking until pudding is tipped with brown and cake tester, inserted midway between rim and center of pudding, comes out clean—15 to 20 minutes longer.

6. Serve hot or warm—New York delis even serve noodle pudding cold.

Steamed Applesauce Pudding

Makes 8 Servings

From my mother's collection of steamed puddings. There are a lot of ingredients, true, but they come together quickly and the finished pudding is supremely moist.

1. Place round cake rack (whatever fits) in bottom of large heavy soup pot and add enough cold water to come just above level of rack. Butter 1½-quart steamed pudding mold well or spritz with nonstick cooking spray and set aside.

2. Whisk first eight ingredients (flour through salt) in large bowl to combine. Add dates and pecans, toss well, and make well in center of dry ingredients.

3. Quickly combine applesauce, melted butter, and egg in small bowl, whisking until smooth. Pour into well in dry ingredients and stir only enough to combine.

4. Spoon batter into pudding mold—it should be no more than three-fourths full. Snap lid on mold.

5. Bring water in soup pot to hard boil, ease pudding mold into pot, centering on rack. Adjust heat so water bubbles gently, cover pot, and steam pudding 2½ hours. Protecting hands with pot holders, remove pudding mold lid, and insert cake tester midway between rim and central tube. If it comes out clean—and it should—pudding is done. If not, re-cover pudding mold and steamer, and steam pudding about 15 to 20 minutes more. When you begin steaming pudding, keep saucepan of boiling water at the ready, check water in steamer now and then, and if it threatens to boil dry, add boiling water until level with top of rack; do not pour water over pudding mold but around edge of steamer.

6. When pudding tests done, remove from steamer and cool 15 minutes right side up in sealed mold on wire baking rack.

7. Remove lid, carefully loosen pudding around edge and central tube with small thin-blade spatula, and invert on heated bright round dessert platter.

8. To serve, cut into wedges at table and if you like, top each portion with whipped cream. Good, too, with Mock Devonshire Cream (page 273) or Crème Fraîche (page 274).

1¾ cups sifted all-purpose flour

1 cup sugar or ½ cup each granulated sugar and raw sugar

1 teaspoon baking powder

1 teaspoon ground cinnamon

½ teaspoon baking soda

½ teaspoon ground ginger

¼ teaspoon ground cloves

¼ teaspoon salt

1 cup finely diced pitted dates or 1 cup dark seedless raisins

1 cup coarsely chopped pecans or walnuts

1 cup firmly packed applesauce (preferably unsweetened and homemade)

½ cup (1 stick) unsalted butter, melted

1 large egg, well beaten

OPTIONAL TOPPING:

1 cup heavy cream, softly whipped

Colonial Suet Pudding

Makes 8 to 10 Servings

If you've never made a steamed pudding, I can't think of a better recipe to try than this one because it contains six ingredients only — Christmas Pudding (page 198) has sixteen.

Note: Because this pudding batter is wetter than most, this pudding takes a little longer to steam.

Tip: For information about suet, see Beef Suet (page xxii).

3 cups sifted all-purpose flour

1 teaspoon baking soda

1 cup (about 4 ounces) finely ground or minced suet (see Tip above)

1 cup finely chopped dark seedless raisins

1 cup unsulfured molasses (not too dark)

1 cup milk

OPTIONAL TOPPING:

1 cup heavy cream, whipped with 2 tablespoons confectioners' (10X) sugar (optional)

1. Place round cake rack (whatever fits) in bottom of large heavy soup pot and add enough cold water to come just above level of rack. Grease 2-quart round-bottomed metal mixing bowl well or spritz with nonstick cooking spray and set aside.

2. Combine flour and baking soda in large mixing bowl, add suet and raisins, and gently work in with hands making sure no clumps stick together. Make well in middle of ingredients.

3. Combine molasses and milk, pour into well in dry ingredients, and stir just enough to incorporate.

4. Scoop batter into bowl — it should be no more than two-thirds full, then cover with oiled foil (oiled side down) and tie round with string to secure.

5. Bring water in soup pot to hard boil, ease pudding into pot foil-side up, and center on rack. Adjust heat so water bubbles gently, cover pot, and steam pudding until cake tester, inserted through foil cover midway between rim and center, comes out clean — about 3¼ hours. Also keep saucepan of boiling water at the ready, check

water in steamer now and then, and if it threatens to boil dry, add boiling water until level with top of rack; do not pour water over pudding mold but around edge of pot.

6. When pudding tests done, remove from steamer and cool 15 minutes in sealed upright bowl on wire baking rack.

7. Remove foil, carefully loosen pudding around edge with small thin-blade spatula, and invert on heated bright round dessert platter.

8. To serve, cut into wedges at table and, if you like, pass bowl of whipped cream so everyone can help himself. I also like this pudding with Hard Sauce (page 287) and Mock Devonshire Cream (page 273).

Steamed Cocoa–Brown Sugar Pudding

Makes 8 to 10 Servings

Though sometimes called "chocolate" steamed pudding, this contains only 2 tablespoons of cocoa powder so the brown sugar dominates. This is the steamed pudding for those who can do without dried or candied fruits. It's also easier to make.

Note: This steamed pudding needs no suet; melted butter works just fine. It also contains no egg.

1. Place round cake rack (whatever fits) in bottom of large heavy soup pot and add enough cold water to come just above level of rack. Butter 2-quart steamed pudding mold well or spritz with nonstick cooking spray and set aside.

2. Whisk flour, cocoa, baking soda, and salt together in large mixing bowl to combine. Add light and dark brown sugars and mix in with fingers, pressing out all lumps. Make well in middle of dry ingredients.

3. Combine buttermilk, melted butter, and vanilla in small bowl, whisking until frothy. Pour into well in dry ingredients and mix only enough to combine.

4. Scoop batter into pudding mold—it should be no more than two-thirds full. Snap lid on mold.

5. Bring water in soup pot to hard boil, ease pudding mold into pot, centering on rack. Adjust heat so water bubbles gently, cover pot, and steam pudding 2½ hours. Protecting hands with pot holders, remove pudding mold lid, and insert cake tester midway between rim and central tube. If it comes out clean—and it should—pudding is done. If not, re-cover pudding mold and steamer, and steam pudding about 15 to 20 minutes more. When you begin steaming pudding, keep saucepan of boiling water at the ready, check water in steamer now and then, and if it threatens to boil dry, add boiling water until level with top of rack; do not pour water over pudding mold but around edge of steamer.

6. When pudding tests done, remove from steamer and cool 10 minutes in sealed upright mold on wire baking rack.

7. Remove lid, carefully loosen pudding around edge and central tube with small thin-blade spatula, and invert on heated bright round dessert platter.

8. To serve, cut into wedges at table and pass bowl of Frothy Egg Sauce. This steamed pudding is equally good with Hard Sauce (page 287).

2 cups sifted all-purpose flour

2 tablespoons unsweetened cocoa powder

1 teaspoon baking soda

¼ teaspoon salt

½ cup firmly packed light brown sugar

½ cup firmly packed dark brown sugar

1 cup buttermilk (not fat-free)

¼ cup (½ stick) unsalted butter, melted

1½ teaspoons vanilla extract

1 recipe Frothy Egg Sauce (page 277)

Christmas Pudding

Makes 8 Servings

The image most of us will forever associate with Christmas Pudding is the one Charles Dickens immortalized in *A Christmas Carol:* "In half a minute Mrs. Cratchit entered—flushed, but smiling proudly—with the pudding, like a speckled cannon ball, so hard and firm—blazing in half of half-a-quarter of ignited brandy, and bedight with Christmas holly stuck into the top." But neither Dickens's Christmas Pudding nor those made today contain plums, only dried and candied fruits.

Christmas puddings originated in England several hundred years before Dickens, some say as early as the early fifteenth century. But those were savory puddings, more like mincemeat. Plum puddings had become a Christmas staple in England as well as in its New World Colony 100 years before Dickens was born, all because the "Pudding King" (George I) demanded that they be served at his lavish Christmas feast in 1714—dessert puddings.

Note: Suet is integral to Christmas Pudding (for details, see Beef Suet, page xxii). Can other fats be used in place of suet? Not if the pudding's to be authentic. My advice: Don't attempt this recipe until you can find genuine suet.

Caveat: Before cutting and serving the pudding, discard the sprigs of holly, placing where neither animals nor children can get at them. If eaten, the berries might make them sick.

1¼ cups sifted all-purpose flour

½ teaspoon ground cinnamon

½ teaspoon ground ginger

½ teaspoon baking powder

¼ teaspoon baking soda

¼ teaspoon freshly grated nutmeg

¼ teaspoon salt

¼ teaspoon ground cloves

⅔ cup coarsely chopped walnuts or pecans

½ cup dark seedless raisins or dried currants

½ cup diced mixed candied fruits (citron, orange and lemon peel, glacéed cherries, etc.)

½ cup firmly packed light brown sugar

1 large egg, lightly beaten with ¼ cup cold water

½ cup (about 2 ounces) firmly packed finely chopped suet (see Note above)

1 tablespoon cold unsalted butter, finely diced

¼ cup brandy (if you intend to flame the pudding)

GARNISH & ACCOMPANIMENT:

Several holly sprigs (see Caveat above)

1 recipe Hard Sauce (page 287)

Recipe continues

1. Place round cake rack (whatever fits) in bottom of large heavy soup pot and add enough cold water to come just above level of rack. Grease 1½-quart steamed-pudding mold well or spritz with nonstick cooking spray and set aside.

2. Whisk first eight ingredients (flour through cloves) in large bowl to combine. Add nuts, raisins, and candied fruits and toss well. Make well in center of mixture.

3. Using hand electric mixer, beat sugar and egg mixture in small bowl until smooth, then by hand fold in suet and butter. Scoop into well in dry ingredients and mix only enough to combine — ignore any bits of flour showing; they will disappear as pudding steams.

4. Spoon batter into pudding mold — it should be no more than two-thirds full. Snap lid on mold.

5. Bring water in soup pot to hard boil and ease pudding mold into pot, centering on rack. Adjust heat so water bubbles gently, cover pot, and steam pudding 2 hours. Protecting hands with pot holders, remove pudding mold lid, and insert cake tester midway between rim and central tube. If it comes out clean — and it should — pudding is done. If not, re-cover pudding mold and steamer, and steam pudding about 15 to 20 minutes more. When you begin steaming pudding, keep saucepan of boiling water at the ready, check water in steamer now and then, and if it threatens to boil dry, add boiling water until level with top of rack; do not pour water over pudding mold but around edge of steamer.

6. When pudding tests done, remove from steamer and cool 15 minutes right-side up in sealed mold on wire baking rack.

7. Remove lid, carefully loosen pudding around edge and central tube with small thin-blade spatula, and invert on heated bright round dessert platter.

8. To blaze, pour brandy over pudding and ignite with a match. Quickly arrange holly sprigs around edge of platter and carry flaming Christmas Pudding into darkened dining room.

9. As soon as flames die, discard holly sprigs (berries are toxic) and cut pudding into wedges. Pass Hard Sauce separately.

Steamed Orange Pudding

Makes 8 to 10 Servings

I hadn't realized how fond my mother was of steamed puddings until I began thumbing through her card file of recipes. I don't remember all of them but this one I definitely do.

Notes: Choose tart oranges with fairly thin rinds for this recipe—you'll line the pudding mold with orange slices. Speaking of which, a plain round-bottomed stainless-steel mixing bowl works best here, a 2-quart one. Most steamed pudding molds are tube molds with fluted sides and therefore bad choices for this particular recipe.

Tip: For information about almond meal, see Other Ingredients, page xxii, and Sources on page 291.

1¼ cups sifted all-purpose flour

½ cup almond meal (see Tip above)

½ teaspoon baking powder

¼ teaspoon salt

¼ teaspoon ground ginger

¼ teaspoon ground cinnamon

¼ teaspoon ground allspice

2⅔ cups sugar

2 cups water

2 medium (about ¾ pound) Valencia oranges (see Notes above), sliced about ⅛ inch thick (rind and all), then seeded

¾ cup (1½ sticks) unsalted butter, softened

3 large eggs

½ cup evaporated milk (not low-fat or fat-free)

¼ cup firmly packed orange marmalade

1 recipe Crème Anglaise (page 270)

1. Place round cake rack (whatever fits) in bottom of large heavy soup pot and add enough cold water to come just above level of rack. Butter 2-quart round-bottomed stainless-steel mixing bowl or spritz with nonstick cooking spray and set aside.

2. Whisk first seven ingredients (flour through allspice) together in second large mixing bowl and set aside.

3. Place 2 cups sugar and water in large nonreactive skillet, set over moderate heat, and bring to a boil. Cook, stirring constantly until sugar dissolves. Reduce heat to low and add orange slices, distributing evenly in sugar syrup. Cover skillet and simmer until orange slices are limp—about 10 minutes.

Recipe continues

Bread Puddings & Steamed Puddings

4. Meanwhile, cover counter with foil and set large wire baking rack on top, preferably one with cross-hatch grids so orange slices aren't likely to slip through. Using mesh skimmer, lift candied orange slices from skillet, arrange flat on rack, and allow to "drip-dry" 10 minutes. Discard sugar syrup.

5. Taking care not to rip orange slices, line bottom and sides of stainless-steel mixing bowl, overlapping as needed and leaving 2-inch space at top. Set bowl aside.

6. Cream remaining ⅔ cup sugar and butter in large electric mixer bowl at high speed until light and fluffy—about 2 minutes. With mixer at low speed, beat eggs in one by one.

7. Quickly combine milk and marmalade, then with mixer still at low speed, add alternately with combined dry ingredients, beginning and ending with dry.

8. Pour batter slowly into orange-lined bowl, taking care not to disturb slices. Cover bowl snugly with heavy-duty foil and tie round with string to seal.

9. Bring water in soup pot to hard boil and ease pudding bowl into pot, centering on rack. Adjust heat so water bubbles gently, cover pot, and steam pudding until cake tester inserted through foil cover midway between rim and center comes out clean—about 2½ hours. Also keep saucepan of boiling water at the ready, check water in steamer now and then, and if it threatens to boil dry, add boiling water until level with top of rack; do not pour water over bowl with pudding but around edge of pot.

10. When pudding tests done, lift to wire baking rack and cool in sealed upright bowl 20 minutes. Remove foil, carefully loosen pudding around edge with thin-blade spatula, and invert on colorful round platter.

11. To serve, carry pudding to dining table, cut into wedges, and pass Crème Anglaise.

Bread Puddings & Steamed Puddings

Steamed Fig and Cranberry Pudding

Makes 8 to 10 Servings

Another steamed pudding from my mother's recipe file, or rather my riff on her recipe. I've substituted dried cranberries—unheard of in my mother's day—for raisins and I think the recipe benefits from the switch. I suspect that dried blueberries would also be good in this recipe in lieu of raisins but have not tried them, although I do use them in the date variation that follows.

Tip: For specifics on suet, see Beef Suet (page xxii). Butter can be substituted for suet in this steamed pudding—not so Christmas Pudding or Colonial Suet Pudding.

1 cup sifted all-purpose flour

1 cup fine dry bread crumbs

½ cup sugar

1 tablespoon baking powder

1 teaspoon ground cinnamon

½ teaspoon ground ginger

¼ teaspoon ground allspice

¼ teaspoon ground cloves

¼ teaspoon salt

1 cup (about 4 ounces) finely chopped beef suet (see Tip above), or ½ cup (1 stick) refrigerator-cold unsalted butter, finely chopped

1 cup finely diced dried figs (about 6½ ounces)

1 cup coarsely chopped dried cranberries

2 large eggs, well beaten

¾ cup milk

1 recipe Hard Sauce (page 287) or Crème Anglaise (page 270)

1. Place round cake rack (whatever fits) in bottom of large heavy soup pot and add enough cold water to come just above level of rack. Butter 2-quart steamed-pudding mold well or spritz with nonstick cooking spray and set aside.

2. Whisk first nine ingredients (flour through salt) in large bowl to combine. Add suet, then using pastry blender, cut in until texture of lentils. Add figs and cranberries and toss well. Make well in center of mixture.

3. Whisk eggs and milk in small bowl until frothy, pour into well in dry ingredients, and mix only enough to combine.

4. Spoon batter into pudding mold—it should be no more than two-thirds full. Snap lid on mold.

5. Bring water in soup pot to hard boil and ease pudding mold into pot, centering on rack. Adjust heat so water bubbles gently, cover pot, and steam pudding 2½ hours. Protecting hands with pot holders, remove pudding mold lid, and insert cake tester midway between rim and central tube. If it comes out clean—and it should—pudding is done. If not, re-cover pudding mold and steamer, and steam pudding about 15 to 20 minutes more. When you begin steaming pudding, keep saucepan of boiling water at the ready, check water in steamer now and then, and if it threatens to boil dry, add boiling water until level with top of rack; do not pour water over pudding mold but around edge of steamer.

6. When pudding tests done, remove from steamer and cool 15 minutes in sealed upright mold on wire baking rack.

7. Remove lid, carefully loosen pudding around edge and central tube with small thin-blade spatula, and invert on heated bright round dessert platter.

8. To serve, cut into wedges at table and accompany with Hard Sauce or Crème Anglaise.

Variation:

Steamed Date and Blueberry Pudding: **Prepare as directed, but substitute moderately finely chopped pitted dates for the figs and dried blueberries for the cranberries (no need to chop blueberries). I also like to use raw sugar in this recipe instead of granulated. Makes 8 to 10 servings.**

Steamed Carrot Pudding

Makes 8 Servings

Noted on this recipe's dog-eared card is a variation Mother planned to develop: "Try with 1 cup drained canned crushed pineapple instead of potatoes and cut sugar." I don't believe she ever came up with that recipe, at least I don't remember it. But I have worked out her variation, which follows. Mother was a bit off on the pineapple measurement but her idea was sound. This tested variation is both delicious and easier than the original—fewer raw potatoes to grate.

Note: It may seem strange that you need only 1 large carrot (about 5 ounces) for 1 cup of grated carrot and twice that amount (10 ounces) for potatoes. Here's why: Carrots grate crisply and contain little water whereas grated potatoes are mushy and ooze lots of water. This should be drained off before you measure the grated potatoes.

1 cup fine dry bread crumbs

½ cup sifted all-purpose flour

1 teaspoon baking powder

1 teaspoon ground cinnamon

½ teaspoon freshly grated nutmeg

¼ teaspoon ground allspice

¼ teaspoon salt

1 cup firmly packed light brown sugar

2 teaspoons finely grated orange zest

½ cup (1 stick) unsalted butter, melted

1 large egg, well beaten

1 cup moderately finely grated peeled raw carrots (about 1 large, about 5 ounces)

1 cup (see Note above) moderately finely grated peeled raw Maine or Eastern potatoes (about 2 medium-small, about 10 ounces)

1 cup moderately coarsely chopped peeled and cored Gala or Granny Smith apple (about 1 large, 6¼ ounces)

½ cup dark seedless raisins or dried currants

1 recipe Hard Sauce (page 287) or Crème Anglaise (page 270)

1. Place round cake rack (whatever fits) in bottom of large heavy soup pot and add enough cold water to come just above level of rack. Butter 1½-quart steamed pudding mold well or spritz with nonstick cooking spray and set aside.

2. Whisk first seven ingredients (bread crumbs through salt) in large bowl to combine. Add sugar and orange zest and mix in, pressing out lumps. Now add all but final ingredient (melted butter through raisins) in order listed, mixing well after each addition.

3. Spoon batter into pudding mold—it should be no more than three-fourths full. Snap lid on mold.

4. Bring water in soup pot to hard boil, ease pudding mold into pot centering on rack. Adjust heat so water bubbles gently, cover pot, and steam pudding 2½ hours. Protecting hands with pot holders, remove pudding mold lid, and insert cake tester midway between rim and central tube. If it comes out clean—and it should—pudding is done. If not, re-cover pudding mold and steamer, and steam pudding about 15 to 20 minutes more. When you begin steaming pudding, keep saucepan of boiling water at the ready, check water in steamer now and then, and if it threatens to boil dry, add boiling water until level with top of rack; do not pour water over pudding mold but around edge of steamer.

5. When pudding tests done, remove from steamer and cool 15 minutes in sealed upright mold on wire baking rack.

6. Remove lid, carefully loosen pudding around edge and central tube with small thin-blade spatula, and invert on heated bright round dessert platter.

7. To serve, cut into wedges at table and accompany with Hard Sauce or Crème Anglaise.

Variation:

Steamed Carrot and Pineapple Pudding: Thoroughly drain 8-ounce can of crushed pineapple packed in 100 percent pineapple juice (you should have about ½ cup crushed pineapple). Prepare pudding as directed, but substitute ½ cup crushed pineapple for the 1 cup potatoes. Also use ½ cup each raw sugar and granulated instead of the light brown sugar. And if you like, substitute ½ cup dried blueberries or coarsely chopped dried cranberries for the raisins. Cool steamed pudding completely, then refrigerate several hours or overnight before cutting. Makes 8 servings.

Bread Puddings & Steamed Puddings

Miscellaneous Puddings

Indian Pudding

Makes 6 Servings

Why "Indian"? Because it's made with meal ground from the flint corn the Wampanoag taught the Pilgrims how to grow, how to harvest, how to dry, how to pulverize, and how to cook. In the beginning, Indian Pudding was little more than sweetened corn mush, but over time it evolved into something more interesting, more flavorful. According to Plimoth Plantation food historian Kathleen Wall, it is the quintessential New England pudding because its three key ingredients were at first available only in New England: Indian corn, milk from imported English cows, and molasses from the Colonists' trade with the West Indies. To quote Wall, Indian pudding "is not an English dish or a Colonial dish. It belongs to all of New England."

Note: This recipe, like the original, contains no eggs and for that reason is soft.

¼ cup yellow cornmeal (not stone-ground)

1 quart (4 cups) milk

⅔ cup unsulfured molasses (not too dark)

⅓ cup firmly packed light brown sugar

¼ cup (½ stick) refrigerator-cold unsalted butter, diced

½ teaspoon ground cinnamon

½ teaspoon ground ginger

¼ teaspoon freshly grated nutmeg

¼ teaspoon salt

OPTIONAL TOPPING:

1 cup heavy cream, whipped to soft peaks with 2 tablespoons confectioners' (10X) sugar, or 1 pint vanilla ice cream

1. Preheat oven to 325°F. Butter shallow 1½-quart casserole well or spritz with non-stick cooking spray and set aside.

2. Combine cornmeal with 1 cup milk in small bowl and set aside. Heat 2 cups remaining milk in double boiler top directly over moderate heat until bubbles appear around edge of pan—3 to 5 minutes.

3. Set double boiler top over simmering water, then whisk in cornmeal-milk mixture and cook, whisking occasionally, until thickened—15 to 20 minutes. Mix in molasses and sugar and cook, whisking often, 3 minutes more.

4. Remove from heat and from double boiler bottom, add butter, cinnamon, ginger, nutmeg, and salt, and whisk until smooth.

5. Scoop into casserole, spreading to edge and smoothing top, then slowly pour fourth and final 1 cup milk evenly on top of pudding.

6. Slide onto middle oven shelf and bake uncovered until pudding begins to pull from sides of baking dish and cake tester, inserted midway between center and rim, comes out clean — about 1½ hours.

7. Remove pudding from oven, set on wire baking rack, and cool 20 minutes.

8. To serve, spoon warm pudding onto colorful dessert plates and, if you like, drift each portion with whipped cream or top with a scoop of ice cream.

Woodford Pudding

Makes 6 Servings

There are many versions of this Kentucky classic, which, as John Egerton writes in his deeply engaging book, *Southern Food: At Home, on the Road, in History*, comes from Woodford County where cooks "have been making it for well over a century." He adds that a Woodford Pudding recipe "appeared in *Housekeeping in the Blue Grass* in 1875, and it was probably not the first." The recipe here was inspired by one I enjoyed at Shakertown at Pleasant Hill, a faithfully restored early nineteenth-century Shaker village deep in the Blue Grass. It came to table with a vanilla sauce, but other recipes specify either a butterscotch sauce or a bourbon one. I've settled for a butterscotch sauce spiked with bourbon.

1. Preheat oven to 350°F. Lightly butter 9 x 9 x 2-inch baking pan or spritz with nonstick cooking spray and set aside.

2. Pudding: Whisk first five ingredients (flour through salt) together in large bowl and set aside.

3. Cream butter in large electric mixer bowl at high speed until light and fluffy—about 1 minute. With mixer at low speed, add sugar gradually, then raise speed to high and beat until again light and fluffy—about 1 minute. Beat eggs in one by one, then add jam and beat only enough to combine.

4. With mixer at low speed, add combined dry ingredients alternately with buttermilk, beginning and ending with dry and beating after each addition only enough to combine. Scoop batter into pan, spreading to corners and smoothing top.

5. Slide onto middle oven shelf and bake until pudding begins to pull from sides of pan and cake tester, inserted midway between rim and center of pan, comes out clean—35 to 40 minutes.

6. Sauce: About 10 minutes before pudding is done, prepare Butterscotch Sauce as directed, but at end of Step 1, add the bourbon.

7. Transfer pudding to wire baking rack and cool 30 minutes; at same time, cool sauce as recipe directs.

8. To serve, cut pudding into squares, triangles, or rectangles and top each portion with generous ladling of sauce.

PUDDING:

1¼ cups sifted all-purpose flour

1 teaspoon ground cinnamon

1 teaspoon baking power

¼ teaspoon baking soda

⅛ teaspoon salt

½ cup (1 stick) unsalted butter

½ cup sugar

3 large eggs

½ cup blackberry jam

½ cup buttermilk (not fat-free)

SAUCE:

1 recipe Butterscotch Sauce (page 268)

2 tablespoons fine Kentucky bourbon

Food for the Gods

Makes 12 Servings

Back in the 1950s, the North Carolina State College Woman's Club (comprised mainly of faculty wives) published a collection of favorite recipes. Among them I found this unusual pudding from Mrs. I.O. Schaub, whose husband had been director of the state's Agricultural Extension Service. My mother had asterisked the recipe in her copy of the little spiral-bound cookbook, though I never remember eating it.

Note: To avoid the sticky job of pitting and chopping dates, use the pre-pitted, chopped dates now available at most supermarkets.

Tip: For best results, use a bright, shiny aluminum or stainless-steel baking pan, not a darkly coated one, which may overbrown the pudding. An ovenproof glass baking dish also works well.

1. Preheat oven to 325°F. Butter 13 x 9 x 2-inch baking pan well (see Tip above) or spritz with nonstick cooking spray and set aside.

2. Whisk together cracker crumbs and baking powder in very large bowl. Add nuts and dates and toss well to mix.

3. Separate 4 eggs; set whites aside. Beat sugar, the 4 yolks, and remaining 2 whole eggs in large electric mixer bowl until smooth—about 1 minute. Add to nut and date mixture and fold in.

4. Using clean bowl and beaters, whip egg whites and salt to soft peaks. Fold about 1 cup beaten whites into nut and date mixture, then gently fold in balance until no streaks of white or brown remain. Scoop batter into pan, spreading to corners.

5. Slide onto middle oven shelf and bake until pudding begins to pull from sides of pan and cake tester, inserted midway between rim and middle of pan, comes out clean—about 1 hour.

6. Remove pudding from oven, set on wire baking rack, and cool 20 minutes.

7. To serve, cut pudding into large squares and top each portion with whipped cream. Good, too, with Mock Devonshire Cream (page 273) or Crème Fraîche (page 274). I've even been known to top Food for the Gods with Butterscotch Sauce (page 268) or Nutmeg Sauce (page 283).

¾ cup graham cracker crumbs

2 teaspoons baking powder

4 cups (about 1 pound) walnuts or pecans, moderately coarsely chopped

1 pound dates, pitted and coarsely chopped (see Note above)

6 large eggs

2 cups (1 pound) firmly packed light brown sugar

¼ teaspoon salt

TOPPING:

1 cup heavy cream, whipped to soft peaks

Miscellaneous Puddings

My Mother's Date-Nut Pudding

Makes 6 Servings

Of all the desserts my mother made when I was a little girl, this one was a favorite. So I went straight to her recipe card file and, to my surprise, found half a dozen different date-nut puddings arranged in chronological order; Mother was meticulous about dating recipes and naming sources. The first, recorded in the early '30s and attributed to "Mother A," surely came from my Grandmother Anderson, skilled with needle and thread but never, as far as I knew, with pot and pan. The next, dated a few years later, came from Gertrude Anderson, one of my father's aunts (his father had seven sisters!). It's a simpler recipe and given the small amount of flour listed (a mere ¼ cup) must have been unusually moist and sticky. Next came three with "Mrs. DBA" printed in the upper right-hand corner (that would be my mother-the-improviser), then one from Flossie Miller (a Raleigh friend) and finally, on the eve of World War II, her last improv.

1. Preheat oven to 350°F. Grease 9 x 9 x 2-inch baking pan well or spritz with nonstick cooking spray and set aside. Sift flour, baking powder, and salt onto piece of wax paper and set aside also.

2. Beat butter and sugar until creamy in large electric mixer bowl, first at low speed and then at high—about 3 minutes. Combine milk and egg mixture in large spouted measuring cup.

3. With mixer at low speed, add dry ingredients to creamed mixture alternately with milk mixture, beginning and ending with dry ingredients and beating after each addition only enough to combine—no matter if floury specks show.

4. By hand fold in dates and walnuts. Scoop batter into baking pan, spreading to corners.

5. Slide onto middle oven shelf and bake until pudding begins to pull from sides of pan and cake tester, inserted midway between rim and middle of pan, comes out clean—40 to 45 minutes.

6. Remove pudding from oven, transfer to wire baking rack, and cool 20 minutes.

7. To serve, cut into large squares and drift each portion with whipped cream. Equally good with Mock Devonshire Cream (page 273).

2 cups sifted all-purpose flour

2 teaspoons baking powder

½ teaspoon salt

¼ cup (½ stick) unsalted butter

¾ cup firmly packed light brown sugar

⅔ cup milk

1 large egg beaten with 1½ teaspoons vanilla extract

1 cup coarsely chopped pitted dates

1 cup coarsely chopped walnuts or pecans

TOPPING:

1 cup heavy cream, whipped to soft peaks

Baked Cranberry Pudding with Hot Butter Sauce

Makes 8 Servings

This recipe, like several others in this book, comes from one of my all-time favorite fund-raisers, *The North Carolina State College Woman's Club Cook Book*. It's perfect for Thanksgiving and Christmas, indeed welcome on any wintry day.

1. Preheat oven to 350°F. Lightly butter 9 x 9 x 2-inch baking pan or spritz with nonstick cooking spray and set aside.

2. Pudding: Whisk flour, sugar, baking powder, and salt together in medium mixing bowl and make well in center of dry ingredients.

3. Whisk milk and egg mixture until smooth in small bowl, pour into well in dry ingredients, and stir only enough to combine—no matter if a few floury specks show. Fold in cranberries. Scoop into baking pan, spreading to corners and smoothing top.

4. Slide onto middle oven shelf and bake until pudding begins to pull from sides of pan and feels springy when touched—35 to 40 minutes.

5. Remove pudding from oven, transfer to wire baking rack, and cool 20 to 30 minutes.

6. Hot Butter Sauce: Meanwhile, using whisk or hand electric mixer at moderate speed, combine all ingredients in small heavy nonreactive saucepan. Set over moderately low heat and cook, stirring constantly, just until sauce thickens a bit—about 2 minutes. Do not allow to boil or sauce may curdle.

7. To serve, cut warm pudding into large squares and ladle a little Hot Butter Sauce over each portion. Pass any remaining sauce in a small pitcher.

PUDDING:

2 cups sifted all-purpose flour

1 cup sugar

2½ teaspoons baking powder

¼ teaspoon salt

⅔ cup milk

1 large egg beaten with 3 tablespoons melted unsalted butter

2 cups (8 ounces) fresh or solidly frozen cranberries, washed, stemmed, and sorted

HOT BUTTER SAUCE:

½ cup (1 stick) unsalted butter

1 cup sugar

¾ cup light cream or half-and-half

Miscellaneous Puddings

Ozark Pudding

Makes 6 Servings

Long popular in the Ozark Mountains of Arkansas, this spicy, thick-enough-to-cut pudding strewn with finely chopped apple and nuts is known in and around Charleston, South Carolina, as Huguenot Torte. But the original comes from Arkansas and make no mistake about that.

Note: Nearly all of my recipes call for flour that's sifted before it's measured. This is one of the exceptions. Exceptional, too, that this rich pudding contains no butter or shortening of any type.

1. Preheat oven to 350°F. Butter 8 x 8 x 2-inch baking pan well or spritz with nonstick cooking spray and set aside. Sift first five ingredients (flour through salt) onto piece of wax paper.

2. Using hand electric mixer at moderate speed, beat sugar, egg, and vanilla in medium bowl about 1 minute. Fold in sifted dry ingredients by hand, then chopped apple, then chopped nuts.

3. Spoon batter into pan, spreading to corners and smoothing top.

4. Slide onto middle oven shelf and bake until pudding begins to pull from sides of pan, is springy when touched, and crusty brown on top—about 30 minutes.

5. Remove pudding from oven, transfer to wire baking rack, and cool 30 minutes.

6. To serve, cut into squares and drift each portion with whipped cream. Good, too, with Mock Devonshire Cream (page 273) or Crème Fraîche (page 274).

¾ cup unsifted all-purpose flour

1½ teaspoons baking powder

¾ teaspoon ground cinnamon

¼ teaspoon ground ginger

¼ teaspoon salt

¾ cup firmly packed light brown sugar

1 large egg

1 teaspoon vanilla extract

¾ cup finely chopped peeled and cored apple (about 1 large)

⅔ cup finely chopped black walnuts, walnuts, or pecans

TOPPING:

1 cup heavy cream, softly whipped with 1 tablespoon confectioners' (10X) sugar and ½ teaspoon vanilla extract

Flossie Miller's Glazed Orange Pudding

Makes 8 Servings

Flossie was one of my mother's best friends, a fellow member of the Raleigh Sewing Club, which as far as I could tell, was more about catching up on local news and swapping favorite family recipes (the only sewing I ever saw was sock-darning). Riffling through my mother's card file of recipes, I found several puddings attributed to Flossie Miller, among them this unusual orange pudding.

Note: Choose a fairly tart orange for this recipe to temper the sweetness—a Valencia is a good choice.

1. Preheat oven to 325°F. Grease 9 x 9 x 2-inch baking pan or spritz with non-stick cooking spray and set aside.

2. Sift flour, baking powder, baking soda, and salt onto piece of wax paper and set aside.

3. Cut unpeeled orange into 6 wedges; remove and discard seeds. Cut orange wedges into 1-inch chunks, rind, pulp, and all, and place in food processor fitted with metal chopping blade. Process until creamy and very finely chopped. Add granulated sugar, egg, and butter; process until combined.

4. Add combined dry ingredients to processor mixture alternately with sour milk, beginning and ending with dry and pulsing after each addition only enough to mix. It's OK if a few floury specks show—they prove you haven't overbeaten the batter. Add raisins and pulse once or twice to combine.

5. Scoop batter into pan, spreading to corners and smoothing top.

6. Slide pan onto middle oven shelf and bake until pudding is nicely browned and cake tester, inserted halfway between rim and center, comes out clean—about 45 minutes.

7. As soon as you remove pudding from oven, pour glaze evenly on top. Transfer pan to wire baking rack and cool pudding 15 to 20 minutes.

8. To serve, cut into four large squares, then halve each diagonally so you have eight triangles, and, if you like, top each portion with whipped cream. I find this pudding equally good with Mock Devonshire Cream (page 273).

2 cups sifted all-purpose flour

1 teaspoon baking powder

½ teaspoon baking soda

½ teaspoon salt

1 large whole orange (see Note above)

1 cup granulated sugar

1 large egg

2 tablespoons softened unsalted butter

1 cup sour milk or buttermilk (not fat-free)

1 cup dark seedless raisins or moderately finely chopped pitted dates (this was Mother's idea)

GLAZE:

¾ cup unsifted confectioners' (10X) sugar mixed with ¼ cup fresh orange juice

OPTIONAL TOPPING:

1 cup heavy cream, whipped to soft peaks

Miscellaneous Puddings

Plantation Molasses Pudding

Makes 8 Servings

Among the little spiral-bound fund-raiser cookbooks I treasure most is *From North Carolina Kitchens: Favorite Recipes, Old & New,* published in the early 1950s. It's a collection of family recipes, some of them more than 100 years old, contributed by farm women who belonged to the state's Federation of Home Demonstration Clubs (administered by the Agricultural Extension Service). There are few cake-mix cakes here, few slice-and-bake cookies, few whipped cream substitutes. But there are many recipes for Molasses Pudding (also called Black Pudding, but in truth a moist gingerbread), made with either cane molasses or sorghum molasses. I use unsulfured cane molasses that's neither too thick nor too dark. No blackstrap.

1. Preheat oven to 350°F. Lightly butter 2-quart baking dish or spritz with nonstick cooking spray and set aside.

2. Sift flour, baking powder, soda, ginger, and salt onto piece of wax paper and set aside.

3. Using electric mixer at moderately high speed, cream butter and sugar until light and fluffy—about 2 minutes. Beat in eggs one by one, then with mixer at low speed, add molasses in slow, steady stream.

4. With mixer still at low speed, add sifted dry ingredients alternately with boiling water, beginning and ending with dry ingredients. Do not over-mix. Pour batter into casserole.

5. Slide onto middle oven shelf and bake until cake tester, inserted midway between rim and center of pudding, comes out clean—about 1 hour.

6. Remove from oven, set on wire baking rack, and cool 15 to 20 minutes.

7. To serve, cut into wedges, rectangles, or squares and spoon topping over each portion.

2½ cups sifted all-purpose flour

1½ teaspoons baking powder

½ teaspoon baking soda

1 teaspoon ground ginger

¼ teaspoon salt

½ cup (1 stick) unsalted butter, softened

½ cup granulated sugar

2 large eggs

1 cup unsulfured molasses (not too dark; see headnote)

1 cup boiling water

TOPPING:

1 cup heavy cream, whipped to soft peaks with 2 tablespoons confectioners' (10X) sugar

Sticky Toffee Puddings

Makes 6 Servings

I'd barely e-mailed friends, relatives, and colleagues for favorite family pudding reci-pes when I heard from New York travel writer/editor/publicist Barbara Gillam saying that she had a fabulous recipe for Sticky Toffee Puddings and would mail it to me as soon as she could find it. In fact, she sent three, one of which *People* magazine had published as the Duchess of Cambridge's favorite. There are countless variations of this popular English dessert, as well as many stories as to when and where it origi-nated, though the consensus seems to be that it was created sometime in the 1960s by Francis Coulson, owner of the Lake District's Sharrow Bay Country House. Or was this, as some suggest, simply his riff on a dessert that he'd tasted elsewhere? I turned to two reliable sources — *The Oxford Companion to Food* by Alan Davidson (published in 1999) and my New York friend Jane Garmey's *Great British Cooking: A Well-Kept Secret* (1981). Neither, to my surprise, even mentions Sticky Toffee Puddings. Nor do any of the cookbooks I picked up while traveling about Britain. Online descriptions of this dessert vary significantly, with some sites calling it a steamed pudding. Wrong. It's a moist pudding-like cake that's baked, cut into squares, rectangles, or wedges, then topped with toffee sauce. I've added another variation here — individual puddings in-stead of a single large one. They're more attractive, I think, and definitely cook faster.

1¼ cups sifted all-purpose flour

1¼ teaspoons baking powder

¼ teaspoon baking soda

⅛ teaspoon salt

¾ cup + 2 tablespoons diced pitted dates (about ½ pound)

⅔ cup water

½ cup firmly packed light brown sugar

2½ tablespoons firmly packed dark brown sugar

3 tablespoons unsalted butter, at room temperature

1 large egg

½ teaspoon vanilla extract

TOFFEE SAUCE:

1½ cups heavy cream

¾ cup granulated sugar

¼ cup (½ stick) unsalted butter, cut into pats and softened slightly

¾ teaspoon vanilla extract

⅛ teaspoon salt

OPTIONAL TOPPING:

1 cup heavy cream, whipped to soft peaks, or 1 pint vanilla ice cream

Recipe continues

1. Preheat oven to 350°F. Spritz six 5- or 6-ounce custard cups or ramekins with nonstick cooking spray and set aside.

2. Sift flour, baking powder, soda, and salt onto piece of wax paper and set aside.

3. Boil dates in water in medium-small heavy nonreactive saucepan over moderate heat until soft and only about ¼ cup water remains—about 7 minutes. Purée in food processor or electric blender and set aside.

4. With electric mixer at medium speed, beat light and dark brown sugars with butter in large mixer bowl just long enough to combine, then beat in egg, add vanilla, and continue beating until smooth.

5. Reduce mixer speed to low and add flour mixture alternately with date purée, beginning and ending with dry ingredients and beating only enough to form a stiff batter.

6. Scoop batter into custard cups, dividing amount evenly, then arrange cups—not touching one another—on rimmed baking sheet.

7. Slide onto middle oven shelf and bake uncovered until cake tester, inserted in middle of pudding, comes out clean—35 to 40 minutes.

8. Toffee Sauce: Meanwhile, bring ¾ cup cream, the granulated sugar, and butter to boil over moderate heat in medium-size heavy saucepan. Adjust heat to low so mixture barely bubbles, and cook, stirring occasionally, until mixture thickens slightly and is the color of pale caramel—about 25 minutes. Remove from heat and stir in remaining ¾ cup cream, vanilla, and salt but keep stirring until smooth.

9. Remove puddings from oven, cool 10 minutes in upright custard cups, then loosen around edge with thin-blade spatula and invert on large round platter lightly spritzed with nonstick cooking spray.

10. To serve, transfer warm puddings to warmed dessert plates, smother with Toffee Sauce, dividing amount evenly, and if you'd like a final flourish, drift with whipped cream or add a scoop of ice cream alongside.

Wild Persimmon Pudding

Makes 8 Servings

Wherever wild persimmons grow—an area that covers the South and much of the southerly Midwest—there are old family recipes for wild persimmon pudding, in truth dozens of variations on the theme. This recipe is an amalgamation of several home-spun recipes, downsized (many begin with a gallon of wild persimmon pulp) and also given a few new spins—like substituting raw sugar for half of the granulated and using finely grated fresh ginger in place of ground ginger.

Note: If you're lucky enough to locate wild persimmons, you'll need to purée them (see page xxi). Can large Asian persimmons be substituted for the wild, which are no bigger than Ping-Pong balls? Yes, but don't expect the flavor and texture of this pudding to be just the same. I find Asian persimmons sweeter and firmer fleshed than the wild. Wild persimmon pulp is quite wet and "loose"—sort of like applesauce. It's difficult to find these days although it occasionally shows up at farmers' markets in the fall. Persimmon pulp is also sometimes available online (see Sources, page 291).

1½ cups sifted all-purpose flour

¾ teaspoon baking powder

½ teaspoon baking soda

½ teaspoon ground cinnamon

½ teaspoon freshly grated nutmeg

¼ teaspoon salt

1½ cups unsweetened wild persimmon purée (see Note above)

½ cup granulated sugar

½ cup raw sugar

2 large eggs, well beaten with 1 tablespoon finely

grated fresh ginger and ¾ teaspoon vanilla extract

3 tablespoons unsalted butter, melted

1½ cups milk

TOPPING:

1 cup heavy cream, whipped to soft peaks

1. Preheat oven to 350°F. Lightly butter 9 x 9 x 2-inch baking dish (ovenproof glass or ceramic) or spritz with nonstick cooking spray and set aside.

2. Whisk first six ingredients (flour through salt) together in small bowl and set aside.

Recipe continues

3. Combine persimmon purée, two sugars, egg mixture, and melted butter in large nonreactive bowl, beating until smooth, then add sifted dry ingredients alternately with milk, beginning and ending with dry ingredients (about three additions for dry ingredients and two for milk).

4. Pour batter into baking dish, spread to corners, and set dish in middle of large roasting pan. Pull middle oven shelf out, center roasting pan on shelf, then add enough boiling water to pan to come about halfway up sides of baking dish.

5. Gently slide shelf back into oven and bake until pudding begins to brown around edges, pull from sides of baking dish, and cake tester, inserted midway between edge and center, comes out clean—45 to 50 minutes.

6. Remove pudding from oven and from water bath. Set on wire baking rack and cool to allow pudding to firm up a bit—about 30 minutes.

7. To serve, cut into large rectangles and top each portion with whipped cream. Good, too, with Mock Devonshire Cream (page 273) or Crème Fraîche (page 274).

Spicy Buttermilk-Glazed Prune Pudding

Makes 12 Servings

Back in the '70s when I criss-crossed the country interviewing good home cooks to feature in my *Grass Roots Cookbook,* this recipe kept turning up among cherished family favorites—or one of the many versions. It's actually a moist date-nut pudding that's baked, cut into squares, then topped with whipped cream or ice cream. The recipe below is an amalgam of several different prune pudding recipes with a few time-saving spins of my own.

Note: Instead of cooking, pitting, and chopping or puréeing the prunes, I use one of the organic prune baby foods now available (an unsweetened one). They come in 2.5-ounce jars; four of them will give you a little more than the 1 cup you need. Treat yourself to the extra ¼ cup—it's good spooned over yogurt.

2 cups sifted all-purpose flour

2 cups sugar, or 1 cup each granulated sugar and raw sugar

1 teaspoon baking powder

1 teaspoon baking soda

1 teaspoon ground cinnamon

½ teaspoon ground allspice

½ teaspoon freshly grated nutmeg

½ teaspoon salt

¼ teaspoon ground cloves

3 large eggs

1 cup puréed or finely chopped cooked pitted prunes (or see Note above)

1 cup vegetable oil

1 cup buttermilk (not fat-free)

¼ cup prune juice

1 teaspoon vanilla extract

½ cup moderately finely chopped black walnuts, walnuts, or pecans

BUTTERMILK GLAZE:

½ cup buttermilk (not fat-free)

½ cup granulated sugar

1½ tablespoons light corn syrup

½ teaspoon vanilla extract

½ teaspoon lemon extract

¼ teaspoon baking soda

TOPPING:

1 cup heavy cream, whipped to soft peaks with 2 tablespoons confectioners' (10X) sugar and 1 teaspoon vanilla extract, or 1 pint vanilla ice cream

1. Preheat oven to 350°F. Spritz 13 x 9 x 2-inch baking pan with nonstick cooking spray and set aside.

Recipe continues

2. Combine first nine ingredients (flour through cloves) in medium mixing bowl; make well in the center. Whisk eggs, prune purée, oil, buttermilk, prune juice, and vanilla extract in second medium bowl until smooth. Pour into well in dry ingredients and stir only enough to combine—floury specks should be visible in batter. Fold in nuts, then scoop batter into pan, spreading to corners.

3. Slide pan onto middle oven shelf and bake until pudding begins to pull from sides of pan and cake tester, inserted in middle of pudding, comes out clean—35 to 40 minutes.

4. Buttermilk Glaze: About 10 minutes before pudding is done, place all ingredients except baking soda in medium-size heavy nonreactive saucepan and bring to a simmer over moderate heat. Adjust heat so mixture barely bubbles and cook 3 minutes, stirring constantly. Remove from heat, add baking soda, and stir until foaming subsides slightly—about 30 seconds.

5. As soon as pudding comes from oven, pour glaze evenly on top, spreading to corners—pudding will sink a bit but this is as it should be. Cool pudding on wire baking rack until glaze sets—about 30 minutes.

6. To serve, cut pudding into large squares and top each portion with whipped cream or ice cream. Good, too, with Mock Devonshire Cream (page 273) or Crème Fraîche (page 274).

Grated Sweet Potato Pudding

Makes 6 to 8 Servings

My home state of North Carolina grows more sweet potatoes than any other, which may explain why sweet potato puddings are so popular here. And why there are so many different versions. This one is a particular favorite. If you've a food processor to grate the sweet potatoes and crumb the bread, you'll find that this recipe goes together zip-quick. And, oh, the aromas wafting through the house as it bakes.

Note: The sweet potatoes I like best are the intensely orange, richly flavored Beauregards or Jewels. Both are widely available.

1. Preheat oven to 350°F. Lightly butter shallow 2-quart baking dish or spritz with nonstick cooking spray and set aside.

2. Place first six ingredients (grated sweet potatoes through salt) in large mixing bowl, toss well, and make well in center.

3. Whisk milk with melted butter and eggs in small bowl until frothy, pour into well in sweet potato mixture, and mix well. Pour into baking dish, spreading to edge.

4. Slide onto middle oven shelf and bake until tipped with brown and cake tester, inserted in pudding midway between center and rims, comes out clean—about 1 hour.

5. Serve hot—as is—or, if you prefer, with drifts of whipped cream. Good, too, with Mock Devonshire Cream (page 273) or Crème Fraîche (page 274).

1 quart (4 cups) moderately coarsely grated peeled raw sweet potatoes (see Note above), about 2 large or 1 to 1¼ pounds

¼ cup raw sugar mixed with 2 tablespoons all-purpose flour

1 cup moderately coarse soft bread crumbs (about 2 slices firm-textured white bread, crusts on)

1½ tablespoons finely grated fresh ginger

½ teaspoon ground cinnamon

¼ teaspoon salt

2 cups milk

2 tablespoons unsalted butter, melted

3 large eggs, well beaten

OPTIONAL TOPPING:

1 cup heavy cream, whipped to soft peaks

Iron Skillet Sweet Potato Pudding

Makes 6 Servings

This is one of the more unusual raw grated potato puddings because it's baked in an iron skillet and is stirred as it bakes. It comes from my long-time friend Kathy McDonald Snead, with whom I worked in *The Ladies' Home Journal* test kitchens in New York. Like me, Kathy was born and brought up in North Carolina. She married Tom Snead soon after leaving the *Journal* and says that this recipe, a particular favorite in her family, came from Tom's mother Mary King Snead. "She was born in Rockingham County (just north of Greensboro) and lived there all her life," Kathy told me. "Mary was an excellent cook—just didn't write things down. So this recipe evolved from my memories of eating grated sweet potato pudding at her house, from various newspaper clippings found in her kitchen, and some notes she'd written on them. I have fiddled and tried to duplicate her pudding for years. Her version was very simple with only a touch of spices and a glazed golden top."

Note: To keep the sweet potatoes from discoloring, Kathy grates them after all the other ingredients have been mixed, measuring them by the cup and mixing in as she grates.

Tip: The iron skillet you use for this recipe should be well seasoned, if not, the pudding may taste slightly of rust.

½ cup sugar

½ teaspoon ground cinnamon

¼ teaspoon ground cloves

¼ teaspoon ground allspice

¼ teaspoon ground nutmeg

¼ teaspoon salt

1 cup milk

3 large eggs, well beaten

½ cup light corn syrup

4 to 5 cups grated peeled raw sweet potatoes (see Note above), about 3 large or 1½ pounds

¼ cup (½ stick) unsalted butter, cut into pats

1. Preheat oven to 350°F.

2. Whisk first six ingredients (sugar through salt) together in large bowl. Gradually whisk in milk, then eggs, then corn syrup and continue whisking until smooth. Fold in grated sweet potatoes.

3. Melt butter in well-seasoned 10-inch cast-iron skillet (see Tip above) or in other heavy ovenproof skillet over moderate heat. Stir in sweet potato mixture, and cook and stir just until hot—about 5 minutes.

4. Slide pudding onto middle oven shelf and bake uncovered, stirring every 15 minutes for first 60 minutes. Bake 15 minutes longer without stirring, allowing pudding to crust over as it thickens and becomes glossy on top.

5. Remove skillet from oven and let pudding stand 15 to 20 minutes.

6. To serve to family, carry skillet to table and dish up pudding. For company, scoop pudding onto bright dessert plates in kitchen.

Mashed Sweet Potato Pudding

Makes 8 Servings

Thumb through any Southern cookbook and you'll see sweet potato puddings galore. Some recipes call for raw grated sweet potatoes (see two preceding recipes) and others for mashed cooked sweet potatoes.

Note: Some cooks peel, chunk, and boil the sweet potatoes, but I prefer to bake them because they're more flavorful and less watery. One hour at 400°F is about right — just be sure that you prick each potato with a kitchen fork before baking so it doesn't explode and leave your oven one unholy mess. I also bake the potatoes on a rimmed baking sheet because they sometimes ooze a bit of liquid. Once the potatoes are tender, cool until easy to handle, then cut an X in the top of each and push the flesh into a large mixing bowl. Then, using a potato masher, mash until silky. Even easier, push the potato flesh into a food processor work bowl, then alternately pulse and churn until smooth. A few seconds is all it takes.

Tip: Grate the ginger on a fine-toothed Microplane, letting the shreds fall onto a piece of wax paper. Because fresh ginger is so widely available these days, I substitute freshly grated ginger for ground because it packs more flavor and less heat.

4 cups mashed baked sweet potatoes (see Note above), about 5 large or 2½ to 3 pounds

½ cup raw sugar

1 (5-ounce) can low-fat or fat-free evaporated milk

¼ cup fresh orange juice

3 large eggs

1 tablespoon finely grated fresh ginger (see Tip above), or ½ teaspoon ground ginger

1 teaspoon finely grated orange zest

1 teaspoon ground cinnamon

¼ teaspoon ground cloves

½ cup coarsely chopped pecans (optional)

OPTIONAL TOPPING:

1 cup heavy cream, whipped to soft peaks with 2 tablespoons confectioners' (10X) sugar and ½ teaspoon vanilla extract

1. Preheat oven to 350°F. Butter 2-quart casserole or spritz with nonstick cooking spray and set aside.

2. Beat all but last ingredient (pecans) in large electric mixer bowl at low speed just long enough to combine, then raise mixer speed to high and beat until absolutely smooth — about 1 minute.

Recipe continues

3. Scoop into casserole, spreading to edge, then if you like, scatter pecans evenly on top.

4. Slide casserole onto middle oven shelf and bake pudding uncovered until cake tester, inserted midway between rim and center, comes out clean—about 50 minutes.

5. To serve, spoon pudding onto dessert plates and, if you like, top each portion with generous helping of whipped cream. Good, too, with Mock Devonshire Cream (page 273) or Crème Fraîche (page 274).

Note: I like this pudding warm as well as hot, and even enjoy it refrigerator-cold (leftovers should be refrigerated).

Surprise Pudding with Orange Sauce

Makes 6 Servings

I'm not sure what the surprise is, but I'm guessing it's the grated carrots stirred into this baked pudding. This recipe, like a few others in this cookbook, comes from a fundraiser published more than fifty years ago by the North Carolina State College Woman's Club. I know the recipes are first-rate because my mother was deeply involved in the writing of the book. I also know that Mrs. W.E. Colwell, whence the recipe comes, was a crackerjack cook.

Note: The Orange Sauce, in truth an orange-flavored butterscotch sauce, is equally delicious ladled over Orange-Walnut Pudding (page 239); the recipe makes 1⅔ cups sauce.

PUDDING:

1¼ cups sifted all-purpose flour

1 teaspoon baking powder

1 teaspoon ground cinnamon

½ teaspoon ground ginger

½ teaspoon baking soda

¼ teaspoon salt

½ cup (1 stick) unsalted butter

½ cup firmly packed light brown sugar

1 teaspoon finely grated lemon zest

1 large egg

1 cup moderately coarsely grated young and tender carrots (about 2 small or 4 ounces)

ORANGE SAUCE (SEE NOTE ABOVE):

1 cup firmly packed light brown sugar

½ cup (1 stick) unsalted butter, softened

½ cup fresh orange juice

1 large egg, well beaten

1. Preheat oven to 350°F. Lightly butter 8 x 8 x 2-inch baking pan or spritz with nonstick cooking spray and set aside.

2. Pudding: Whisk first six ingredients (flour through salt) together in medium mixing bowl.

3. Cream butter, sugar, and lemon zest at high speed in large electric mixer bowl until light—about 2 minutes. Beat in egg, then by hand, fold in combined dry ingredients, then grated carrots. Scoop into baking pan, spreading to corners and smoothing top.

Recipe continues

Miscellaneous Puddings

4. Slide onto middle oven shelf and bake until pudding begins to pull from sides of pan, brown lightly, and feels springy when touched—about 25 minutes.

5. Remove pudding from oven, set on wire baking rack, and cool 20 to 30 minutes.

6. Orange Sauce: Meanwhile, using whisk or hand electric mixer at moderate speed, combine all ingredients in small heavy nonreactive saucepan. Set over moderately low heat and cook, stirring constantly, just until sauce thickens—about 3 minutes.

7. To serve, cut warm pudding into large squares and ladle a little hot Orange Sauce over each portion. Pass any remaining sauce in a small pitcher.

Grandmother Anderson's Streusel Pudding

Makes 6 to 8 Generous Servings

When I sent relatives an SOS for favorite family pudding recipes, this one came from my Wisconsin cousin Dotty Tookey along with this note: "I'm not very talented in the kitchen but do have this recipe from our Grandmother Anderson. It was given to her by the woman in whose home she and Grandfather were boarding while in Germany. It's not fancy but it's a family favorite."

To be honest, I never heard of this recipe, in fact never knew that my grandparents had ever lived in Germany or if so, when this might have been—late nineteenth century I'm guessing. In fact, I don't remember eating anything my Grandmother Anderson cooked. She lived in a big Charles Addams-y Victorian house in Columbus, Ohio's Upper Arlington neighborhood not so far from Ohio State University where Grandfather had been Dean of the School of Education. My family lived in Raleigh, NC—a "fer piece" from Columbus, as Southerners like to say. I wondered if Cousin Dotty might have confused our grandparents with my own mother and father who lived in Vienna early in their married life while Daddy was teaching botany at the university there. My mother was an excellent cook and did bring home several recipes that her Viennese landlady had given to her, but this streusel pudding wasn't among them. I've searched Mother's two recipe files—twice—and no streusel pudding. The mystery deepens but one day Dotty and I will solve it. This pudding, like so many our mothers made, is cake-like, cut into portions, and topped with plenty of whipped cream or ice cream. My own favorite is My Mother's Date-Nut Pudding (page 214).

Note: Use a shiny silver aluminum or stainless-steel baking pan for this recipe. Darkly coated pans tend to overbrown, or even burn, puddings as rich as this one.

1½ cups sifted all-purpose flour

¾ cup granulated sugar

1 teaspoon baking powder

¾ teaspoon salt

¼ cup (½ stick) refrigerator-cold unsalted butter, cut into pats

½ cup milk

1 large egg, well beaten with 1 teaspoon vanilla extract

MIDDLE LAYER:

½ cup firmly packed light brown sugar

2½ tablespoons unsifted all-purpose flour

2 tablespoons unsalted butter, melted

¾ cup moderately coarsely chopped pecans or walnuts

TOPPING:

1 cup heavy cream, whipped to soft peaks, or 1 pint vanilla ice cream (or my new favorite, dulce de leche ice cream)

Recipe continues

1. Preheat oven to 375°F. Generously butter stainless-steel or other bright metal 8 x 8 x 2-inch baking pan or spritz with nonstick cooking spray and set pan aside.

2. Sift flour, granulated sugar, baking powder, and salt into large mixing bowl and scatter butter on top. Using pastry blender, cut butter into dry ingredients until size of lentils.

3. Combine milk and egg mixture in large measuring cup, then forking dry ingredients briskly, add combined liquids slowly and continue forking just till everything holds together and forms a batter. Spread half of this mixture over bottom of baking pan and set aside.

4. For Middle Layer: Using fork, combine brown sugar and flour in small bowl, add butter, and stir just until butter melds with brown sugar and flour—about 1 minute.

5. Crumble evenly over batter in pan, then scatter ½ cup pecans on top. Finally, cover all with remaining batter, spreading to corners, and sprinkle with remaining ¼ cup pecans.

6. Slide onto middle oven shelf and bake until dappled with brown and pudding begins to pull from sides of pan—about 25 minutes.

7. Remove pan from oven, transfer to wire baking rack, and cool pudding 20 to 30 minutes.

8. To serve, cut into rectangles and top each portion with whipped cream or ice cream.

Orange-Walnut Pudding

Makes 6 Servings

My mother had many European friends who'd fled Hitler's regime and landed in Raleigh because of the big state university there. Their husbands, many of them scientists like my father, joined the faculty and became distinguished professors. Having lived in Austria as a bride, my mother knew the loneliness of being a stranger in a foreign land. So she did what she could to welcome these refugees and make them feel at home. Many became lifelong friends. This unusual pudding made with candied orange rind came from one of them, a German, and I'm ashamed to say I don't remember her name—Frau von-something-or-other.

Note: I like to ladle a little orange sauce over this pudding; the one accompanying Surprise Pudding (page 235) is particularly good and makes as much as you'll need (1⅔ cups). I offer it as an option to the more routine whipped cream topping below.

2 cups sifted all-purpose flour

½ cup sugar

1 tablespoon baking powder

¼ teaspoon salt

½ cup coarsely chopped walnuts

1 cup milk

1 large egg, beaten

3 tablespoons moderately finely chopped candied orange rind

2 tablespoons unsalted butter, melted

TOPPING:

1 cup heavy cream, whipped to soft peaks with 2 tablespoons confectioners' (10X) sugar and 1 teaspoon vanilla extract, or 1 recipe Orange Sauce (see page 235)

1. Preheat oven to 350°F. Lightly butter 9 x 9 x 2-inch baking pan or spritz with nonstick cooking spray and set aside.

2. Whisk flour, sugar, baking powder, and salt together in medium mixing bowl. Add walnuts, toss to mix, then make well in center of dry ingredients.

3. Whisk milk and egg until smooth in small bowl, then mix in candied orange rind and melted butter. Pour into well in dry ingredients and stir only enough to combine—no matter if bits of flour show. Scoop batter into baking pan, spreading to corners and smoothing top.

Recipe continues

Miscellaneous Puddings

4. Slide pan onto middle oven shelf and bake until pudding begins to brown, pull from sides of pan, and feels springy when touched—20 to 25 minutes.

5. Remove pudding from oven, set pan on wire baking rack, and cool pudding 10 minutes.

6. To serve, cut warm pudding into large squares and drift each portion with whipped cream topping—be generous. Or skip the whipped cream and top instead with hot Orange Sauce.

Layered Gratin of Buttered Crumbs, Peaches, and Quark

Makes 6 Servings

Quark? It's a tart, creamy unripened cheese so popular in Germany it's not only stirred into main dishes, sides, salads, and desserts but also eaten right out of the container just as we do yogurt. Increasingly available here, quark can be found in upscale or specialty groceries; and, to my surprise, it turned up recently in the wellness department of my Walmart.

Note: If quark is unavailable, you have three options: Substitute fine-curd ricotta (a little less tart), order quark online (see Sources, page 291), or make your own (see page xxx).

Tip: For a richer gratin, substitute challah or brioche crumbs for the soft white bread crumbs.

PEACHES:

1½ pounds (about 4 large) firm-ripe peaches, peeled, pitted, and thinly sliced

¼ cup Grand Marnier or other orange liqueur

1½ tablespoons fresh lemon juice

CRUMBS:

¼ cup (½ stick) unsalted butter, cut into pats

3 cups moderately coarse soft bread crumbs (see Tip above), about 6 slices firm-textured white bread, crusts on

2 tablespoons granulated sugar

2 tablespoons raw sugar

¼ teaspoon freshly grated nutmeg

QUARK FILLING:

1½ cups firmly packed quark or fine-curd ricotta (not low-fat or fat-free), see Note above

⅓ cup granulated sugar combined with 2 tablespoons cornstarch

2 large eggs

1 large egg yolk

1 teaspoon finely grated lemon zest

½ teaspoon finely grated orange zest

1. Preheat oven to 400°F. Generously butter 2-quart nonreactive gratin pan or shallow casserole no more than 1¾ inches deep and set aside.

2. Peaches: Place all ingredients in large nonreactive bowl, toss well, and set aside while you proceed with recipe.

3. Crumbs: Melt butter in heavy 12-inch skillet over moderate heat, add crumbs and both sugars, and cook, tossing mixture constantly, until golden brown—2 to 3 minutes. Remove from heat, add nutmeg, toss well, and reserve.

4. Quark Filling: Place all ingredients in medium bowl and using hand electric mixer, beat at moderate speed until smooth and creamy—about 1 minute.

5. Drain peaches well, reserving liquid. Pat crumb mixture over bottom of gratin pan and drizzle evenly with reserved peach liquid. Spread quark filling over crumbs, then arrange peaches on top in decorative rows, overlapping slices as needed.

6. Slide onto middle oven shelf and bake uncovered just until quark mixture is softly set—35 to 40 minutes.

7. Transfer gratin to wire baking rack and cool 15 to 20 minutes.

8. To serve, dish up at table. Some people like to top this gratin with vanilla ice cream but I don't find this necessary.

Ricotta Pudding with Dark Sweet Red Cherries

Makes 6 Servings

I've always preferred ricotta to cottage cheese because of its finer texture and mellower flavor and for those reasons have been substituting it for cottage cheese in this and other recipes. This particular recipe is equally delicious made with quark (see page xxx), though this tart and creamy fresh cheese is less available than ricotta. Every supermarket I know carries several brands of ricotta, including full-fat, low-fat, and no-fat versions of each.

Note: This recipe also calls for semolina (hard wheat) — the grain, not the flour. Specialty food stores usually sell semolina, but if you can't find it, simply substitute couscous (it's 100 percent semolina). Even quick-cooking Cream of Wheat works well here — it contains semolina.

Tip: If fresh cherries are out of season, no problem. Substitute frozen pitted, unsweetened dark sweet cherries. Sold in 12-ounce packages, they're carried by nearly every supermarket. For this recipe, you'll need one-and-a-half 12-ounce packages. Thaw cherries before using, then drain as dry as possible (add the cherry juice to your morning OJ).

1 pound firm-ripe dark sweet red cherries, stemmed and pitted (or see Tip above)

¾ cup sugar

3 tablespoons fresh lemon juice

1 (15-ounce) container ricotta (not low-fat or fat-free) blended with 2

tablespoons sour cream or 1⅞ cups firmly packed quark (see headnote)

¼ cup quick-cooking semolina (see Note above) or couscous (not a mix) or Cream of Wheat

2 teaspoons finely grated lemon zest

3 large eggs, separated

1 large egg yolk

1½ teaspoons baking powder

¼ teaspoon salt

1 tablespoon refrigerator-cold unsalted butter, diced

1. Preheat oven to 375°F. Lightly butter 2½-quart soufflé dish or spritz with non-stick cooking spray and set aside.

2. Place cherries, 2 tablespoons sugar, and lemon juice in large nonreactive bowl, toss well, and set aside.

3. Place ricotta, ½ cup of remaining sugar, semolina, and lemon zest in food processor and alternately churn and pulse until absolutely smooth—about 1 minute but pause to scrape work bowl at half time. Pulse in egg yolks one by one, then add baking powder and pulse quickly to incorporate. Scoop all into large mixing bowl.

4. Using hand electric mixer at moderate speed, beat egg whites with salt in medium bowl until frothy. Raise mixer speed to high and beat egg whites to stiff peaks, adding remaining 2 tablespoons sugar gradually.

5. Fold about one-fourth beaten whites into ricotta mixture to lighten it, then fold in remaining whites until no streaks of white or yellow remain. Easy does it. Fold in cherries and all accumulated cherry juice.

6. Pour into soufflé dish and dot with bits of butter.

7. Slide onto middle oven shelf and bake until pudding is richly browned and set like custard—50 to 60 minutes.

8. Transfer pudding to wire baking rack and cool 25 minutes—pudding will fall somewhat as it cools but this is as it should be.

9. To serve, dish ricotta pudding up at table using your most colorful dessert plates. Nothing more needed.

Rote Grütze (Red Berry Pudding)

Makes 6 to 8 Servings

Shortly after my *Food of Portugal* was published in the late '80s, Hedy Würz, a German friend then working at the New York City branch of The German National Tourist Office, said, "We must do a German cookbook." I thought a minute, then said, "Why not?" I had visited Germany countless times, written about it for *Bon Appétit, Food & Wine,* and *Travel & Leisure,* and had even produced a portfolio of German food, fashion, and handicrafts for *Family Circle* magazine. Before long, Hedy and I were deep into *The New German Cookbook,* which HarperCollins published in 1993 (it's still in print). My job was to organize the book and test and write the recipes. Hedy's was to find all the recipes we'd considered essential and translate them into English. She'd arrive at my apartment with a sheath of papers written not only in German but often in flowery German script. I marveled at Hedy's language facility. With me at my computer taking dictation, she sat nearby translating recipes into English. She never hesitated or stumbled as she read, even when it came to obtuse culinary terms. Of the several hundred recipes that I tested for the book, this one remains a party favorite. I shared the Rote Grütze recipe tests with friends in my Gramercy Park co-op and in no time got notes begging for the "red glop" recipe. An accommodating make-ahead, Rote Grütze continues to wow dinner guests, especially when layered into tall goblets with Mock Devonshire Cream. For an even showier dessert that will serve ten, I layer the "red glop" with Swedish Cream (page 141).

Tip: Use berries frozen in light syrup. As for the wine, any good red table wine will do—Cabernet Sauvignon, Valpolicella, even a smooth Chianti, Spanish Rioja, or Portuguese Dão or Douro.

2 (10-ounce) packages frozen raspberries (see Tip above), thawed, drained, and juice reserved

1 (16-ounce) package frozen strawberries, thawed and puréed with their juice

1 (16-ounce) can pitted dark sweet cherries with their liquid

1 quart (4 cups) sweetened cranberry juice (about)

¾ cup granulated sugar

1 tablespoon finely grated lemon zest

¼ cup fresh lemon juice

1 cup dry red table wine (see Tip above) blended into smooth paste with ⅔ cup unsifted cornstarch

TOPPING:

1 recipe Mock Devonshire Cream (page 273), or 1 cup heavy cream, whipped to soft peaks with 2 tablespoons confectioners' (10X) sugar and ½ teaspoon vanilla extract

Recipe continues

1. Combine juice from raspberries, strawberry purée, and cherries and their liquid in 1-quart glass measuring cup, then add enough cranberry juice to total 1 quart.

2. Transfer all to large heavy nonreactive saucepan and add 2 more cups cranberry juice, the sugar, and lemon zest and juice. Bring to boiling over moderate heat, stirring often.

3. As soon as mixture boils, add wine-cornstarch paste, stirring vigorously. Cook and stir until mixture thickens and clears—about 3 minutes. Stir in reserved raspberries and cook and stir 1 minute—no longer or mixture will begin to thin.

4. Pour all into large nonreactive bowl and cool to room temperature, stirring often. Cover and chill 24 hours. Use this time to prepare Mock Devonshire Cream; it, too, must be well chilled before it's served.

5. To serve, spoon Rote Grütze into dessert dishes and drift with Mock Devonshire Cream or whipped cream. Or for a showier presentation, layer into tall glass goblets with the topping of your choice, beginning with berry pudding and ending with topping.

Heavenly Hash

Makes 6 Servings

I debated long and hard about including this recipe in this book, even queried colleagues for their opinions. I've always preferred from-scratch, fresh-ingredient recipes to big food-company ones that were created to push products I don't like — in this case faux whipped cream and sometimes maraschino cherries. I'm not sure when this recipe surfaced, but I suspect that it might have been during World War II when sugar was severely rationed but super-sweet marshmallows were not. Heavenly Hash (also called Lush Mush) was an instant hit. Like it or not, it's a part of American culinary history and its popularity has never waned in deepest America. The version here is not the original, but my more healthful spin on it. I've omitted the maraschino cherries and substituted fresh berries or peaches. Though the marshmallows and canned crushed pineapple remain, the cream I use is strictly fresh.

Note: To keep the fresh fruit from watering down the pudding, use only firm-ripe berries or peaches and drain them well.

1 (8-ounce) can crushed pineapple packed in pineapple juice (not syrup), well drained and juice reserved

1 cup mini marshmallows

1 cup diced hulled firm-ripe strawberries (about 5 large berries) or 1 cup diced pitted peeled peaches (about 2 medium), see Note above

½ cup lightly toasted coarsely chopped pecans (6 to 8 minutes in a 350°F oven)

1 cup refrigerator-cold heavy cream, stiffly whipped with 1 tablespoon confectioners' (10X) sugar and ½ teaspoon vanilla extract

OPTIONAL GARNISH:

6 small sprigs fresh mint, lemon verbena, or lemon geranium

1. Place pineapple, marshmallows, and ¼ cup reserved pineapple juice in large nonreactive bowl and toss well to mix. Cover and refrigerate about 1 hour.

2. Remove marshmallow mixture from refrigerator and fold in strawberries, pecans, and stiffly whipped cream — easy does it.

3. To serve, spoon into stemmed goblets and, if you like, sprig each portion with fresh mint, lemon verbena, or lemon geranium.

Miscellaneous Puddings

Eton Mess

Makes 8 Servings

To be honest, I'd forgotten all about this pudding until my New York friend Barbara Gillam e-mailed, "Don't forget Eton Mess." It's a traditional English dessert that deserves to be remembered.

Why Eton? It's believed to have been created at Eton back in the 1930s. Why Mess? Because it's a hodge-podge of broken meringues, whipped cream, and strawberries.

Note: The meringues to use for this pudding are crisp meringue cookies — not macaroons sometimes confused with meringues, and heaven forbid, not any containing coconut. I have used the Italian amaretti in Eton Mess with good results. Still, plain old-fashioned meringue cookies — the super-crisp ones that many supermarkets sell — work best. You can also use commercially baked meringue nests, which can be ordered online as can meringue cookies and amaretti (see Sources, page 291).

Tip: If the meringues are to be crisp, you must serve Eton Mess straight away. After an hour, most of the meringues will have softened, leaving only a few crunchy bits in the cream. Leftovers the next day were delicious but different — the meringues had completely "melted" into the cream — now pinkish thanks to the strawberries.

1. Place strawberries, granulated sugar, and lemon juice in large nonreactive bowl and macerate 10 minutes.

2. Meanwhile, using hand electric mixer, whip cream, confectioners' sugar, and vanilla to soft peaks in nonreactive bowl. Fold in crumbled meringues. Scoop out ½ cup berries and reserve to ladle over each portion of pudding. Fold remaining strawberries into whipped cream mixture.

3. To serve, mound whipped cream mixture in stemmed goblets and spoon reserved strawberries on top, dividing amount evenly.

1 pound (about 3 cups) red-ripe strawberries, hulled and coarsely diced

1 tablespoon granulated sugar

1 tablespoon fresh lemon juice

2 cups refrigerator-cold heavy cream

2 tablespoons confectioners' (10X) sugar

1 teaspoon vanilla extract

2 cups very coarsely crumbled crisp meringue cookies (about 8 cookies or 4 meringue nests; see Note above).

Pudim Molotov

Makes 8 Servings

The majority of Portugal's beloved egg sweets are yolks only, but this one's a dramatic departure — whites whipped into an airy meringue that's baked in an angel food cake or tube pan. Why Molotov? None of the chefs I've interviewed over the years could explain why a Portuguese classic carries a Russian name.

Note: Making burnt sugar syrup is a bit tricky so watch the pot carefully; note, too, that the syrup will continue to darken after the pot's taken off the heat.

Tip: You must use a one-piece tube pan for this recipe because pans with removable bottoms may not seal tightly enough to keep the batter from leaking out as the pudding bakes.

1. To prepare pan: Butter bottom, sides, and central tube of 10-inch angel food cake pan (see Tip above). Add sugar, tilt pan from side to side till bottom, sides, and central tube are lightly coated, then tap out excess sugar and set pan aside.

2. Burnt Sugar Syrup: Place sugar in medium-size heavy saucepan, set over moderate heat, and cook, swirling pan or stirring often, until sugar melts and turns color of caramel — about 3 minutes. Remove from heat, add boiling water — it will sputter wildly — and when sputtering stops, mix in lemon juice. Return to moderate heat and cook, stirring often, until syrupy and color of dark caramel — about 10 minutes (see Note above). Remove from heat.

3. Pudding: Preheat oven to 350°F. Place egg whites and salt in large electric mixer bowl and beat at moderate speed until foamy — 10 to 15 seconds. Reduce mixer speed to low, add sugar gradually, then drizzle in ½ cup of burnt sugar syrup. Raise mixer speed to high and beat until egg whites peak softly — about 2 minutes.

4. Carefully transfer meringue to prepared tube pan, rap once or twice on counter to expel large air bubbles, then set pan in middle of roasting pan that's about 2 inches larger all around than tube pan.

5. Pull lower oven shelf out, center roasting pan on shelf, then add boiling water to pan to depth of 1 inch. Tube pan should not float, but if it does, just let it float — the pudding will be insulated from direct contact with the oven shelf and that's key.

TO PREPARE PAN:

1 teaspoon unsalted butter, at room temperature

2 tablespoons sugar

BURNT SUGAR SYRUP:

½ cup sugar

⅔ cup boiling water

1 tablespoon fresh lemon juice

PUDDING:

10 large egg whites

⅛ teaspoon salt

½ cup sugar

6. Gently slide shelf back into oven and bake pudding uncovered until cake tester, inserted midway between rim and central tube, comes out clean—35 to 40 minutes.

7. Remove pudding from oven and from water bath. Carefully loosen around edge and central tube with small thin-blade spatula dipped in hot water. Invert pudding onto colorful large round rimmed platter.

8. To serve, drizzle remaining hot burnt sugar syrup (about 1 tablespoon) over pudding, carry to table, then cut into large wedges—this pudding is mostly air. Does Pudim Molotov need a sauce? Not really, though I do sometimes pass a pitcher of Quick Cardinal Sauce (page 284) or Butterscotch Sauce (page 268).

Miscellaneous Puddings

Finnish Cranberry Pudding

Makes 6 Servings

I've eaten this pudding in Helsinki where it's made with lingonberries, a rarity here so I've substituted cranberries — equally red, equally tart. With six ingredients only, this pudding couldn't be easier to make.

Note: A few supermarkets still sell the old-fashioned Cream of Wheat that takes 10 minutes to cook, but nearly all of them sell three quicker versions: Original — Instant, Original — 1-Minute cook time, and Original — 2½-Minute cook time, the one I used here.

Tip: When puréeing the berries, use a large sieve that's neither too coarse nor too fine — "medium" is just right.

1. Place cranberries and water in large nonreactive saucepan, set over moderately high heat, and boil uncovered until cranberries burst — about 10 minutes.

2. Empty cranberries and cooking water into large sieve (see Tip above), set over large nonreactive saucepan, and let juices drip through, pressing cranberries gently to extract as much juice and pulp as possible.

3. Add sugar and salt to cranberry juice and pulp in pan and bring to boil over moderate heat. Whisking briskly, add Cream of Wheat in slow, steady stream to prevent lumping. Reduce heat to moderately low and cook, whisking often, until mixture thickens and no starchy taste lingers — 3 to 5 minutes.

4. Pour mixture into large heatproof nonreactive bowl (preferably large electric mixer bowl) and beat at high speed until pale pink, light, and fluffy — 15 to 20 minutes.

Note: You could serve this pudding straight away, but I prefer to cover it and refrigerate 2 hours.

5. To serve, scoop pudding into dessert dishes or stemmed goblets, and trickle a little heavy cream over each portion.

1 pound (about 1 quart or 4 cups) fresh or solidly frozen cranberries

1½ cups water

¾ cup sugar

¼ teaspoon salt

½ cup uncooked 2½-minute Cream of Wheat (see Note above)

¾ cup heavy cream

Zuppa Inglese

Makes 8 to 10 Servings

Translated literally, *zuppa Inglese* means "English soup." But it is nothing of the kind. It's a showy, party-perfect Italian version of an English trifle, in this case a melange of custard (half vanilla, half chocolate) and leftover cake spiked with wine (usually a sweet Italian Marsala) or, on occasion, dark rum. I prefer Marsala.

Tip: The fancy, expensive imported chocolates are too thin to shave neatly into curls, so I use the domestic chocolate my supermarket sells. To make chocolate curls, simply run a swivel-bladed vegetable peeler across a one-ounce square of room-temperature chocolate, letting the shavings fall onto a piece of wax paper, then chill until ready to use.

Note: Soft ladyfingers are a good substitute for cake. Each 3-ounce package contains 12 split ladyfingers (24 pieces), or 72 pieces from 3 packages—exactly what you need for this Zuppa Inglese.

CUSTARD:

2 cups half-and-half

2 cups milk

1⅔ cups sugar

4 large eggs

2 large egg yolks

½ cup sifted all-purpose flour

¼ cup sifted unsweetened cocoa powder

½ teaspoon ground cinnamon

2 to 2½ tablespoons boiling water

2 teaspoons vanilla extract

MARSALA SYRUP:

½ cup water

⅓ cup sugar

½ cup sweet Marsala wine or Malmsey (sweet Madeira wine)

CAKE, TOPPING, AND GARNISH:

3 (3-ounce) packages ladyfingers (see Note above)

1 cup heavy cream, whipped to soft peaks

1 ounce bittersweet or semisweet chocolate, at room temperature, shaved into curls (see Tip above)

1. Custard: Bring half-and-half, milk, and 1 cup sugar to boil in medium-size heavy saucepan over moderate heat, stirring constantly. Remove from heat.

2. Using hand electric mixer, beat eggs, egg yolks, and remaining ⅔ cup sugar at high speed until thick and lemony—about 2 minutes. With mixer at low speed, mix in flour, then add about 1 cup hot milk mixture and beat only enough to combine.

Recipe continues

Miscellaneous Puddings

3. Stir egg-milk mixture back into pan, set over moderate heat, and cook, stirring constantly, just until mixture is as thick as stirred custard and no raw floury taste lingers—30 seconds to 1 minute. Do not boil or custard may curdle.

4. Pour half of custard into medium heatproof bowl and remainder into second bowl. Blend cocoa and cinnamon in small bowl and stir in enough boiling water to make thick, smooth sauce. Blend sauce into one bowl of custard. Mix vanilla into second bowl of custard. Cover both custards and set aside while you prepare Marsala Syrup.

5. Marsala Syrup: Bring water and sugar to boil in small heavy saucepan over moderate heat, stirring until sugar dissolves completely. Reduce heat to low and simmer 1 minute. Remove syrup from heat and cool to room temperature. Mix in Marsala.

6. To assemble, cover bottom of deep 3-quart glass bowl or soufflé dish with 14 ladyfinger halves, breaking as needed to fill spaces. Brush ladyfingers with Marsala syrup, using about 3 tablespoons. Now build up layers this way, brushing each ladyfinger layer with 3 tablespoons Marsala syrup: half of vanilla custard, 14 ladyfinger halves, half of chocolate custard, 14 ladyfinger halves, remaining vanilla custard, 14 ladyfinger halves, remaining chocolate custard, remaining 16 ladyfinger halves brushed with remaining ¼ cup Marsala syrup. Cover pudding and chill overnight.

7. To serve, remove pudding from refrigerator, swirl whipped cream on top, then sprinkle with chocolate shavings and present at table.

Tipsy Parson

Makes 6 to 8 Servings

This eighteenth-century odds-and-ends English dessert (wine-soaked cubes of left-over sponge or pound cake layered in a bowl with berry jam, custard sauce, and whipped cream) arrived in the Colonial South early on and remains popular to this day. Also called a trifle, it soon became better known as Tipsy Parson because it was said that the preachers treated to Sunday dinner after church had no problem devouring the spirited dessert, a few of them even taking seconds.

Tip: To save time, I use a frozen pound cake. For this recipe, you'll need 5½ cups of 1½-inch cubes of cake—exactly what a 10.75-ounce frozen pound cake delivers.

1. Place cake cubes in large nonreactive mixing bowl, drizzle with sherry, and toss well to mix. Cover and let stand at room temperature while you prepare and cool Crème Anglaise—it should cool 10 to 15 minutes before you proceed.

2. To assemble Tipsy Parson, build up layers of cake cubes, Crème Anglaise, jam, and whipped cream in 2-quart crystal or glass bowl in order listed, using half of each ingredient each time, and beginning each layer with cake and ending with whipped cream. For a final flourish, swirl top layer of whipped cream into hills and valleys. Garnish top, if you like, with strategically placed mint sprigs and strawberry fans.

3. To serve, carry Tipsy Parson to dining table and get ready for "oohs," "aahs," and recipe requests.

1 (10.75-ounce) frozen pound cake (crust on), thawed and cut in 1½-inch cubes (see Tip above)

½ cup cream sherry, tawny port, or sweet Madeira (Malmsey or Bual)

1 recipe Crème Anglaise (page 270)

1 cup firmly packed strawberry or raspberry jam, stirred well

1 cup heavy cream, whipped to soft peaks with 2 tablespoons confectioners' (10X) sugar and ½ teaspoon vanilla extract

OPTIONAL GARNISH:

5 small sprigs fresh mint or lemon geranium

5 medium-size firm-ripe strawberries, cut into fans (see Tip, page 139)

Sauces
&
Toppings

Homemade Biscuit Mix

Makes 5⅓ Cups

Or should I call this All-Purpose Topping, something to make ahead and keep in the freezer? I seal it in a plastic zipper freezer bag so it's ready to dip into whenever I need an "instant" topping for a crisp, cobbler, or other fruit pudding. A New York friend tells me that a couple of Brooklyn restaurants are now baking and serving cobblers in small wide-mouth preserving jars — each enough for one serving. Not that I'm recommending that you try that — it's risky unless you have perfect jars and spot-on ovens and timers. I, myself, prefer to bake crisps and cobblers the old-fashioned way.

Note: Once you've spooned the mix into a freezer bag, press out all the air before sealing — or resealing — and don't forget to label and date the bag. Stored this way, the biscuit mix should keep well for several months, meaning that the baking powder won't lose its "oomph."

Tip: You must use a double-acting baking powder for this mix, one that reacts first when exposed to liquid and second when it's heated.

1. Place flour, baking powder, sugar, and salt in large bowl and whisk well to combine.

2. Add butter and using pastry blender, cut butter into flour mixture until texture of lentils.

3. Scoop mixture into labeled and dated sturdy plastic zipper bag, press out all air, seal, and store in freezer where it won't get lost.

4. Use mix as individual recipes direct — So Easy Blueberry-Pecan Crunch (page 2) to name one.

4½ cups unsifted all-purpose flour

2 tablespoons double-acting baking powder (see Tip above)

4 teaspoons sugar

1 teaspoon salt

10 tablespoons (1 stick + 2 tablespoons) refrigerator-cold unsalted butter

Butter Crumb Streusel

Makes 8 Cups

Following my mother's lead, I keep a stash of ready-to-use streusel in the freezer, so whenever I want to rustle up a crisp, crumble, crunch, or cobbler, I've only to prepare the fruit. Saves worlds of time.

Note: Also see Gluten-Free Streusel Topping (page 266).

Tip: For this recipe, the crumbs should be about the size of small garden peas — roughly ⅛ inch across.

1. Place flour and brown sugar in large bowl and toss well to combine. Add butter, then using fingers, work in until uniformly crumbly and the texture of garden peas. Mix in bread crumbs.

2. Scoop streusel into four 1-pint freezer containers, dividing amount evenly, or spoon 2 cups streusel into each of four small plastic zipper bags and press out air. Seal, date, label, and store in freezer. Streusel will remain "fresh" for about a month.

3. To use, thaw streusel, then scatter over betties, crisps, crumbles, or cobblers as recipes direct.

Variation:

Whole-Wheat Butter Crumb Streusel: Prepare as directed, but substitute 3 cups moderately coarse whole-wheat bread crumbs for the white (see Tip above). Makes 8 cups.

3 cups sifted all-purpose flour

1½ cups firmly packed light brown sugar

1½ cups (3 sticks) refrigerator-cold unsalted butter, diced

3 cups coarse bread crumbs (about 6 slices firm-textured white bread, crusts on; see Tip above)

Sauces & Toppings

Gluten-Free Granola Topping

Makes 8 Cups

This handy make-ahead is delicious, in fact a good topping for any crisp, crumble, or cobbler whether you must avoid gluten (wheat, rye, and barley protein) or not. So, make a batch and freeze. Also be sure to try Fresh Fig–Granola Crumble (page 51). The topping's entirely gluten-free *if* you use pure (uncontaminated) rolled oats (see Gluten-Free Flours & Meals, page xxvii, and Sources, page 291).

Note: The amount of granola needed to top a crisp, crumble, or cobbler varies from recipe to recipe, but as a rule, 2 cups is about right. If you plan to substitute this granola for the topping called for in a recipe in the Crisps & Cobblers chapter, to make sure that the recipe is entirely gluten-free you must also eliminate any other wheat flour called for—usually the small amount needed to thicken a filling. But that's as easy as substituting 1 tablespoon cornstarch for each 2 tablespoons flour (cornstarch being the more effective thickener). Cook the cornstarch mixture, stirring constantly, only until it thickens—about 3 minutes. Further cooking will thin the cornstarch mixture, so get it off the heat immediately. That's the cardinal rule of cornstarch cookery.

Tip: Candied or glacéed fruits (sometimes called "fruitcake mix") usually only appear in supermarkets as the Thanksgiving-Christmas holidays approach, but they can be ordered off-season online (see Sources, page 291).

5¼ cups uncooked pure (gluten-free) old-fashioned rolled oats

⅔ cup sliced almonds

1 teaspoon ground cinnamon

¼ teaspoon freshly grated nutmeg

¼ teaspoon salt

½ cup honey

6 tablespoons (½ stick + 2 tablespoons) unsalted butter, melted

1 cup diced mixed glacéed or candied fruits (see Tip above)

3 tablespoons moderately finely chopped crystallized ginger

1. Preheat oven to 350°F. Line large rimmed baking sheet with baking parchment and set aside.

2. Place first five ingredients (rolled oats through salt) in large mixing bowl and toss well to mix. Whisk honey and melted butter in small bowl until well blended. Drizzle over oat mixture and toss well to mix. Spread evenly over baking sheet.

3. Slide onto middle oven shelf and bake, stirring every 5 minutes and moving browner portions around edges in toward center—this is essential. Re-spread mixture after each stir, and continue baking until uniformly crumbly and lightly toasted—about 15 minutes.

4. Remove from oven and mix in glacéed fruits and crystallized ginger. Once again, spread evenly over baking sheet. Set on wire baking rack and cool to room temperature.

5. Scoop granola into large zipper freezer bag and press out all air. Seal, label, and date, then store in freezer; granola will keep well for 4 to 6 weeks.

6. Use in place of other crisp, crumble, or cobbler toppings, following directions spelled out in recipe headnote opposite as well as in individual recipe instructions.

Gluten-Free Streusel Topping

Makes about 5¼ Cups

Good to have on hand when orchards hang out the "Y'all come" signs. Pick your own home-grown peaches, pears, apples, and all manner of berries—or buy them at your farmers' market. This streusel can be frozen, then dipped into any time a betty, crisp, or crumble needs a jiffy topping. This one, as its title promises, is gluten-free. But to make any recipe in the Crisps & Cobblers chapter entirely gluten-free, you must remove all other wheat flour called for—usually the small amount used to thicken the filling. Fortunately, that requires nothing more complicated than substituting 1 tablespoon cornstarch for each 2 tablespoons flour. But cornstarch, unlike flour, does break down if overcooked—see headnote for Gluten-Free Granola Topping recipe, which precedes.

Notes: Some high-end supermarkets sell soy flour and almond meal, ditto specialty groceries and health food stores. Both, moreover, are available online (see Sources, page 291). When making berry betties, crisps, and crumbles, I omit the optional spices in the streusel, which tend to mask the berries' delicate flavors. But for apple, peach, and pear cobblers, spices are welcome—sometimes cinnamon only, sometimes cinnamon plus nutmeg and/or allspice. What I add depends on whether I'm in the mood for something delicate or something spicy.

1 cup unsifted natural or full-fat soy flour (see Notes above)

1 cup unsifted stone-ground white or yellow cornmeal

1 cup firmly packed light brown sugar

½ cup almond meal (see Notes above)

½ teaspoon salt

½ teaspoon ground cinnamon (optional, see Notes above)

½ teaspoon freshly grated nutmeg (optional, see Notes above)

¼ teaspoon ground allspice (optional, see Notes above)

¾ cup (1½ sticks) refrigerator-cold unsalted butter (no substitute), diced

1. Whisk first five ingredients (soy flour through salt) and any optional spices together in large bowl until well combined. Using pastry blender, cut in butter until crumbly and texture of lentils.

2. Scoop streusel into large zipper freezer bag and press out all air. Seal, date, and label, then store in freezer. Streusel will keep well for about a month.

3. Use in place of other betty, crisp, or crumble toppings, following directions spelled out in recipe headnote opposite as well as those in individual recipe instructions.

Butterscotch Sauce

Makes about 1¼ Cups

As easy as it is rich, this golden brown sauce will dress up a simple custard or crisp as well as almost any bread pudding — except those that call for specific sauces.

1. Place all ingredients in medium-size heavy saucepan, set over moderately low heat, and cook, whisking often, until butter melts and sauce thickens slightly — about 5 minutes.

2. Remove from heat and cool about 30 minutes, whisking often.

3. Pour into small pitcher and serve at room temperature with a favorite apple crisp, simple custard, or bread pudding.

Note: If there are any leftovers, cover and refrigerate; bring to room temperature before serving.

½ cup (1 stick) unsalted butter, cut into pats

½ cup firmly packed light brown sugar

½ cup heavy cream

¼ teaspoon salt

Thin Chocolate Sauce

Makes about 2 Cups

Though traditionally served with Kiss Pudding (page 98), I also like this chocolate sauce over simple bread or rice puddings, tapioca pudding, even Pudim Molotov (page 252).

1. Whisk sugar, cocoa, cornstarch, and salt together in small heavy saucepan, then whisking hard, add milk slowly and continue beating until smooth.

2. Set over moderately low heat and cook, stirring constantly, until sauce thickens—about 3 minutes.

3. Blend about ½ cup hot sauce into beaten egg, then stir back into pan. Cook, stirring constantly over low heat, until instant-read thermometer, inserted in middle of sauce, reads 160°F. Do not allow sauce to boil—it will curdle. Remove from heat and mix in vanilla.

4. Cool sauce to room temperature, stirring often to prevent top from "skinning over," then serve with Kiss Pudding or other favorite dessert. Refrigerate any leftover sauce.

½ cup granulated sugar or raw sugar, or ¼ cup of each

2 tablespoons unsweetened cocoa powder

2 teaspoons cornstarch

¼ teaspoon salt

1¾ cups milk

1 large egg, well beaten

1 teaspoon vanilla extract

Crème Anglaise (Custard Sauce)

Makes about 2 Cups

This classic—equally good hot or cold—is delicious spooned over steamed puddings, fruit-nut puddings, bread puddings, even crisps and cobblers.
   Tip: The water boiling in the bottom of the double boiler should never touch the double boiler top.

1. Combine milk, sugar, and salt in medium double boiler top, set directly over moderate heat, and cook, stirring frequently, until mixture simmers—about 5 minutes.

2. Whisking beaten eggs briskly, blend in about ½ cup hot milk mixture, then stir back into double boiler top.

3. Set double boiler top over bottom containing 2½ to 3 inches boiling water (see Tip above). Cook, stirring constantly, just until custard thickens and coats metal spoon—about 5 minutes. Remove from heat and stir in vanilla.

4. Serve hot, warm, or well chilled—whatever individual recipes suggest.

2 cups milk (or for richer sauce, 1 cup each milk and half-and-half)

⅓ cup sugar

⅛ teaspoon salt

2 large eggs, well beaten

1 teaspoon vanilla extract

Mock Devonshire Cream

Makes about 1½ Cups

Devonshire Cream, some say, has been popular in England ever since the thirteenth century. It's made by steaming heavy cream, then setting it aside till the cream clots softly and the clots float. The flavor is mellow and slightly sweet. Serving Devonshire Cream with fresh strawberries has become an annual ritual at Wimbledon. My mock version approaches the original in taste if not texture (mine's smoother). I like mine with almost any fruit cobbler or crisp as well as with Summer Pudding (page 172) and that glorious German red berry dessert called Rote Grütze (page 246).

1. Combine all ingredients in small nonreactive bowl, whisking until smooth.

2. Cover and refrigerate several hours or until ready to serve.

3. Whisk briskly until smooth, then serve as a topping for crisps, cobblers, bread puddings, and more.

¾ cup heavy cream whipped to soft peaks with 2 tablespoons confectioners' (10X sugar) and ¼ teaspoon vanilla extract

½ cup firmly packed sour cream

Sauces & Toppings

Crème Fraîche

Makes about 1½ Cups

Slightly sweeter than sour cream, this French favorite—translation: "fresh cream"—couldn't be easier to make. With only two ingredients—three at most—it goes together in about a minute. But it must be covered with cheesecloth and set aside to "work" at room temperature for about 12 hours, until slightly thicker than stirred custard but not as thick as sour cream. Crème fraîche is a good substitute for whipped cream toppings and many of my recipes offer it as an option.

1. Whisk cream and sour cream together in small nonreactive bowl until smooth. Cover with double thickness of cheesecloth, set in cool draft-free spot, and let stand for at least 12 hours or overnight.

2. Remove cheesecloth, whisk mixture until smooth, then scoop into 1-pint preserving jar. Screw lid down tight and store in refrigerator for up to 1 week.

3. Use as a topping for crisps, cobblers, bread puddings, and more.

1½ cups heavy cream

3 tablespoons sour cream or buttermilk (not low-fat or fat-free), or 1½ tablespoons of each

Frothy Egg Sauce

Makes about 2½ Cups

This is the sauce to serve with Steamed Cocoa–Brown Sugar Pudding (page 197). I also like it spooned over crisps and cobblers as well as with any pudding that calls for Crème Anglaise.

Note: Because the eggs in this recipe are not cooked, use pasteurized eggs, which many supermarkets now sell, or eggs from a local source you trust.

Tip: Because this delicate sauce deflates a bit on standing, make it just before serving.

2 large pasteurized eggs (see Note above)

¾ cup sifted confectioners' (10X) sugar

1 teaspoon vanilla extract, or 1 tablespoon brandy, bourbon, or rum

1. Using hand electric mixer, beat eggs at high speed in small bowl until color and consistency of mayonnaise—about 2 minutes.

2. Reduce mixer speed to low and add confectioners' sugar gradually. Add vanilla, then with mixer speed at high, beat until light and frothy—about 5 minutes.

3. Serve at once.

Quick Raspberry Sauce

Makes about 1¼ Cups

Just the thing to jazz up a simple custard, rice pudding, Bavarian cream, even scoops of vanilla ice cream or fruit sherbet.

Note: Stored tightly covered in a 1-pint preserving jar, this raspberry sauce keeps well for several days — in other words, it's a good make-ahead.

1. Place all ingredients in food processor or electric blender and alternately pulse and churn until smooth.

2. Scoop all into fine sieve set over small nonreactive bowl and using bottom of ladle, force purée into bowl. Discard solids left in strainer.

3. Transfer sauce to 1-pint preserving jar, screw lid down tight, and refrigerate several hours or up to 3 or 4 days.

4. To serve, ladle over custards, rice puddings, or Bavarians or, if you prefer, pass separately so that everyone can help himself to as much as he likes.

1 (10-ounce) package frozen unsweetened raspberries, thawed (do not drain)

1 cup unsifted confectioners' (10X) sugar

½ teaspoon finely grated orange or lemon zest

Blueberry Maple Sauce

Makes about 1½ Cups

This is the recipe Judy Berek, a New Yorker writing a Hudson Valley cookbook, serves with her luscious Maple Bread Pudding (page 184). She also ladles the sauce over slices of her maple pound cake, even over vanilla ice cream. Check out her website: hudsonvalleycooking.com.

1. Heat 1 cup blueberries, maple syrup, lemon zest, and juice in small, heavy nonreactive saucepan over moderate heat, stirring occasionally, until berries begin to pop—about 5 minutes.

2. Remove from heat, stir in remaining blueberries, and cool to room temperature.

3. Serve with Maple Bread Pudding. Good, too, with almost any custard or rice pudding.

2 cups fresh or solidly frozen blueberries

¼ cup pure maple syrup (use the darker, more flavorful grade B)

Finely grated zest of 1 medium lemon

¼ cup fresh lemon juice

Whiskey Sauce

Makes 2 Cups

Perfect with all manner of bread puddings, but especially delicious with French Bread Pudding (page 183).

1. Whisk sugar, cornstarch, and salt together in small, heavy nonreactive saucepan, gradually add water, and continue whisking until smooth.

2. Set over moderate heat and cook, stirring constantly, until mixture thickens and clears and no starchy flavor lingers—about 3 minutes. Do not boil or sauce will thin.

3. Remove from heat, add whiskey, butter, and nutmeg, and stir until butter melts. Cool 15 to 20 minutes, stirring often to prevent sauce from "skinning over."

4. Pour into small pitcher and serve with any bread or steamed pudding you fancy. I also like this sauce trickled over apple crisps or cobblers that aren't overly spicy.

½ cup sugar

2 tablespoons cornstarch

¼ teaspoon salt

1½ cups water

¼ cup bourbon, dark rum, or rye whiskey

1 tablespoon unsalted butter, softened

½ teaspoon freshly grated nutmeg

Nutmeg Sauce

Makes about 1¼ Cups

Instead of topping every apple or peach crisp and cobbler with whipped cream, why not go "rogue" and put out a pitcher of this spicy sauce? Only freshly grated nutmeg will do here because the commercially ground tends to be bitter. Certainly, it lacks the lemony delicacy of nutmeg you grate yourself.

Note: Several back-and-forths on a fine-toothed Microplane, set at a 45-degree angle on a double thickness of wax paper, will give you just the amount of nutmeg you need. And oh, the aroma. Once you've used freshly grated nutmeg, you're not likely to settle for the pre-ground.

1. Whisk two sugars, flour, and nutmeg in small, heavy nonreactive saucepan until smooth, then add water, vinegar, and lemon juice and whisk to combine.

2. Set over moderate heat and cook, stirring constantly, until thickened, smooth, and no raw floury taste lingers—about 5 minutes.

3. To serve, pour hot sauce into small pitcher, then set on table as an accompaniment to fresh-from-the-oven peach or apple crisps and cobblers. Just a trickle or two is all that's needed.

1 cup minus 2 tablespoons granulated sugar

2 tablespoons raw sugar or loosely packed light brown sugar

2 tablespoons all-purpose flour

1 teaspoon freshly grated nutmeg (see Note above)

1 cup water

2 teaspoons cider vinegar

1 teaspoon fresh lemon juice

Quick Cardinal Sauce

Makes about 2½ Cups

So easy, so good. I like this sauce ladled over custards, rice puddings, even Swedish Cream (page 141).

Tip: If red currant jelly is unavailable, substitute any bright red berry jelly or jam—any seeds will be sieved out.

1. Place all ingredients in food processor, then purée by buzzing 10 to 15 seconds, pausing at half time to scrape processor bowl and blade.

2. Scoop all into fine sieve set over large nonreactive bowl and using bottom of ladle, force purée into bowl. Taste sauce and adjust sugar as needed. Discard solids left in sieve.

3. Transfer sauce to 1-quart preserving jar, screw lid down tight, and store in refrigerator (sauce keeps well for several days).

4. Serve over whatever custards and creams you fancy.

1 (10-ounce) package frozen unsweetened raspberries, thawed (do not drain)

1 (10-ounce) package frozen unsweetened strawberries, thawed (do not drain)

¼ cup sugar, or to taste

2 tablespoons red currant jelly (see Tip above)

1 tablespoon fresh lemon juice

Hard Sauce

Makes about 1½ Cups

Just the thing for steamed pudding—any steamed pudding. Also note the vanilla variation that follows. Why the name "hard sauce"? No one knows for sure, but it may be because this is more of a spread than a sauce, i.e., harder or firmer. Or it may be because the sauce is spiked with hard liquor. Either explanation is believable. Take your pick.

1. Cream butter at high speed in small electric mixer bowl until fluffy and almost white—about 2 minutes.

2. With machine off, add 1 cup confectioners' sugar, then beat at low speed until smooth. Add remaining 2 cups sugar the same way, 1 cup at a time with the machine off, then beat until smooth at low speed. This way the powdery sugar won't fly out of the bowl and dust everything in sight.

3. Add brandy and salt, then beat at high speed until fluffy and light—about 2 minutes.

4. Transfer to 1-pint container, snap on lid, and refrigerate until ready to serve.

5. Just before serving, beat hard sauce at high speed with hand electric mixer until fluffy, then scoop into small colorful bowl and set out as an accompaniment to steamed pudding.

¾ cup (1½ sticks) unsalted butter, at room temperature

3 cups sifted confectioners' (10X) sugar

3 tablespoons brandy or dark rum

⅛ teaspoon salt

Variation:

Vanilla Hard Sauce: Prepare as directed, but omit brandy or rum. Instead, add 1½ tablespoons warm water and 1½ teaspoons vanilla extract in Step 3 along with salt. Makes about 1½ cups.

Sauces & Toppings

Brown Sugar Hard Sauce

Makes about 1¼ Cups

I don't remember my mother ever making this unusual hard sauce though I found the recipe in her recipe file. It's easy enough and would, I think, be delicious with almost any steamed pudding. Ditto date-nut pudding.

1. Combine brown sugar and water in small saucepan. Bring to boil over high heat, then cook, stirring constantly, until all sugar has dissolved—about 30 seconds. Transfer to small electric mixer bowl and cool to room temperature—about 20 minutes.

2. Add butter, confectioners' sugar, rum, and vanilla to cooled brown sugar mixture and beat at low speed just long enough to combine. Raise mixer speed to high and continue beating until light and fluffy—about 1 minute.

3. Serve at once with any steamed pudding or, if you prefer, chill well and serve cold. This hard sauce is delicious either way.

¼ cup firmly packed dark brown sugar

2 tablespoons water

½ cup (1 stick) unsalted butter, at room temperature

½ cup unsifted confectioners' (10X) sugar

2 tablespoons dark rum, bourbon, or cold strong dark coffee

1 teaspoon vanilla extract

SOURCES

Note: For more information about the ingredients, bakeware, and cook's tools listed here, go to the Pudding Primer, page xv.

Almond Meal
(also called Natural Almond Flour):
bobsredmill.com
justalmonds.com

Amaretti:
zabars.com
supermarketitaly.com
sahadifinefoods.com

Apples (dried and freeze-dried):
nuts.com
shop.honeyville.com

Bakeware and Pudding Molds:
fantes.com
foodservicewarehouse.com
duchessprovisions.com
kitchenworksinc.com
surlatable.com
webstaurantstore.com
williams-sonoma.com

Black Walnuts (shelled and ready-to-use):
earthy.com
black-walnuts.com

Cajeta (Mexican caramelized goat milk):
mexgrocer.com

Chef's Torches and Other Cook's Tools:
kitchenworksinc.com
fantes.com
foodservicewarehouse.com
surlatable.com
webstaurantstore.com
wayfair.com
williams-sonoma.com

Chocolate (premium baking chocolates):
worldwidechocolate.com
duchessprovisions.com
chocolatesource.com

Cornmeal (stone-ground):
ansonmills.com
oldmillofguilford.com

Dulce de Leche:
mexgrocer.com
olivenation.com

Extracts and Flavorings (including vanilla beans and rose water). Pure almond extract, also butterscotch, coconut, hazelnut, lemon, maple, orange, rum, vanilla, etc.:
olivenation.com
duchessprovisions.com
savoryspiceshop.com
penzeys.com

Glacéed or Candied Fruits (mixed and individual):
nuts.com

Gluten-Free Flours and Meals:
arrowheadmills.com
bobsredmill.com
nuts.com

Herbs and Spices:
penzeys.com

Hickory Nuts (shelled and ready-to-use):
rayshickorynuts.com
pinenut.com

Ladyfingers (both soft and crisp):
gourmetfoodworld.com
worldmarket.com
amazon.com (half a dozen varieties)

Maple Sugar (granulated):
vermontpuremaplesyrup.com
vermontcountrystore.com
sugarbushfarm.com

Maple Syrup (grade B):
gradebmaplesyrup.org
piecesofvermont.com
vermontpuremaplesyrup.com

Meringue Cookies and Nests:
missmeringue.com

Peaches (tree-ripened):
carolinapeach.com
gapeaches.com

Pecans (orchard-fresh):
doubletreepecan.com
pearsonfarm.com

Pistachios (blanched, unsalted, raw, and roasted):
nuts.com

Quark:
murrayscheese.com

Rose Water:
See Extracts & Flavorings (page 291).

Soy Flour:
bobsredmill.com
hodgsonmillstore.com

Wild Persimmons:
localharvest.org/persimmon-pulp-C14148
(Two-pint containers of frozen unsweetened
wild persimmon pulp is generally — but not
always — available from late September through
January, sometimes later. It's so scarce that I stock
up and keep a good supply in my freezer.)

INDEX

Page numbers in *italics* indicate illustrations

A

Almond(s), xxxiii. *See also* Granola Topping, Gluten-Free, 264–265
    -Orange-Apricot Crisp, 49–50
Almond meal, xxii, 201, 266, 291
Almond milk, xxii
Amaretti, xxii, 291
    -Peach Crisp (variation), 44
    -Pear Crisp, 43–44
Angel food cake pan, xviii
Apple(s), 291
    Betty, -Blueberry (variation), 33
    Betty, -Cranberry (variation), 33
    Betty, Golden Delicious–Butter Crumb, *34*, 35–36
    Betty, Golden Delicious–Butter Crumb, Gluten-Free (variation), 36
    Bread Pudding with Fresh Apples (variation), 186
    Brown Betty, Antebellum, 28–29
    Brown Betty, Spicy, *30*–32, *31*
    in Carrot Pudding, Steamed, 206–207
    Cran-Apple Casserole with Oatmeal Crust, 40
    Crisp, -Cheddar, 26–27
    Crumble, Pear 'n', with Pecan-Oatmeal Crust, 41–42
    Crumble, Three-Fruit Pecan-Oatmeal (variation), 42
    Dried Fruits, Wine-Poached, Cobbler of, 66–67
    "Dutch Baby", *22*, 23–24
    Eve's Pudding, 38–39
    Green Tomato Crumble with Raisins and, 64–65
    Handy Dandy Apple Pudding (variation), 33
    in Noodle Pudding, 191–192
    October Pudding, 25
    Ozark Pudding, 218
    Pandowdy, Old Pennsylvania, 37
    preparing, xx
    Scallop, -Pecan, 15
    Slump, 20–21
Applesauce Pudding, Steamed, 193
Apricot(s)
    Dried Fruits, Wine-Poached, Cobbler of, 66–67
    Fluff, 156
    -Orange-Almond Crisp, 49–50
    preparing, xxi

B

Bacon, in Pudding of the Abbot of Priscos (Pudim Abade de Priscos), 103–104
Bakeware, xv, xvii–xviii, 291
Baking sheets, rimmed, xvii
Banana Pudding, Old-Timey Tar Heel, 92, *93*–94
Bavarian Cream
    Raspberry, 114
    Showstopper, 116, *117*
    Vanilla, 115
Beef Suet, xxii
    in Christmas Pudding, 198–200, *199*
    in Fig and Cranberry Pudding, Steamed, 204–205
    Suet Pudding, Colonial, 194–195
Berry(ies). *See also specific berries*
    Biscuits 'n', 18, *19*
    Cardinal Sauce, Quick, 284, *285*
    Cobbler, Berries of Summer, with Rye Biscuit Topping, 13–14
    Jam Custards, Blue Ridge, 76
    preparing, xx–xxi
    Rote Grütze (Red Berry Pudding), 246–248, *247*
    Slump or Grunt, Yankee, 8–9
    Summer Pudding, 172–173
    Berry Patch Cobbler with Pecan Shortbread Crust, *16*, 17
Betty(ies)
    Apple-Blueberry (variation), 33
    Apple Brown, Antebellum, 28–29
    Apple Brown, Spicy, 30–32, *31*
    Apple-Cranberry (variation), 33
    Golden Delicious–Butter Crumb, *34*, 35–36
    Golden Delicious–Butter Crumb, Gluten-Free (variation), 36
    Peach (variation), 33
Bill Smith's Butterscotch Pudding, 126–127
Biscuit-Buttermilk Pudding, 176
Biscuit Topping
    Apple Slump, 20–21
    Berry Slump or Grunt, Yankee, 8–9
    Biscuits 'n' Berries, 18, *19*
    Blueberry-Pecan Crunch, So Easy, 2, *3*
    Cobbler, Peach Tree, 45
    Cobbler of Wine-Poached Dried Fruits, 66–67
    Homemade Biscuit Mix, 262
    Rye, Berries of Summer Cobbler with, 13–14
Blackberry(ies)
    Cobbler, Berry Patch, with Pecan Shortbread Crust, *16*, 17

preparing, xx–xxi
Pudding, Bread-and-Butter, 174, *175*
Trifle, 143
Woodford Pudding, 212
Black Walnuts, xxii, xxxiii, 291
October Pudding, 25
Ozark Pudding, 218
Prune Pudding, Spicy Butter-
milk-Glazed, 227–228
Blueberry(ies)
-Apple Betty (variation), 33
Buckle, Down East, 4–5
Cobbler, Red, White, and Blue
Berry–Corn Bread, *10*, 11–12
Cream (variation), 139
and Date Pudding, Steamed (varia-
tion), 205
Eve's Pudding (variation), 39
Maple Sauce, *280*, 281
-Oatmeal Crumble, 6, *7*
-Pecan Crunch, So Easy, 2, *3*
preparing, xx
Pudding, French Canadian, 171
Blue Ridge Jam Custards, 76
Bread, xxii–xxiii
in Apple Brown Betty, Antebellum,
28–29
in Apple Brown Betty, Spicy, 30, *31*
-and-Butter Blackberry Pudding,
174, *175*
Buttered Crumbs, Peaches, and
Quark, Layered Gratin of,
242–243
Bread puddings
Blackberry Pudding, Bread-and-
Butter, 174, *175*
Blueberry Pudding, French Cana-
dian, 171
Buttermilk-Biscuit Pudding, 176
Chocolate Bread Pudding, The Best,
164–166, *165*
Date-Nut-Bread Crumb Pudding,
Mother's, 177
Days-of-Yore Bread Pudding, 162
French Bread Pudding with Whis-
key Sauce, 183
Graham Cracker Pudding, 189–190
Lemon Meringue Bread Pudding,
168, 169–170
Maple Bread Pudding, 184–186, *185*
Maple Bread Pudding with Dried
Fruits (variation), 186

Maple Bread Pudding with Fresh
Apples (variation), 186
Martha Washington Pudding, 163
New Mexican Bread Pudding (Cap-
irotada), *178*, 179–180
Peach Cups, Upside-Down, with
Spicy Peach Sauce, 187–188
Queen of Puddings, 181–182
Rum-Raisin Bread Pudding, 167
Summer Pudding, 172–173
Brown Betty
Apple, Antebellum, 28–29
Apple, Spicy, 30–32, *31*
Brown Sugar, xxxi
–Cocoa Pudding, Steamed, *196*, 197
Hard Sauce, *288*, 289
Buckle, Blueberry, Down East, 4–5
Burnt Sugar Syrup, 252
Butane torch, xix, 87
Butter, melting, xxiii
Butter Crumb
–Golden Delicious Betty, *34*, 35–36
–Golden Delicious Betty, Glu-
ten-Free, 36
Streusel, 263
Streusel, Whole-Wheat (variation),
263
Buttermilk, xxiii
-Biscuit Pudding, 176
Cocoa–Brown Sugar Pudding,
Steamed, *196*, 197
Corn Bread Cobbler, Red, White,
and Blue Berry–, *10*, 11–12
in Crème Fraîche, 274, *275*
-Glazed Prune Pudding, Spicy,
227–228
Green Tomato–Corn Bread Crisp,
62–63
Orange Pudding, Glazed, Flossie
Miller's, 219
Woodford Pudding, 212
Butter Sauce, Hot, Baked Cranberry
Pudding with, *216*, 217
Butterscotch extract, 126
Butterscotch Pudding, Bill Smith's,
126–127
Butterscotch Sauce, 268

C

Cajeta, 291
Candied Fruit, xxiii, 291
Christmas Pudding, 198–200, *199*

Granola Topping, Gluten-Free,
264 265
Rice à l'Impératrice, 96–97
Rum Pudding with Fruit and Nuts,
Grandma Anna Weigl's,
136–137
Capirotada (New Mexican Bread Pud-
ding), *178*, 179–180
Caramel
Cornstarch Pudding (variation),
125
Crème Caramel, Feliciana Parish
Sweet Potato, 100–102, *101*
Dulce de Leche Pots de Crème,
106, 107
Flan, River of Gold, 81
Pudding of the Abbot of Priscos
(Pudim Abade de Priscos),
103–104
Caramelized Topping, in Crème Brûlée,
88
Cardamom, xxiii, 95
Cardinal Sauce, Quick, 284, *285*
Carrot(s)
and Pineapple Pudding, Steamed
(variation), 207
Pudding, Steamed, 206–207
Surprise Pudding with Orange
Sauce, 235–236
Casserole dishes, xvii
Cast-iron skillet, xvii
Charlotte, Orange, Mummy's, 150–151
Cheddar-Apple Crisp, 26–27
Cheese, xxiii, xxxiii.
Bread Pudding, New Mexican (Cap-
irotada), *178*, 179–180
Cheddar-Apple Crisp, 26–27
Cottage Cheese, in Noodle Pud-
ding, 191–192
grating, xxiv
quark, making, xxx
Quark, Peaches, and Buttered
Crumbs, Layered Gratin of,
242–243
Ricotta Pudding with Dark Sweet
Red Cherries, 244–245
Ricotta, in Tiramisu, 153
Cherry(ies)
Clafoutis, *56*, 57
Cobbler, 55
preparing, xxi
Rice à l'Impératrice, 96–97

Ricotta Pudding with Dark Sweet
Red Cherries, 244–245
Rote Grütze (Red Berry Pudding),
246–248, *247*
Cherry pitter, xix
Chocolate
Bread Pudding, The Best, 164–166,
165
Cocoa–Brown Sugar Pudding,
Steamed, *196*, 197
Cornstarch Pudding (variation),
125
curls, 255
Mousse, 128–129
Mousse, Mexican Chocolate (varia-
tion), 129
Panna Cotta, Hazelnut, 105
Pots de Crème, 99
Pudding Cake, 134–135
Pudding, Perfectly Silky, 130
Sauce, in Kiss Pudding, 98
Sauce, Thin, 269
Soufflé, 108–109
sources, 291
Christmas Pudding, 198–200, *199*
Cinnamon
-Dusted Baked Custard (Sericaia),
82–84, *83*
and Milk Pudding (Manjar de Leche
y Canela), Sandra Gutierrez's,
132, *133*
Citrus juice, xv, xxiv
Citrus zest, xxiv
Clafoutis, Cherry, *56*, 57
Clementines, xxiv
Sweet Potato Panna Cotta with, in
Lemongrass Syrup, *118*,
119–120
Cobbler(s). *See also* Betty(ies); Crisp(s)
Apple Pandowdy, Old Pennsylva-
nia, 37
Apple-Pecan Scallop, 15
Apple Slump, 20–21
Berries of Summer, with Rye Biscuit
Topping, 13–14
Berry Patch, with Pecan Shortbread
Crust, *16*, 17
Berry Slump or Grunt, Yankee, 8–9
Biscuit Mix, Homemade, 262
Biscuits 'n' Berries, 18, *19*
Blueberry Buckle, Down East, 4–5
Cherry, 55

Cherry Clafoutis, *56*, 57
of Dried Fruits, Wine-Poached,
66–67
"Dutch Baby", *22*, 23–24
Eve's Pudding, 38–39
Handy Dandy Pudding, Apple (vari-
ation), 33
Handy Dandy Pudding, Peach (vari-
ation), 33
Handy Dandy Pudding, Pear, 33
October Pudding, 25
Peach Pudding, Pinehurst, 48
Peach Tree, 45
Plum, Fresh, with Whole-Wheat
Topping, 52–54, *53*
Red, White, and Blue Berry–Corn
Bread, *10*, 11–12
Rhubarb, Roasted, with Whole-
Wheat Topping, 58–59
Cocoa–Brown Sugar Pudding, Steamed,
196, 197
Coconut, xxiv
Custards, 75
Tapioca Pudding (variation), 89
Coconut milk, xxiv, 75
Coffee, instant espresso, xxiv
Condensed milk, sweetened, xxix
Confectioners' sugar, xxxi
Corn Bread
Cobbler, –Red, White, and Blue
Berry, *10*, 11–12
–Green Tomato Crisp, 62–63
Green Tomato Crumble with Apples
and Raisins, 64–65
Cornmeal
Corn Bread Cobbler, –Red, White,
and Blue Berry, *10*, 11–12
Corn Bread–Green Tomato Crisp,
62–63
Indian Pudding, 210–211
stone-ground, xxiv–xxv
Streusel Topping, Gluten-Free,
266–267
sources, 291
Cornstarch
in gluten-free fillings, 264
as thickener, xxv
Cornstarch puddings
Butterscotch Pudding, Bill Smith's,
126–127
Caramel Cornstarch Pudding (vari-
ation), 125

Chocolate Cornstarch Pudding
(variation), 125
Chocolate Pudding, Perfectly Silky,
130
Cinnamon and Milk Pudding (Man-
jar de Leche y Canela), Sandra
Gutierrez's, 132, *133*
Classic Cornstarch Pudding,
125
Rum Pudding with Fruit and Nuts,
Grandma Anna Weigl's,
136–137
Strawberry Cream, 139
Trifle, Blackberry, 143
Cranberry(ies)
-Apple Betty (variation), 33
Cobbler, Red, White, and Blue
Berry–Corn Bread, *10*, 11–12
Cran-Apple Casserole with Oatmeal
Crust, 40
and Fig Pudding, Steamed, 204–
205
preparing, xx
Pudding, Baked, with Hot Butter
Sauce, *216*, 217
Pudding, Finnish, 254
Cream, types of, xxv
Creams. *See* Custards and creams
Crème Anglaise (Custard Sauce), 270,
271
Crème Brûlée, *86*, 87–88
Crème Caramel, Feliciana Parish Sweet
Potato, 100–102, *101*
Crème Fraîche, 274, *275*
Crisp(s). *See also* Cobbler(s); Crum-
ble(s)
Apple-Cheddar, 26–27
Blueberry-Pecan Crunch, So Easy,
2, *3*
Cran-Apple Casserole with Oatmeal
Crust, 40
Green Tomato–Corn Bread, 62–63
Orange-Almond-Apricot, 49–50
Peach-Amaretti (variation), 44
Pear-Amaretti, 43–44
Crumble(s). *See also* Crisp(s)
Blueberry-Oatmeal, 6, *7*
Fig-Granola, Fresh, 51
Green Tomato, with Apples and Rai-
sins, 64–65
Peaches, Pick-Your-Own, with Gin-
ger Shortbread, 46–47

Pear 'n' Apple, with Pecan-Oatmeal
    Crust, 41–42
R & R, 60–61
Three-Fruit Pecan-Oatmeal (varia
    tion), 42
Crunch, Blueberry-Pecan, So Easy, 2,
    3
Custard cups, xvii
Custards and creams. *See also* Corn-
    starch puddings; Soufflé(s)
Banana Pudding, Old-Timey Tar
    Heel, *92*, 93–94
Bavarian Cream, Raspberry, 114
Bavarian Cream, Showstopper, 116,
    117
Bavarian Cream, Vanilla, 115
Charlotte, Orange, Mummy's,
    150–151
Cinnamon-Dusted Baked Custard
    (Sericaia), 82–84, *83*
Classic Baked Custard, 70, *71*
Coconut Custards, 75
Crème Anglaise (Custard Sauce),
    270, *271*
Crème Brûlée, *86*, 87–88
Crème Caramel, Sweet Potato, Feli-
    ciana Parish, 100–102, *101*
Crème Fraîche, 274, *275*
Devonshire Cream, Mock, *272*,
    273
Flan, River of Gold, 81
Floating Island, 74
Fluff, Apricot, 156
Fluff, Peach, 156
Fool, Gooseberry, 146
Jam Custards, Blue Ridge, 76
Kiss Pudding, 98
Lemon Sponge, Honeyed, 154–155
Molasses Custard, 77
Mousse, Chocolate, 128–129
Mousse, Mexican Chocolate (varia-
    tion), 129
Mousse, Mocha (variation), 129
Orange Pudding (Pudim de Lar-
    anja), Enca Mello Lameiro's,
    148–149
Panna Cotta, Chocolate-Hazelnut,
    105
Panna Cotta, Dulce de Leche,
    121–122
Panna Cotta, Lemon Verbena,
    123–124

Panna Cotta, Sweet Potato, with
    Clementines in Lemongrass
    Syrup, *118*, 119–120
Potato Pudding, Irish, 147
Pots de Crème, Chocolate, 99
Pots de Crème, Dulce de Leche,
    106, 107
Pots de Crème, Mocha (variation),
    99
Pudding Cake, Chocolate, 134–135
Pudding Cake, Lemon, 138
Pudim Abade de Priscos (Pudding of
    the Abbot of Priscos), 103–104
Pumpkin Pudding, Ina Lieb's,
    144–145
Rice à l'Impératrice, 96–97
Rice Pudding, 85
Rice Pudding, Indian (Kheer), 95
Rum Cream with Sliced Peaches,
    142
Slight Pudding, 152
Snow Pudding, Sara's, 158–159
Spanish Cream, 131
Swedish Cream, *140*, 141
Syllabub, 157
Tapioca Pudding, Coconut (varia-
    tion), 89
Tapioca Pudding, Mama's, 89
Tapioca Pudding, Pecan (variation),
    89
Tea Custard, *78*, 79–80
Tiramisu, 153
Vanilla Bean Custard, Baked, 72–73
Vanilla Bean Custard, Individual
    (variation), 73
Zabaglione, 90, *91*
Zuppa Inglese, 255–256, *257*

D

Date(s)
    and Blueberry Pudding, Steamed
        (variation), 205
    Food for the Gods, 213
    -Nut–Bread Crumb Pudding, Moth-
        er's, 177
    -Nut Pudding, My Mother's, 214, *215*
    Orange Pudding, Glazed, Flossie
        Miller's, 219
    Sticky Toffee Puddings, *222*,
        223–224
Days-of-Yore Bread Pudding, 162
Devonshire Cream, Mock, *272*, 273

Dewberries, preparing, xx–xxi
Double boiler, xvii
Dried Fruit(s)
    Cobbler of, Wine-Poached, 66–67
    Maple Bread Pudding with (varia-
        tion), 186
Dulce de Leche
    commercial, 121, 291
    Panna Cotta, 121–122
    Pots de Crème, *106*, 107
    sweetened condensed milk in, xxix
"Dutch Baby", *22*, 23–24

E

Eggs, pasteurized, xxv–xxvi, 96, 131, 143,
    150, 157
Egg Sauce, Frothy, *276*, 277
Enco Mello Lameiro's Pudim de Laranja
    (Orange Pudding), 148–149
Equipment and tools
    bakeware, xv, xvii–xviii
    ovens, xvi
    sources for, 291
    types of, xix–xx
Espresso, instant, xxiv
Eton Mess, *250*, 251
Evaporated milk, xxix
Eve's Pudding, 38–39
Extracts/flavorings, xv, xxvi, 291

F

Feliciana Parish Sweet Potato Crème
    Caramel, 100–102, *101*
Fig(s)
    and Cranberry Pudding, Steamed,
        204–205
    -Granola Crumble, Fresh, 51
    preparing, xxi
Finnish Cranberry Pudding, 254
Flan, River of Gold, 81
Floating Island, 74
Flossie Miller's Glazed Orange Pudding,
    219
Flours
    all-purpose, xxvi–xxvii
    blends, xxvii
    gluten-free, xxvii–xxviii, 292
    soy, xxvi, 266, 292
    whole-wheat, xxvii
Fluff
    Apricot, 156
    Peach, 156

Food for the Gods, 213
Food mill, xix
Food processor, xix–xx
Fool, Gooseberry, 146
French Bread Pudding with Whiskey
    Sauce, 183
French Canadian Blueberry Pudding,
    171
Frothy Egg Sauce, *276*, 277
Fruit(s). *See also* Berry(ies); Candied
    Fruit; *specific fruits*
    Dried, Maple Bread Pudding with
        (variation), 186
    Dried, Wine-Poached Cobbler of,
        66–67
    equivalents table, xxxiii
    preparing, xx–xxii
    Rum Pudding with Nuts and,
        Grandma Anna Weigl's,
        136–137
    Snow Pudding, Sara's, 158–159

G

Gelatin, xxvii, xxxiii
Geranium, lemon, xxviii
Ginger
    fresh, xxvii, 232
    Shortbread, Pick-Your-Own Peaches
        Crumble with, 46–47
Gluten Free
    Fig-Granola Crumble, Fresh, 51
    flours/meals, xxvii–xviii, 292
    Golden Delicious–Butter Crumb
        Betty (variation), 36
    Granola Topping, 264–265
    Streusel Topping, 266–267
Golden Delicious–Butter Crumb Betty,
    34, 35–36
    Gluten-Free (variation), 36
Gooseberry(ies)
    Fool, 146
    preparing, xx
Graham Cracker(s), xxxiii
    Food for the Gods, 213
    Lemon Sponge, Honeyed, 154–155
    Pudding, 189–190
Grandma Anna Weigl's Rum Pudding
    with Fruit and Nuts,
    136–137
Grand Marnier Soufflé (variation), 112
Grandmother Anderson's Streusel Pud-
    ding, 237–238

Granola
    -Fig Crumble, Fresh, 51
    Topping, Gluten-Free, 264–265
Gratin of Buttered Crumbs, Peaches,
    and Quark, Layered, 242–
    243
Green Tomato
    –Corn Bread Crisp, 62–63
    Crumble with Apples and Raisins,
    64–65
Grunt, Berry, Yankee, 8–9
Gutierrez, Sandra, Manjar de Leche y
    Canela (Cinnamon and Milk
    Pudding), 132, *133*

H

Half-and-half, xxv
Handy Dandy Pudding
    Apple (variation), 33
    Peach (variation), 33
    Pear, 33
Hard Sauce, *286*, 287
    Brown Sugar, *288*, 289
    Vanilla (variation), 287
Hazelnut(s), xxxiii
    -Chocolate Panna Cotta, 105
    in Rum Pudding with Fruit and
        Nuts, Grandma Anna Weigl's,
        136–137
    toasting, xxviii
Hazelnut extract, xxvi, 105
Heavenly Hash, 249
Heavy cream, xxv
Hickory nuts, xxviii, 292
Honey
    Fig-Granola Crumble, Fresh, 51
    Granola Topping, Gluten-Free,
        264–265
    Lemon Sponge, Honeyed,
        154–155
    selecting, xxviii
    Wine-Poached Dried Fruits, Cob-
        bler of, 66–67

I

Ina Lieb's Pumpkin Pudding, 144–145
Indian Pudding, 210–211
Indian Rice Pudding (Kheer), 95
Ingredients. *See also* Flours
    "dos" and "don'ts", xv
    equivalents table, xxxiii
    fruits, xx–xxii

listed, xxii–xxxii
    sources for, 291–292
Irish Potato Pudding, 147
Iron Skillet Sweet Potato Pudding,
    230–231

J

Jam
    Custards, Blue Ridge, 76
    Tipsy Parson, *258*, 259
    Woodford Pudding, 212

K

Kheer (Indian Rice Pudding), 95
Kiss Pudding, 98

L

Ladyfingers
    Italian, xxviii
    Orange Charlotte, Mummy's, 150–151
    Rum Pudding with Fruit and Nuts,
        Grandma Anna Weigl's,
        136–137
    sources, 292
    Tiramisu, 153
Lemon
    Meringue Bread Pudding, *168*,
        169–170
    Pudding Cake, 138
    Snow Pudding, Sara's, 158–159
    Sponge, Honeyed, 154–155
Lemon geranium, xxviii
Lemongrass, xxviii
    Syrup, Sweet Potato Panna Cotta
        with Clementines in, *118*,
        119–120
Lemon Verbena, xxix, 123
    Panna Cotta, 123–124
Lieb, Ina, Pumpkin Pudding, 144–145
Light cream, xxv
Liquor/liqueur, xxix. *See also* Rum
    Christmas Pudding, 198–200,
        199
    Egg Sauce, Frothy, *276*, 277
    Grand Marnier Soufflé (variation),
        112
    Hard Sauce, *286*, 287
    Hard Sauce, Brown Sugar, *288*, 289
    Snow Pudding, Sara's, 158–159
    Sweet Potato Crème Caramel, Feli-
        ciana Parish, 100–102, *101*
    Whiskey Sauce, 282

M

Mama's Tapioca Pudding, 89

Mandolines, xx

Mangoes, preparing, xxi

Manjar de Leche y Canela (Cinnamon and Milk Pudding), Sandra Gutierrez's, 132, *133*

Maple (Syrup/Sugar), xxix, 292

    Blueberry Sauce, *280*, 281

    Bread Pudding, 184–186, *185*

    Bread Pudding with Dried Fruits (variation), 186

    Bread Pudding with Fresh Apples (variation), 186

    Eve's Pudding, 38–39

Marsala Syrup, 255, 256

Marshmallows, in Heavenly Hash, 249

Martha Washington Pudding, 163

Mello Lameiro, Enco, Pudim de Laranja (Orange Pudding), 148–149

Meringue(s)

    Banana Pudding, Old-Timey Tar Heel, *92*, 93–94

    Blackberry Trifle, 143

    browning, xxvi

    cookies/nests, xxix, 292

    Eton Mess, *250*, 251

    Floating Island, 74

    Jam Custards, Blue Ridge, 76

    Lemon Meringue Bread Pudding, *168*, 169–170

    Martha Washington Pudding, 163

    Pudim Molotov, 252–253

Mexican Chocolate Mousse (variation), 129

Microplanes, xx

Milk, canned, xxix

Milk Pudding, Cinnamon and (Manjar de Leche y Canela), Sandra Gutierrez's, 132, *133*

Mocha

    Mousse (variation), 129

    Pots de Crème (variation), 99

Molasses, xxx, 126

    in Butterscotch Pudding, Bill Smith's, 126–127

    Custard, 77

    Indian Pudding, 210–211

    Plantation Pudding, 220, *221*

    in Pumpkin Pudding, Ina Lieb's, 144–145

    in Suet Pudding, Colonial, 194–195

Mousse

    Chocolate, 128–129

    Mexican Chocolate (variation), 129

    Mocha (variation), 129

Mummy's Orange Charlotte, 150–151

N

Nectarines, preparing, xxi

New Mexican Bread Pudding (Capirotada), *178*, 179–180

Nonreactive bakeware, xv

Noodle Pudding, 191–192

Nut(s). *See also specific nuts*

    equivalents table, xxxiii

Nutmeg, xxx, 162

    Sauce, 283

O

Oatmeal, xxvii

    Crisp, Orange-Almond-Apricot, 49–50

    Crumble, -Blueberry, 6, *7*

    Crumble, R & R, 60–61

    Crust, Cran-Apple Casserole with, 40

    Granola Topping, Gluten-Free, 264–265

    -Pecan Crumble, Three-Fruit (variation), 42

    -Pecan Crust, Pear 'n' Apple Crumble with, 41–42

October Pudding, 25

Orange(s)

    -Almond-Apricot Crisp, 49–50

    Charlotte, Mummy's, 150–151

    clementines, xxiv

    Pudding (Pudim de Laranja), Enca Mello Lameiro's, 148–149

    Pudding, Glazed, Flossie Miller's, 219

    Sauce, Surprise Pudding with, 235–236

    Soufflé, 112–113

    Steamed Orange Pudding, 201–203, *202*

    Sweet Potato Panna Cotta with Clementines in Lemongrass Syrup, *118*, 119–120

    Syllabub, 157

    -Walnut Pudding, 239–241, *240*

Oven temperature, xvi

Ozark Pudding, 218

P

Pandowdy, Apple, Old Pennsylvania, 37

Panna Cotta

    Chocolate-Hazelnut, 105

    Dulce de Leche, 121–122

    Lemon Verbena, 123–124

    Sweet Potato, with Clementines in Lemongrass Syrup, *118*, 119–120

Parmigiano-Reggiano, grating, xxiv

Peach(es)

    -Amaretti Crisp (variation), 44

    Betty (variation), 33

    Cobbler, Peach Tree, 45

    Crumble, Pick-Your-Own, with Ginger Shortbread, 46–47

    Cups, Upside-Down, with Spicy Peach Sauce, 187–188

    Dried Fruits, Wine-Poached, Cobbler of, 66–67

    Fluff (variation), 156

    Handy Dandy Peach Pudding (variation), 33

    Heavenly Hash, 249

    Pinehurst Peach Pudding, 48

    preparing, xxi

    Quark, and Buttered Crumbs, Layered Gratin of, 242–243

    Rum Cream with Sliced Peaches, 142

    Sauce, Spicy, Upside-Down Peach Cups with, 187–188

    Soufflé, Fresh, 110–111

    sources, 292

Pear(s)

    -Amaretti Crisp, 43–44

    Crumble, 'n' Apple, with Pecan-Oatmeal Crust, 41–42

    Crumble, Three-Fruit Pecan-Oatmeal (variation), 42

    Handy Dandy Pear Pudding, 33

    preparing, xx

Pecan(s)

    Applesauce Pudding, Steamed, 193

    -Apple Scallop, 15

    -Blueberry Crunch, So Easy, 2, *3*

    Christmas Pudding, 198–200, *199*

    Cran-Apple Casserole with Oatmeal Crust, 40

Date-Nut Pudding, My Mother's, 214, *215*
equivalents, xxxiii
Food for the Gods, 213
Graham Cracker Pudding, 189–190
Heavenly Hash, 249
-Oatmeal Crumble, Three-Fruit (variation), 42
-Oatmeal Crust, Pear 'n' Apple Crumble with, 41–42
October Pudding, 25
Ozark Pudding, 218
Prune Pudding, Spicy Butter-milk-Glazed, 227–228
Shortbread Crust, Berry Patch Cobbler with, *16*, 17
sources, 292
Streusel Pudding, Grandmother Anderson's, 237–238
Tapioca Pudding (variation), 89
toasting, xxx
Pennsylvania Apple Pandowdy, Old, 37
Persimmons, Wild
    preparing, xxi–xxii
    Pudding, 225–226
    sources, xxxii, 292
Pie pans, xvii
Pineapple
    and Carrot Pudding, Steamed (variation), 207
    in Heavenly Hash, 249
    in Rum Pudding with Fruit and Nuts, Grandma Anna Weigl's, 136–137
Pinehurst Peach Pudding, 48
Pistachios, xxx, 95, 292
Plantation Molasses Pudding, 220, *221*
Plum(s)
    Cobbler, Fresh, with Whole-Wheat Topping, 52–54, *53*
    in Crumble, Three-Fruit Pecan-Oatmeal (variation), 42
Potato(es)
    Pudding, Irish, 147
    in Steamed Carrot Pudding, 206–207
Pots de Crème
    Chocolate, 99
    Dulce de Leche, *106*, 107
    Mocha (variation), 99
Prune Pudding, Spicy Butter-milk-Glazed, 227–228

Pudding(s). *See also* Bread puddings; Custards and creams; Steamed puddings
Cranberry, Baked, with Hot Butter Sauce, *216*, 217
Cranberry, Finnish, 254
Date-Nut, My Mother's, 214, *215*
defined, xiii
"dos" and "don'ts", xv–xvi
equipment for. *See* Equipment and tools
Eton Mess, *250*, 251
Food for the Gods, 213
Heavenly Hash, 249
Indian, 210–211
ingredients for. *See* Ingredients
Layered Gratin of Buttered Crumbs, Peaches, and Quark, 242–243
Molasses, Plantation, 220, *221*
Orange, Glazed, Flossie Miller's, 219
Orange-Walnut, 239–241, *240*
Ozark, 218
Persimmon, Wild, 225–226
Prune, Spicy Buttermilk-Glazed, 227–228
Pudim Molotov, 252–253
Ricotta, with Dark Sweet Red Cherries, 244–245
Rote Grütze (Red Berry Pudding), 246–248, *247*
Sticky Toffee, *222*, 223–224
Streusel, Grandmother Anderson's, 237–238
Surprise, with Orange Sauce, 235–236
Sweet Potato, Grated, 229
Sweet Potato, Iron Skillet, 230–231
Sweet Potato, Mashed, 232–234, *233*
Tipsy Parson, *258*, 259
Woodford, 212
Zuppa Inglese, 255–256, *257*
Pudding of the Abbot of Priscos (Pudim Abade de Priscos), 103–104
Pudding Cake
    Chocolate, 134–135
    Lemon, 138
Pudding molds, xviii, 291
Pudim Abade de Priscos (Pudding of the Abbot of Priscos), 103–104
Pudim de Chá (Tea Custard), *78*, 79–80

Pudim de Laranja (Orange Pudding), Enca Mello Lameiro's, 148–149
Pudim Molotov, 252–253
Pumpkin Pudding, Ina Lieb's, 144–145

Q

Quark
    making, xxx
    Peaches, and Buttered Crumbs, Layered Gratin of, 242–243
    sources, 292
Queen of Puddings, 181–182

R

R & R Crumble, 60–61
Raisins
    in Applesauce Pudding, Steamed, 193
    in Bread Pudding, New Mexican (Capirotada), *178*, 179–180
    in Christmas Pudding, 198–200, *199*
    Green Tomato Crumble with Apples and, 64–65
    in Martha Washington Pudding, 163
    in Noodle Pudding, 191–192
    in Orange Pudding, Glazed, Flossie Miller's, 219
    in Rice Pudding, 85
    Rum-Raisin Bread Pudding, 167
    in Suet Pudding, Colonial, 194–195
    Wine-Poached Dried Fruits, Cobbler of, 66–67
Ramekins, xvii
Raspberry(ies)
    Bavarian Cream, 114
    Bavarian Cream, Showstopper, 116, *117*
    Cardinal Sauce, Quick, 284, *285*
    Cream (variation), 139
    Crumble, R & R, 60–61
    preparing, xx–xxi
    Rote Grütze (Red Berry Pudding), 246–248, *247*
    Sauce, Quick, 278, *279*
Red Berry Pudding (Rote Grütze), 246–248, *247*
Red, White, and Blue Berry–Corn Bread Cobbler, *10*, 11–12
Rhubarb
    Cobbler, Roasted, with Whole-Wheat Topping, 58–59

Crumble, R & R, 60–61
preparing, xxi
Rice
    arsenic in, xxviii, xxx–xxxi
    long-grain, xxx
Rice à l'Impératrice, 96–97
Rice Pudding, 85
    Indian (Kheer), 95
    Rice à l'Impératrice, 96–97
Ricotta
    Pudding with Dark Sweet Red Cher-
        ries, 244–245
    in Tiramisu, 153
Ring molds, xviii
River of Gold Flan, 81
Roasting pans, xviii
Rose water, xxvi, 95, 292
Rote Grütze (Red Berry Pudding),
    246–248, *247*
Rum
    Cream with Sliced Peaches, 142
    Egg Sauce, Frothy, *276*, 277
    Hard Sauce, *286*, 287
    Hard Sauce, Brown Sugar, *288*, 289
    Pudding with Fruit and Nuts,
        Grandma Anna Weigl's,
        136–137
    -Raisin Bread Pudding, 167
    Sweet Potato Crème Caramel, Feli-
        ciana Parish, 100–102, *101*
    Whiskey Sauce, 282
Rye Biscuit Topping, Berries of Summer
    Cobbler with, 13–14

S

Salmonella, and eggs, xix, xxv, 89, 96,
    131, 143, 150, 157
Salt, un-iodized, xxxi
Sandra Gutierrez's Manjar de Leche y
    Canela (Cinnamon and Milk
    Pudding), 132, *133*
Sara's Snow Pudding, 158–159
Sauce(s). *See also* Topping(s)
    Blueberry Maple, *280*, 281
    Butter, Hot, Baked Cranberry Pud-
        ding with, *216*, 217
    Butterscotch, 268
    Cardinal, Quick, 284, *285*
    Chocolate, Thin, 269
    Crème Anglaise (Custard Sauce),
        270, *271*
    Egg, Frothy, *276*, 277

Hard, *286*, 287
Hard, Brown Sugar, *288*, 289
Hard, Vanilla (variation), 287
Nutmeg, 283
Orange, Surprise Pudding with,
    235–236
Peach, Spicy, Upside-Down Peach
    Cups with, 187–188
Raspberry, Quick, 278, *279*
Toffee, *222*, 223, 224
Whiskey, 282
Savarin molds, xviii
Semolina, 244
Sericaia (Cinnamon-Dusted Baked Cus-
    tard), 82–84, *83*
Shortbread
    Ginger, Pick-Your-Own Peaches
        Crumble with, 46–47
    Pecan Crust, Berry Patch Cobbler
        with, *16*, 17
Slight Pudding, 152
Slump
    Apple, 20–21
    Berry, Yankee, 8–9
Smith, Bill, Butterscotch Pudding,
    126–127
Snow Pudding, Sara's, 158–159
Soufflé(s)
    Chocolate, 108–109
    Grand Marnier (variation), 112
    Orange, 112–113
    Peach, Fresh, 110–111
    Strawberry, Fresh (variation), 111
Sour Cream
    in Crème Fraîche, 274, *275*
    in Devonshire Cream, Mock, *272*,
        273
    Rum Cream with Sliced Peaches,
        142
Soy flour, xxvi, 266, 292
Spanish Cream, 131
Spice grinder, electric, xix
Steamed pudding molds, xviii, 291
Steamed puddings. *See also* Hard
    Sauce
    Applesauce Pudding, Steamed, 193
    Carrot and Pineapple Pudding,
        Steamed (variation), 207
    Carrot Pudding, Steamed, 206–207
    Christmas Pudding, 198–200, *199*
    Cocoa-Brown Sugar Pudding,
        Steamed, *196*, 197

Date and Blueberry Pudding,
    Steamed (variation), 205
Fig and Cranberry Pudding,
    Steamed, 204–205
Noodle Pudding, 191–192
Orange Pudding, Steamed, 201–
    203, *202*
Suet Pudding, Colonial, 194–195
Sticky Toffee Puddings, *222*, 223–224
Strawberry(ies)
    Biscuits 'n' Berries, 18, *19*
    Cardinal Sauce, Quick, 284, *285*
    Cream, 139
    Eton Mess, *250*, 251
    Heavenly Hash, 249
    preparing, xx–xxi
    Rote Grütze (Red Berry Pudding),
        246–248, *247*
    Soufflé, Fresh (variation), 111
    in Swedish Cream, *140*, 141
Streusel
    Butter Crumb, 263
    Butter Crumb, -Golden Delicious
        Betty, *34*, 35–36
    Butter Crumb, -Golden Delicious
        Betty, Gluten-Free (variation), 36
    Butter Crumb, Whole-Wheat (vari-
        ation), 263
    Gluten-Free Streusel Topping,
        266–267
    Pudding, Grandmother Anderson's,
        237–238
Suet. *See* Beef Suet
Sugar
    Brown Sugar-Cocoa Pudding,
        Steamed, *196*, 197
    Brown Sugar Hard Sauce, *288*, 289
    Burnt Sugar Syrup, 252
    caramelizing, 87, 88
    types of, xxxi–xxxii
Summer Pudding, 172–173
Surprise Pudding with Orange Sauce,
    235–236
Swedish Cream, *140*, 141
Sweet Potato(es)
    baking, 232
    Crème Caramel, Feliciana Parish,
        100–102, *101*
    Panna Cotta with Clementines in
        Lemongrass Syrup, *118*,
        119–120
    Pudding, Grated, 229

Pudding, Iron Skillet, 230–231
Pudding, Mashed, 232–234, *233*
Syllabub, 157
Syrup
    Burnt Sugar, 252
    Lemongrass, *118*, 119
    Marsala, 255, 256

T

Tapioca, xxxii
Tapioca Pudding
    Coconut (variation), 89
    Mama's, 89
    Pecan (variation), 89
Tar Heel Banana Pudding, Old-Timey,
    92, 93–94
Tea Custard, *78*, 79–80
Thermometers, xvi, xix
Tipsy Parson, *258*, 259
Tiramisu, 153
Toffee Pudding, Sticky, *222*, 223–224
Toffee Sauce, *222*, 223, 224
Tomato. *See* Green Tomato
Topping(s). *See also* Biscuit Topping;
       Oatmeal; Sauce(s); Streusel
    Caramelized, in Crème Brûlée,
        87–88
    Corn Bread Cobbler, Red, White,
        and Blue Berry–, *10*, 11–12
    Corn Bread Crisp, –Green Tomato,
        62–63
    Crème Fraîche, 274, *275*
    Devonshire Cream, Mock, *272*, 273
    Granola-Fig Crumble, Fresh, 51
    Granola, Gluten-Free, 264–265
    Whipped Cream, 13, 15
    Whole-Wheat, Fresh Plum Cobbler
        with, 52–54, *53*
    Whole-Wheat, Roasted Rhubarb
        Cobbler with, 58–59
Trifle, Blackberry, 143
Tube cake pan, xviii

U

Upside Down Peach Cups with Spicy
    Peach Sauce, 187–188

V

Vanilla
    Banana Pudding, Old-Timey Tar
        Heel, *92*, 93–94
    Bavarian Cream, 115

beans, xxvi
Crème Brûlée, *86*, 87–88
Custard, Classic Baked, 70, *71*
Custards, Vanilla Bean, Individual
    (variation), 73
Custard, Vanilla Bean, Baked, 72–73
Floating Island, 74
Hard Sauce (variation), 287
Potato Pudding, Irish, 147

W

Walnut(s), xxxii, xxxiii. *See also* Black
       Walnuts
    Applesauce Pudding, Steamed, 193
    Bread Crumb–Date-Nut Pudding,
        Mother's, 177
    Christmas Pudding, 198–200, *199*
    Cran-Apple Casserole with Oatmeal
        Crust, 40
    Date-Nut Pudding, My Mother's,
        214, *215*
    Food for the Gods, 213
    Graham Cracker Pudding, 189–190
    October Pudding, 25
    -Orange Pudding, 239–241, *240*
    Ozark Pudding, 218
    Prune Pudding, Spicy Butter-
        milk-Glazed, 227–228
    Streusel Pudding, Grandmother An-
        derson's, 237–238
    toasting, 191
Weigl, Anna, Rum Pudding with Fruits
       and Nuts, Grandma, 136–137
Whipped Cream Topping, 13, 15
Whipping cream, xxv
Whiskey Sauce, 282
    French Bread Pudding with, 183
Whole Wheat
    Butter Crumb Streusel (variation),
        263
    Topping, Fresh Plum Cobbler with,
        52–54, *53*
    Topping, Roasted Rhubarb Cobbler
        with, 58–59
Whole-wheat flour, xxvii
Wine, xxxii
    Dried Fruits, -Poached, Cobbler of,
        66–67
    Flan, River of Gold, 81
    Martha Washington Pudding, 163
    Rote Grütze (Red Berry Pudding),
        246–248, *247*

Syllabub, 157
Tipsy Parson, *258*, 259
Tiramisu, 153
Zabaglione, 90, *91*
Zuppa Inglese, 255–256, *257*
Woodford Pudding, 212

Z

Zabaglione, 90, *91*
Zuppa Inglese, 255–256, *257*

NOTES

Day of the Dead

ABDO
Publishing Company

A Buddy Book
by
Julie Murray

Buddy BOOKS
Holidays

Coordinating Series Editor: Rochelle Baltzer
Editor: Sarah Tieck
Contributing Editors: Megan M. Gunderson, Bridget O'Brien, Marcia Zappa
Graphic Design: Denise Esner
Cover Photograph: *Shutterstock*: tipograffias.
Interior Photographs/Illustrations: *AP Photo*: The Orange County Register, Michael Goulding (p. 15), Rex Features via AP Images (pp. 17, 21), Corpus Christi Caller-Times, Michael Zamora (p. 5); *Getty Images*: Mark D Callanan (p. 13), Claudio Cruz/LatinContent (p. 11), DEA / G. DAGLI ORTI (p. 8), Ronaldo Schemidt/AFP (p. 5); *Glow Images*: H. Tom Hall/National Geographic Image Collection (p. 7); *iStockphoto*: ©iStockphoto.com/ sf_foodphoto (p. 15); *Shutterstock*: AGCuesta (p. 19), bikeriderlondon (p. 22), jejim (p. 9).

Library of Congress Cataloging-in-Publication Data

Murray, Julie, 1969-
 Day of the dead / Julie Murray.
   pages cm. -- (Holidays)
 ISBN 978-1-62403-182-3
 1. All Souls' Day--Juvenile literature. I. Title.
 GT4995.A4M88 2014
 394.266--dc23
                         2013027431

Table of Contents

What Is Day of the Dead? 4

The Story of Day of the Dead...........6

Changing Dates 9

Traditions and Customs 10

Altars 12

Skulls 14

Graves 16

Day of the Dead Foods 18

Day of the Dead Today 20

Remember Loved Ones...............22

Important Words 23

Web Sites 23

Index....................................24

What Is Day of the Dead?

Day of the Dead is a Mexican holiday. It is also **celebrated** in parts of the United States and Latin America. On this day, people honor the dead.

Day of the Dead falls on November 2 and sometimes November 1. Spanish **conquerors** moved the celebration to these dates. They were **Christians** and wanted it to be on All Souls' Day and All Saints' Day.

Day of the Dead is called *Día de los Muertos* in Spanish.

The Story of Day of the Dead

Day of the Dead began more than 2,000 years ago in what is now Mexico. In late summer, native people spent about a month honoring the dead.

The ancient city of Tenochtitlán was the Aztec capital. It is believed that 140,000 people lived there at its peak.

In the 1400s and early 1500s, the Aztecs were an important people in Mexico. They became famous for their way of life. They were powerful **warriors** and ruled a large area.

The goddess Mictecacihuatl was an important part of the **celebration**. She was known as "Lady of the Dead."

Aztecs believed she was the queen of the underworld. Stories say she ruled the bones of those who had died.

Mictecacihuatl (meek-tay-kah-SEE-wahtl) was honored in Aztec art.

Changing Dates

Day of the Dead started out as a month-long **celebration**. The dates were chosen based on the Aztec calendar.

In the 1500s, the Spanish **conquered** the Aztecs. They introduced **Christianity** and changed the Aztec way of life. This included moving Day of the Dead to Christian holy days.

The Aztec calendar was based on the sun.

Traditions and Customs

On Day of the Dead, people spend time honoring their dead loved ones. They visit graves. They may have picnics or parades. They also think about death, so they won't be afraid of it.

In some places, people remember *angelitos*, or dead children, on November 1. They honor dead adults on November 2.

Altars

During Day of the Dead, families build **altars** in their homes. This is a special act to honor their dead loved ones.

They place certain objects around the altar to remember the person. These include flowers, food, and pictures. They also light candles next to it.

Altars are called *ofrendas*. They may include offerings that stand for earth, fire, wind, and water.

13

Skulls

Skulls are an important **symbol** of Day of the Dead. People wear wooden skull masks or paint their faces like skulls. They place wooden skulls on **altars**. And, they eat candy skulls.

Candy skulls are often bright and colorful. This reminds people the holiday is about love and happiness.

Skull masks and other decorations are called *calacas*.

15

Graves

In some areas, families clean and decorate graves. They use candles, marigolds, and favorite foods of the dead. They hope the spirits of loved ones will return for a visit. In this way, they remember people who have died.

Grave decorations are often colorful. They stand for special things about the person who has died.

Day of the Dead Foods

Some families have picnics at the graves of their loved ones. They may eat a loved one's favorite foods.

People also eat *pan de muerto*. This is a sweet bread made with eggs and sometimes a plant called anise. People also eat chocolate and a spicy sauce called mole (MOH-lay).

Pan de muerto is baked in different shapes. Often, it is round with dough on top shaped like a skull and bones.

Day of the Dead Today

Day of the Dead is a popular Mexican holiday. People attend parties and parades. Some gather at graves for picnics. They eat breads and candies in the shape of skulls and skeletons.

On Day of the Dead, people honor their lost loved ones. They are reminded that death is a part of life.

People dress up to
take part in parades.

Remember Loved Ones

If you have lost a loved one, you could honor them on Day of the Dead. Get flowers and place them in a special part of your home. Or, play that person's favorite music and eat his or her favorite food.

Some people also place flowers on graves.

Important Words

altar a raised structure, such as a table, that holds objects meant to honor someone or something.

celebrate to observe a holiday with special events. These events are known as celebrations.

Christian (KRIHS-chuhn) a person who practices Christianity, which is a religion that follows the teachings of Jesus Christ.

conquer (KAHN-kuhr) to take control using military force.

symbol (SIHM-buhl) an object or mark that stands for an idea.

warrior a soldier or fighter.

Web Sites

To learn more about Day of the Dead,
visit ABDO Publishing Company online. Web sites about Day of the Dead are featured on our Book Links page. These links are routinely monitored and updated to provide the most current information available.

www.abdopublishing.com

Index

All Saints' Day 4

All Souls' Day 4

altars **12, 13, 14**

Aztecs **7, 8, 9**

Christianity **4, 9**

food **10, 12, 14, 15, 16, 18, 19, 20, 22**

graves **10, 16, 17, 18, 20, 22**

Mexico **4, 6, 7, 20**

Mictecacihuatl **8**

parades **10, 20, 21**

skulls **14, 15, 19, 20**

Spain **4, 9**

Tenochtitlán **7**

United States **4**